The Perception of Multiple Objects

Neural Network Modeling and Connectionism
Jeffrey L. Elman, Editor

Connectionist Modeling and Brain Function: The Developing Interface
Stephen José Hanson and Carl R. Olson, editors

Neural Network Design and the Complexity of Learning
J. Stephen Judd

Neural Networks for Control
W. Thomas Miller, Richard S. Sutton, and Paul J. Werbos, editors

The Perception of Multiple Objects: A Connectionist Approach
Michael C. Mozer

The Perception Of Multiple Objects:

A Connectionist Approach

Michael C. Mozer

A Bradford Book
The MIT Press
Cambridge, Massachusetts
London, England

This book was printed and bound in the United States of America.

Library of Congress Cataloging-in-Publication Data

Mozer, Michael C.
  The perception of multiple objects : a connectionist approach / Michael C. Mozer.
      p.   cm. — (Neural network modeling and connectionism)
  "A Bradford book."
  Includes bibliographical references and index.
  ISBN 0-262-13270-2 (hc)
  1. Neural networks (Computer science) 2. Connection machines. 3. Perception. I. Title. II. Series.
QA76.87.M69 1991
006.3—dc20   90-13549
                                                                  CIP

Contents

Series Foreword

The goal of this series, Neural Network Modeling and Connectionism, is to identify and bring to the public the best work in the exciting field of neural network and connectionist modeling. The series includes monographs based on dissertations, extended reports of work by leaders in the field, edited volumes and collections on topics of special interest, major reference works, and undergraduate and graduate-level texts. The field is highly interdisciplinary, and works published in the series will touch on a wide variety of topics ranging from low-level vision to the philosophical foundations of theories of representation.

Jeffrey L. Elman, Editor

Associate Editors:

James Anderson, Brown University
Andrew Barto, University of Massachusetts, Amherst
Gary Dell, University of Illinois
Jerome Feldman, University of California, Berkeley
Stephen Grossberg, Boston University
Stephen Hanson, Princeton University
Geoffrey Hinton, University of Toronto
Michael Jordan, MIT
James McClelland, Carnegie-Mellon University
Domenico Parisi, Instituto di Psicologia del CNR
David Rumelhart, Stanford University
Terrence Sejnowski, The Salk Institute
Paul Smolensky, University of Colorado
Stephen P. Stich, Rutgers University
David Touretzky, Carnegie-Mellon University
David Zipser, University of California, San Diego

Acknowledgements

Now that I've experienced life on the other side of the prison walls, I can sincerely express my gratitude to Donald Norman and David Rumelhart for their support and guidance during my stay at UC San Diego. Many thanks are also due to Geoffrey Hinton, James McClelland, and Paul Smolensky for helpful discussions about this work, and to Marlene Behrmann, Harold Pashler, and David Touretzky for their careful critique and suggestions on an earlier draft. Mark Wallen, Sondra Buffett, Kathy Farrelly, and Rachel Mann were indispensable in just about every other department.

This work was supported by NSF Presidential Young Investigator Award IRI-9058450, grant 90-21 from the James S. McDonnell Foundation, and an IBM Graduate Fellowship to the author; Contract N00014-85-C-0133 NR 667-541 with the Personnel and Training Research Programs of the Office of Naval Research and a grant from the System Development Foundation to Donald Norman and David Rumelhart; and grant 87-2-36 from the Sloan Foundation to Geoffrey Hinton.

The Perception of Multiple Objects

1 Introduction

As one looks around the world, many objects fall into view at once. Intuitively, one has the impression that a great deal of information about these objects is immediately available. For instance, as I stare at my computer terminal, I am aware not only of the terminal but also of many words printed on the screen, a blue book and a small yellow notepad sitting on my desk, the shiny metal rim of the desk, and even the texture of the wooden desktop. Is this merely an illusion? Am I simply switching rapidly among the various objects, or is there some sense in which I can truly apprehend many objects simultaneously? If the former, how is the switching controlled? If the latter, what are the limits on parallel processing of sensory information?

A rich body of experimental data has accumulated that hints at answers to these questions: Psychologists have examined the amount of information required to overload the perceptual system, errors produced when the system is overloaded, factors that influence the difficulty of perception, and the breakdown of the perceptual system as exhibited by neurological patients. This book describes a computational model that can explain a broad spectrum of such data. In doing so, the model makes concrete predictions as to what sorts of information the visual system can process in parallel and what sorts must be processed serially. The model is called *MORSEL* for its ability to perform multiple object recognition and attentional selection. MORSEL is a working computational model that, in its present implementation, is primarily directed at letter and word recognition and early stages of reading. MORSEL goes beyond most psychological theories in that it is a fully mechanistic account, not just a functional-level theory. It is further distinguished by addressing an extremely wide scope of data.

MORSEL integrates and builds upon many of the recent developments in the perceptual and attentional literature (Duncan & Humphreys, 1989; Fukushima, 1987; Fukushima & Miyake, 1982; Hinton, 1981b; LaBerge & Brown, 1989; Marcel, 1983a,b; McClelland, 1985,

1986a; McClelland & Rumelhart, 1981; Pashler & Badgio, 1987; Treisman & Gelade, 1980). In fact, it can be viewed as a synthesis of these various theoretical perspectives. Surprisingly, the conglomeration fits together reasonably well, and addresses some important issues in representation, including the type-token distinction.

The book is divided into seven chapters. The remainder of chapter 1 presents a brief introduction to the class of connectionist models and sketches a rough overview of MORSEL. Chapters 2–5 describe each of MORSEL's components in detail. Chapter 6 reports on simulation experiments using MORSEL to replicate phenomena in the experimental literature and discusses other phenomena that MORSEL is well-equipped to account for. Finally, chapter 7 provides a summary evaluation of the model and notes several unresolved problems.

1.1 Connectionist Models

Massively parallel models of computation have shown promising results in the areas of pattern recognition, memory, learning, and language comprehension (Anderson & Hinton, 1981; Feldman & Ballard, 1982; McClelland, Rumelhart, & Hinton, 1986). These models, called *connectionist* or *parallel distributed processing* models, offer a new approach to the representation and manipulation of knowledge. They consist of a large number of simple neuron-like processing units operating in parallel. In most cases, each unit represents a possible hypothesis; for example, in the perceptual domain the hypotheses concern the presence or absence of features in the environment. Units have varying degrees of "confidence" in the truth of their hypotheses. The degree of confidence is quantified by an internal state variable of the unit, its *activation level*. Units can transmit their activation levels to one another through connecting links. Links may be either excitatory or inhibitory. When two units represent mutually compatible hypotheses, they are connected by an excitatory link. Excitatory links cause the confidence in one hypothesis to increase the confidence in the other hypothesis. When two units represent mutually incompatible hypotheses, they are connected by an inhibitory link. Inhibitory links cause the confidence in one hypothesis to decrease the confidence in the other hypothesis. The outcome of any computation in a connectionist network is thus the result of cooperation and competition among a large number of simple processors.

To be concrete, consider an early and often cited connectionist model, the *interactive activation (IA) model of word perception* (McClelland & Rumelhart, 1981; Rumelhart & McClelland, 1982), sketched in figure 1.1. The model consists of three levels: feature, letter, and word levels. Each unit at the feature and letter levels represents the hypothesis that a particular feature or letter is present in a given position; each word unit represents the hypothesis that the letters form a particular word. The model "sees" a visual input pattern by having a subset of its feature units activated. Feature units then excite their corresponding letter units, and letter units their corresponding word units. Connections between levels are bidirectional, so that word units excite their corresponding letter units and letters their features. Additionally, units within a rectangle in figure 1.1 are mutually inhibitory. Once set into motion, activation flows through this network until a stable interpretation of the perceptual input is settled upon.

1.1.1 Local and Distributed Representations

The question of how to represent entities, whether they be hypotheses, objects, concepts, or schemata, is critical in connectionist modeling.

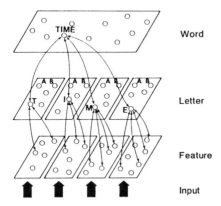

Figure 1.1 A sketch of the interactive activation model of word perception. Connections are shown for a single word and its constituents. (Reprinted with permission from "Putting knowledge in its place: A scheme for programming parallel processing structures on the fly" by J. L. McClelland, in *Cognitive Science*, 9, p. 115. Copyright 1985 by Ablex Publishing.)

At one extreme, an entity may be represented by the activity of a single unit, in which case the representation is said to be *local*. For example, in the IA model, the representation at the word level is local, with one unit per word. Traditional semantic network models also adopt a local representation scheme (e.g., Collins & Quillian, 1969). In contrast, an entity may be represented by the activity of more than one unit and each unit may be involved in the representation of more than one entity, in which case the representation is said to be *distributed* and the active units are said to form a *pattern of activity* across the set of available units. Distributed representations may be *sparse* or *dense*, depending on the proportion of active units. For example, the letter level of the IA model specifies a sparsely distributed representation of a word in that each word is represented by the activity of 4 out of 4 × 26 letter-level units. The feature level of the model specifies a somewhat denser representation, with about 16 of 56 feature-level units active for each word.

Local and distributed representational schemes differ along several functional dimensions, the primary ones being: (1) the number of entities that can be veridically represented simultaneously, and (2) the degree to which the representations facilitate generalization.

1.1.1.1 Representing Multiple Entities

Local representations allow as many entities to be represented at once as there are units. For instance, multiple words can be activated simultaneously at the word level of the IA model because there is one unit for each word. This representation is *faithful* (Smolensky, 1990), meaning that a one-to-one mapping exists between sets of words and patterns of activity. Distributed representations, in contrast, have difficulty in faithfully representing multiple entities. For instance, at the letter level of the IA model, the simultaneous activation of several words leads to ambiguity: **BOOR** and **HEAT** yield the same activity pattern as **BOOT** and **HEAR**, or **BEAR** and **HOOT** for that matter. To represent multiple entities without confusion in a distributed representation, the representation must specify which units participate in the representation of which entity—in the above example, which letters belong in which word. Smolensky (1990) discusses a class of representations that are able to solve this difficult problem, formally known as the *binding problem*. Examples of this class can be found in

St. John and McClelland (1986) and Touretzky and Hinton (1985, 1988). In chapter 2, I present a representation of this class that has a limited ability to encode multiple words simultaneously without confusing which letters belong in which word.

1.1.1.2 Generalization

Whereas local representations are better suited to the representation of multiple entities than distributed representations, distributed representations often have the advantage when it comes to generalization. *Generalization* is the ability to respond appropriately to an unfamiliar entity based on experience with a set of familiar entities. In distributed connectionist networks, this desirable property occurs naturally, and takes the form of similar responses being made to entities having similar representations (Hinton, 1980; McClelland, Rumelhart, Hinton, 1986). Similarity of representation is defined in terms of the distance or angle between the activity vectors representing the entities. In many cases, this is equivalent to the number of active units shared by the representations of the entities. Because a local representation of one entity shares no units with that of another, local representations do not facilitate generalization. On the other hand, it is a logical consequence of most distributed representations that two entities with properties in common will have overlapping patterns of activity. For instance, the encodings of **BEAT** and **BEAR** at the letter level overlap on three of four features—**B**, **E**, and **A**. With this representation, it is easy to construct or train a network to respond in a certain way to all words beginning with **B** or all words with a vowel in the second position; such generalizations will not readily emerge using local representations of words.

1.1.2 Types and Tokens in Connectionist Models

An apparent weakness of the connectionist approach is its difficulty in handling the *type-token distinction* (Norman, 1986). The problem here is how to represent different instances (tokens) of the same entity (type) in a manner that will uphold their similarity yet allow them to be treated as distinct. For example, consider how one might represent two visual stimuli: a green neon **WALK** sign at a pedestrian crossing and a flashing red **WALK** sign (the latter indicating that the sign will shortly change to **DON'T WALK**). On the one hand, it is desirable for the two representations to be identical so that the appropriate response will be produced in either situation—walking across the street. On the other hand, it is important to encode the color of the sign so that one situation can be treated differently than the other—perhaps the walker should be more vigilant if the sign is flashing red.

A natural way of characterizing tokens of a given type is through the use of *similar-but-distinct* distributed representations. Imagine a pool of units in which one subset of the units represents a green **WALK** sign and another subset a flashing red **WALK** sign. The overlap between the two patterns of activity represents the type "walk," while the nonoverlap is what allows one token to be distinguished from the other. Viewing tokens in this manner, the problem of representing types and tokens seems only an extreme case of the more general problem of representing similarity. Two tokens are an extreme case because they are highly similar.[1]

Assuming then that tokens are represented as similar-but-distinct activity patterns, the next concern is how to handle multiple tokens simultaneously, or more generally, how to handle similar items simultaneously. The problem here is that two similar items will have highly overlapping patterns of activity, and it will be difficult to disentangle one pattern from the other. Thus, specialized processing structures are required to operate on these representations.

1.2 MORSEL: An Overview

With the preceding discussion, I hope to have raised several general issues in connectionist modeling, issues particularly pertinent to building a model of multiple-object recognition. I will return to these issues later as they come to bear on the work. In the remainder of this chapter, I present a brief overview of MORSEL.

Figure 1.2 shows a sketch of MORSEL. The heart of MORSEL is a set of processing subsystems or *modules* that analyze a visual input

---

[1] An obvious localist representation of types and tokens would be to have one unit for each token, and to represent the type by the union of the token units. However, as with any local representation, this scheme has serious limitations due to the number of token units required in high-dimensional feature spaces and the fact that similarity is not explicitly encoded.

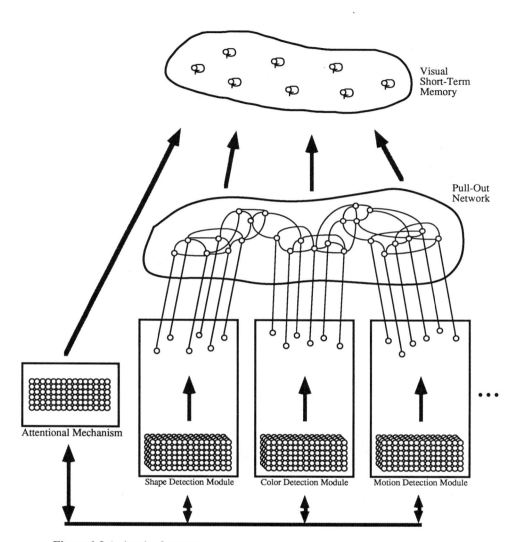

Figure 1.2 A sketch of MORSEL.

along independent attribute dimensions. The figure depicts three modules which detect object shape, color, and motion. These modules have the capacity to analyze multiple objects in parallel, but resource limitations cause a degradation in the quality of analysis as the amount of information to be processed increases. Consequently, two additional components are required: a "clean up" mechanism (called the *pull-out network* or *PO net*) that constructs a consistent interpretation of the somewhat noisy perceptual data produced by the modules, and an *attentional mechanism* (or *AM* for short) that guides the efforts of the modules and prevents them from attempting to process too much information at once. The AM works by selectively gating the flow of activity through the various modules. The final component of MORSEL is a *visual short-term memory* that bundles together attributes of an object and holds on to many object descriptions simultaneously.

To describe the typical operation of the model, consider a simple example in which MORSEL is shown a display containing two colored letters, a red X and a blue T. These letters will cause a pattern of activity on MORSEL's "retina," which serves as input to each of the processing modules as well as to the attentional system. The attentional system then focuses on one retinal region, say the location of the red X. Information from that region is processed by each module. The module that extracts shape information might identify the object as an "x" or, if the stimulus is noisy or processing is insufficient, possibly a "y"; the module that extracts color information might identify the object as being red. The PO net then selects the most plausible interpretation produced by each module, in this case "x" and "red." The representation at this level of the system (and at the outputs of the modules) encodes attributes of the visual form *without regard to location*. Location information is recovered from the AM, which indicates the current location and breadth of focus. Shape, color, and location information can then be bound together and stored in the short-term memory or used as desired by higher-level systems. Next, attention shifts to the blue T, and this process is repeated. I defer further details until later, but note that if attention is not focused on a particular region of the retina, all items in the retina are processed in parallel and crosstalk among the items can ensue. This crosstalk can cause one item to interfere with the perception of another.

1.2.1 Modular Organization

My use of the term "module" is consistent with that of Fodor (1983) and Marr (1982), and roughly corresponds to the *feature-registration stage* of Treisman and Gelade's (1980) feature-integration theory. The primary properties of these modules are: (a) they encode perceptually independent information, and consequently, the computations performed by one module are irrelevant with respect to those performed by other modules; (b) they receive no "top-down" input from higher levels of the system; and (c) they operate automatically in the sense that allocation of processing resources is not necessary. These properties allow the modules to operate quickly and efficiently.

The modules could be anatomically distinct entities in the brain or merely functionally independent. Both possibilities are likely: the visual system may be prewired to analyze color and motion information along different pathways (Van Essen & Maunsell, 1983); other stimulus dimensions, such as letter shape and letter case, may be analyzed independently (Friedman, 1980) but specialized processing channels as these are surely experience dependent.

My focus has been on constructing a module that performs letter and word recognition, described in chapter 2. This is the only module I have implemented, though the others can be viewed as operating in a similar manner. It seems somewhat presumptuous to bill MORSEL as a model of multiple-*object* perception when only letter and word perception is discussed. However, my aim is to focus on *multiple*-object perception; hence, the particular objects are of secondary interest. The model generalizes quite readily to arbitrary two-dimensional line drawings, a point I return to in chapter 7.

2 Multiple Word Recognition

In this chapter, I describe a network capable of simultaneously recognizing multiple words appearing in arbitrary locations in the visual field. There is a dual problem that goes hand in hand with this one: the network must also recognize a single word as being the same, independent of its location, despite the fact that different locations may give rise to quite different patterns of activity on the retina. This problem is variously known as *translation-invariant recognition* or *stimulus equivalence* (Hebb, 1949; Neisser, 1967), and is an instance of the more general problem of shape constancy under any set of transformations such as translation, dilation, and rotation.

2.1 Prior Connectionist Models of Multiple Word Recognition

McClelland and Rumelhart's IA model of word perception did not have to face either the problem of multiple-word recognition or translation-invariant recognition because it was designed to deal with *single* words in a *prespecified* position. That is, input to the model consisted of a set of features corresponding to the first letter in a word, to the second letter, and so forth; retinal position was not considered. How might such a model be extended to deal with the registration of multiple words distributed spatially across a visual image? Two approaches have been suggested.

2.1.1 The Hardware-Replication Approach

The simplest possibility is to have an independent word recognition subsystem, essentially a copy of the IA model, operating at each region of the retina. This approach requires extreme redundancy, because all knowledge implicit in the network—the connections that specify how features combine to form letters and letters to form words—must be replicated for each local subsystem. Further, the approach is inflexible if connection strengths need to be adaptively updated. To avoid the problems associated with replicated hard-wired connections, McClelland (1985, 1986a) has suggested a mechanism, the *connection information distributor*, in which all connections are dynamically programmed from a central knowledge source.

Using this mechanism, McClelland developed a model called PABLO that is able to process several words simultaneously and exhibits crosstalk when the network is overloaded. Basically, the model works as follows: When a set of words is presented, local position-specific letter detectors become activated and feed their activity into a common central pool of letter units. These central letter units serve as input to a central word analyzer, which identifies all words that can be formed from the letters currently reaching it, preserving some information about relative within-string position. The central word analyzer then feeds information back to local word analyzers, setting up temporary connections that allow the detection of all words currently active in the central analyzer. The letters that are present on each set of local detectors combine with the top-down input to allow identification of the appropriate words.

PABLO has been tested on a small lexicon consisting of two to four letter words. Given the nature of the representations used, it is not entirely clear how well the model will function with longer words. Also, PABLO has not been implemented in a form that will handle words translated along a continuous retina; input to the model is at the letter level, not the feature level. PABLO has several more serious limitations.

- Although this mechanism avoids the replication of knowledge across local subsystems, replication of hardware is necessary. Specifically, each subsystem requires a sufficient number of dedicated units and connections to perform the letter-to-word mapping, and one subsystem is required for each possible location in which a word might appear. To handle a reasonable-sized visual field, the amount of hardware needed is inelegant, if not unwieldy. Hardware requirements of PABLO and the word recognition system described below are compared in appendix A. Conservatively, PABLO requires an order of magnitude more connections and processing units.

- The output of PABLO, which is simply the concatenation of the outputs of the local subsystems, contains no explicit translation-invariant representation of a recognized word. Thus, the system does not achieve translation invariance without an additional component that combines outputs of the various subsystems.

- PABLO seems to be too powerful as a model of human information processing, particularly with regard to its ability to maintain item-location bindings precisely and to process multiple items without proximity-based interference effects. Experimental reports of human perceptual errors (see chapter 6) suggest in fact that precise location information is not maintained in the visual system, and that interference is dependent on proximity. PABLO may not produce comparable errors. As a simple example, McClelland notes that PABLO has "no difficulty processing the same word twice if it occurred in two different locations." (McClelland, 1986a, p. 165). However, people do not have a corresponding ability to keep track of multiple tokens of the same type, at least in brief displays (Mozer, 1989).

- The connectivity of PABLO is somewhat baroque. Extremely specific connections are required, consisting primarily of one-to-one reciprocal mappings: Inputs from the local subsystems converge to the central knowledge store, and outputs from the central knowledge store diverge back to the local subsystems.

2.1.2 The Normalization Approach

An alternative suggestion for processing multiple entities is a normalization scheme, proposed by, among others, Hinton (1981a,b; Hinton & Lang, 1985), McCulloch and Pitts (1943), and Palmer (1984). The basic idea is to apply transformations to a portion of the retinal image in an attempt to "normalize" an object in position, scale, and orientation. The normalization procedure effectively factors out any transformational differences between two instances of the same object in the retinal image. Once normalized, an image can be analyzed by a rigid template-matching system like the IA model.

This approach requires a set of units representing the retinal image and another set representing the normalized image, as well as a means of selecting which region of the retina to normalize. In Hinton's scheme, selection is performed by a set of *mapping* units, each of which represents one possible mapping between the retinal image and the normalized image. The mapping units gate the flow of activity between the retinal-image units and the normalized-image units (i.e., activity can flow along a connection only if the mapping unit is active). Connections are symmetric, so that retinal-image units gate the flow of activity between normalized-image and mapping units, and normalized-image units gate the flow of activity between retinal-image and mapping units. This allows predetermined values on any two sets of units to fill in the value of the third. Appendix A compares hardware requirements of this scheme and my model. The normalization approach requires roughly the same number of connections and units as my model.

This approach provides a means of achieving translation-invariant recognition. The price paid is that only one object can be recognized at a time. [1] Another objection that has been raised to this approach is that it demands a rigidity of connection and a type of functional specificity of units quite different from that observed in the brain (Singh, 1966).

2.2 The Linearity-Nonlinearity Dilemma

While PABLO is able to recognize multiple words in parallel, it does not yield translation-invariant representations because its outputs are tied to the local processing structures. Conversely, while the normalization approach achieves a translation-invariant representation, it is unable to operate on multiple words in parallel. An ideal solution would be a network that could perform both multiple-word recognition and translation-invariant recognition. Unfortunately, these dual goals are conflicting. To illustrate the conflict, consider the visual system in terms of its input-output properties. If the system is to process multiple words, its response to simultaneously presented words should be identical to the sum of its responses to each word presented

---

[1] Although object recognition is serial, the approach does not deny a considerable amount of early parallel processing of the retinal image. That is, the "retinal-image" units could represent higher-order retinotopic features that are computed in parallel from the image itself.

in isolation. That is, the processing of one word should not interact with the processing of another.[2] If the visual system is to achieve this independence, it must operate linearly. Linear systems have the property of superposition, namely that the combined response to several stimuli is the sum of the responses to the individual stimuli.

However, if the system is to achieve a translation-invariant response, nonlinearities are required. A translation-invariant system that is purely linear cannot detect letter arrangements. For instance, compare the response of such a system to the words ON and NO. Because the system is linear, the response to ON is simply the sum of the responses to O in the first position and N in the second; likewise, NO is the sum of N in the first position and O in the second. Further, because of translation invariance, the response to a given letter will be independent of its position; hence the system will respond identically to ON and NO. Thus, the property of superposition will prevent the system from responding to position-dependent interactions within a word.

To summarize, nonlinearities are important for encoding meaningful relations among letters, but when distinct words are to be identified simultaneously, interactions caused by nonlinearities represent only noise. Thus, the issue of linearity versus nonlinearity presents a major dilemma for any model that attempts to perform both multiple-word recognition and translation-invariant recognition. The letter and word recognition module of MORSEL proposes one solution to this dilemma. Essentially, the solution is to include nonlinearities at early stages of the system where the relations among letters are encoded, but to make later stages of the system, where the responses to multiple words are combined, linear.

2.3 BLIRNET

The letter and word recognition module of MORSEL is a network whose purpose is to detect information concerning the identities of one or more letter strings appearing on its "retina," regardless of the strings' locations. This network is called *BLIRNET* because it builds

---

[2] At later semantic stages of analysis such interactions are to be expected, but presumably not in a system that is concerned with visual pattern recognition.

location invariant representations of multiple letter strings (also because the operation of the network "blurs" the input via a coarse-coded representation). BLIRNET is a multilayered hierarchical network, the bottom layer of which serves as input and the top layer as output. Before describing the architecture of BLIRNET, it is useful to consider the representations at the input and output layers.

2.3.1 Input Representation

Presentation of a visual display causes a pattern of activity on MORSEL's "retina." In the current implementation, the retina is a feature map arranged in a 36×6 spatial array, with detectors for five feature types at each point in the array. The input pattern is thus composed of 1,080 ($= 36 \times 6 \times 5$) units. The input feature types, inspired by Julesz's (1981) textons, are oriented line segments at $0°$, $45°$, $90°$, and $135°$, and line-segment terminator detectors. I assume that the registration of these simple visual features occurs via some parallel, unlimited capacity process (see Folk & Egeth, 1989, for experimental confirmation).

To present letters and words, I designed a font in which each letter is encoded as a binary activity pattern over a 3×3 retinal region. The letters are all upper case, and visually similar letters yield similar activity patterns. This can be seen in the confusion matrix of figure 2.1, where each entry is the normalized dot product of the 45-element activity patterns corresponding to the given pair of letters, $\mathbf{p}_1$ and $\mathbf{p}_2$:

$$\frac{\mathbf{p}_1^T \mathbf{p}_2}{\|\mathbf{p}_1\| \; \|\mathbf{p}_2\|} .$$

This is a measure of the proportion of features two letters share. Pairs like **P** and **R** or **O** and **Q** share many features, whereas pairs like **E** and **Y** or **M** and **T** share few if any.

Letter strings can be encoded as a sequence of letters placed in horizontally adjacent 3×3 regions. Figure 2.2 depicts the retinal representation of the phrase **OUR NATION**. An empty 3×3 region separates one word from the other. The retina can be packed with up to 24 letters by forming two rows, each containing 12 letters.

	A	B	C	D	E	F	G	H	I	J	K	L	M	N	O	P	Q	R	S	T	U	V	W	X	Y
B	.54																								
C	.45	.67																							
D	.46	.82	.76																						
E	.46	.69	.76	.64																					
F	.52	.57	.54	.48	.81																				
G	.60	.76	.83	.80	.74	.62																			
H	.72	.52	.36	.44	.52	.59	.51																		
I	.24	.39	.57	.44	.59	.42	.45	.31																	
J	.24	.33	.50	.37	.44	.50	.45	.31	.77																
K	.48	.33	.36	.22	.52	.59	.32	.69	.31	.31															
L	.31	.50	.64	.57	.66	.32	.49	.49	.49	.29	.49														
M	.50	.34	.30	.46	.31	.35	.33	.64	.16	.16	.64	.41													
N	.44	.36	.31	.48	.32	.45	.42	.67	.17	.25	.59	.32	.78												
O	.51	.77	.84	.94	.60	.45	.86	.42	.42	.42	.21	.53	.43	.45											
P	.64	.78	.50	.59	.59	.75	.57	.62	.31	.38	.46	.29	.40	.42	.55										
Q	.56	.69	.81	.84	.65	.44	.78	.47	.47	.40	.34	.60	.49	.51	.91	.54									
R	.65	.71	.52	.53	.60	.68	.52	.62	.35	.35	.62	.35	.51	.53	.50	.90	.61								
S	.53	.76	.71	.61	.61	.55	.79	.45	.51	.45	.32	.32	.20	.28	.69	.57	.61	.52							
T	.10	.24	.34	.27	.36	.40	.31	.18	.74	.74	.18	.12	.00	.10	.25	.28	.24	.25	.31						
U	.32	.59	.64	.74	.52	.33	.70	.62	.38	.38	.38	.69	.48	.59	.76	.31	.67	.28	.51	.18					
V	.18	.30	.24	.34	.25	.29	.29	.53	.18	.26	.35	.34	.37	.48	.32	.35	.31	.32	.22	.21	.53				
W	.33	.34	.30	.46	.31	.35	.40	.64	.16	.24	.64	.41	.67	.78	.43	.32	.49	.43	.20	.19	.64	.55			
X	.18	.00	.16	.00	.17	.19	.07	.35	.35	.26	.70	.22	.55	.48	.00	.09	.15	.32	.15	.21	.18	.20	.55		
Y	.00	.00	.09	.00	.09	.10	.08	.18	.37	.37	.46	.12	.38	.30	.00	.00	.00	.08	.08	.56	.18	.21	.38	.63	
Z	.17	.43	.54	.48	.56	.27	.42	.17	.67	.42	.33	.53	.26	.00	.45	.25	.51	.30	.42	.40	.33	.10	.26	.48	.30

Figure 2.1 Confusion matrix for pairs of upper-case letters presented to BLIRNET.

2.3.2 Output Representation

Units in the output layer of BLIRNET have been trained to detect the presence of particular sequences of letters. These units, called *letter-cluster* units, respond to local arrangements of letters but are not sensitive to the larger context or the absolute retinal location of the letters. For example, there might be a unit that detects the sequence **NAT**, and it would become activated by words like **NATION** or **DOMINATE** presented in any location on the retina, though not by **BOTANY** or **GRANITE**, which contain **N**, **A**, and **T** but in a different order. Thus, the only location information retained at the output level consists of the relative positions of letters within a cluster. This representation

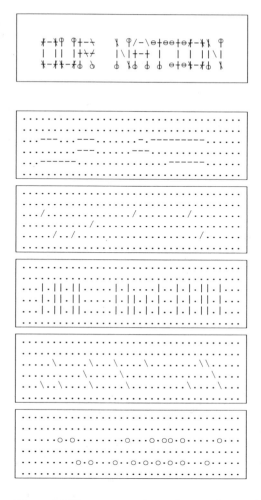

Figure 2.2 The top array shows the superimposed feature activations for a sample input, the phrase OUR NATION, positioned on the model's retina. The remaining arrays represent the individual retinotopic feature maps. Each character in an array represents the activity of a single unit. A "." indicates that the unit is off. A "−", "/", "|", "\" indicates activity of the corresponding unit in the 0°, 45°, 90°, 135° line segment map, respectively, and "o" indicates activity in the line segment terminator map.

contrasts with ones in which absolute letter position is encoded (e.g., the letter level of McClelland and Rumelhart's IA model). Recent psychological data favor a relative positional encoding (Humphreys, Evett, & Quinlan, 1990).

The letter-cluster units respond to triples of letters in four consecutive slots, either a sequence of three adjacent letters, such as NAT, or two adjacent letters and one nearby letter, such as NA_I or N_TI, where the underbar indicates that any single letter—but not an empty space—may appear in the corresponding position.[3] An asterisk is used to signify an empty space; for example, **N is an N with two spaces to its left. (Double asterisks are used simply to keep all names in the form *XXX*, *XX_X*, or *X_XX*.) Presentation of **NATION** should result in the activation of the following letter-cluster units: **N, **_A, *NA, *_AT, *N_T, NAT, N_TI, NA_I, ATI, A_IO, AT_O, TIO, T_ON, TI_N, ION, I_N*, IO_*, ON*, O_**, and N**. Note that the first two and last two letters of a string are explicitly encoded as such—here, **N, **_A, O_**, and N**. If a string has more than four letters, however, the positions of the string's inner letters can be determined only by examining the ensemble of letter-cluster activations and reconstructing the original arrangement of letters.

While strings with fewer than four letters can be packed into a single letter-cluster unit, these strings are still represented by the set of all appropriate units. Thus, short strings are in principle no different than longer strings: each is represented by a distributed *pattern* of activity across the letter-cluster units. Even isolated letters can be represented with triples of the form **X, *X*, and X**. Thus, the letter-cluster level of representation can substitute for both the letter and word levels found in many other models (e.g., McClelland & Rumelhart, 1981).

The letter-cluster coding scheme is analogous to Wickelgren's (1969) context-dependent allophone code used to represent the pronunciation of a word. The interesting thing about this scheme is that the unordered set of codes is generally sufficient to reconstruct the ordered components of the word. Thus, the set of units activated by a word uniquely determines that word: the representation is faithful. Pinker and Prince (1988; Prince & Pinker, 1988) point to several limitations of this representation; for instance, if the codes consist of triples, they are inadequate to represent strings containing repeated digraphs. However, the representation can generally be expanded to

---

[3] It is not critical to the behavior of the model that the units represent letter triples. The important property is that they encode chunks of information larger than isolated letters and smaller than entire words. Any sort of *conjunctive coding* (Smolensky, 1990) will suffice.

overcome this limitation; indeed, this is why I included clusters of the form _XX_X_ and _X_XX_ as well as consecutive letter triples. Further, the representation need not be constructed by hand; connectionist learning procedures can be used to discover representations of this sort that are guaranteed to be faithful (Mozer, 1989, 1990).

The letter-cluster coding scheme is interesting in another important respect. It allows for the simultaneous representation of multiple words, up to certain limits on the number of words and the amount of overlap among words. For example, if the letter-cluster units appropriate for the words **PINT** and **TOAD** are simultaneously activated, there is sufficient information in the letter-cluster activity pattern to reconstruct the identities of the two words. The problem of reconstruction becomes increasingly difficult with increasing similarity among words. For example, if **PINT** and **HUNT** are presented, only three units—*PI, PIN, and PI_T—can help determine which letter follows the **P**, whereas with **PINT** and **TOAD**, units such as P_NT and INT jointly provide supporting evidence. The problem of reconstruction also grows with the number of words, because large sets of words inevitably contain some overlap.

2.3.2.1 How Many Letter-Cluster Units are Necessary?

There are 56,966 possible letter clusters of the form described above. With this set of clusters, virtually any word of any length can be represented, an improvement over a local representation that would require one unit per word. The situation is better still. With only the 1,000 most common letter clusters, over 50% of all clusters that appear in English words are accounted for; with the top 6,000, over 95% of all clusters are accounted for when word frequency is taken into consideration (result based on Kučera & Francis, 1967). I therefore take 6,000 as the approximate number of clusters required in a full-scale simulation model.

This relatively small set of clusters is clearly capable of representing orthographically regular nonwords as well as English words. Of course, the ultimate validity of the letter-cluster representation is determined not by the number of strings than can be represented but by the ease with which later stages of processing can use the information contained in the representation. It turns out, as I discuss in chapters 3 and 5, that this distributed representation of a word can be as effective as a local representation. In fact, there are no "word units" to be found in MORSEL; they simply aren't necessary. The letter-cluster representation is far more flexible, given properties mentioned above.

2.3.3 Architecture

I now consider how BLIRNET achieves the desired input-output mapping, that is, the transformation from low-level position-specific features into high-level position-invariant features. The architecture to accomplish this transformation is diagramed in figure 2.3. BLIR-NET consists of a series of layers, the bottom layer (L_1) being the

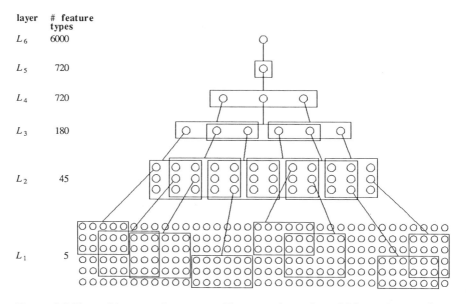

Figure 2.3 The architecture of BLIRNET. The network consists of 6 layers, arranged in retinotopic maps of decreasing dimensions. At each point within a map, indicated by a circle, there is one unit for each feature type. The number of feature types is shown in the column on the left. The receptive field of a unit is depicted by a box around its set of input units. To simplify the sketch, only some connections from L_1 to L_2 are shown. (Reprinted with permission from "Early parallel processing in reading: A connectionist approach" by M. C. Mozer, in M. Coltheart, Ed., *Attention and performance XII: The psychology of reading*, p. 89. Copyright 1987 by Erlbaum Associates.)

"retina" described previously and the top layer (L_6) the letter-cluster detectors. Intermediate layers (L_2-L_5) register successively higher-order features with decreasing spatial resolution. Each layer can be thought of as a retinotopic map of certain dimensions, with detectors for a certain number of feature types at each point in the map. L_1 has a 36×6 map with five *elementary* feature types. At each successive layer, the map dimensions decrease and the number of feature types increases. L_6 has a 1×1 map, meaning that there is no encoding of location, with approximately 6,000 feature types—the letter-cluster units.

The network is strictly feedforward: activations flow unidirectionally from the input to the output layer. Figure 2.3 also shows the pattern of connectivity among units. The general rule of connectivity is that each unit in layer $i+1$ (L_{i+1}) may potentially receive input from all units of all feature types in a local spatial region of layer i (L_i). This region is indicated by a box drawn around the L_i units and connected to the L_{i+1} unit.

The operation of the network can be divided into two distinct stages. The L_1-L_5 mapping aims to recode the input into a translation-invariant representation. The L_5-L_6 mapping then recodes this representation into the letter-cluster representation. The distinction between these two parts of the network is reflected in the fact that connection strengths between units are set differently in each part: in L_1-L_5, weights are prewired and fixed, whereas in L_5-L_6, weights are learned (see Widrow, Winter, & Baxter, 1987, for a related two-stage model).

2.3.4 Connection Strengths

The connections between L_1 and L_5 are set up such that units in each layer detect conjunctions of features from the layer below. The motivation underlying this mapping is roughly as follows: If units in L_{i+1} encode relations among n-tuples of features in L_i, spatial resolution in L_{i+1} can be cut by a factor of n without losing the information required to reconstruct the relative spatial arrangement of the L_i features. To illustrate this point, consider a two-layer network with two spatial positions in the lower layer (L_1) and one in the upper (L_2). In each L_1 position are 26 units, one for each letter of the alphabet; in L_2 are 26×26 units, one for each pairing of letters. By encoding conjunctions of letters in L_2, information about the ordering of letters is retained even without an explicit spatial representation.

The idea, then, is for L_1-L_5 to factor out explicit spatial information entirely, and instead maintain spatial information in terms of the relative positions of features. The problem with a straightforward realization of this idea is that the number of features needed at each level grows exponentially: given α_i features in L_i, α_i^n features are needed in L_{i+1} to encode all combinations of size n. However, exponential growth can be avoided if, instead of encoding each L_{i+1} feature by a single unit, each is represented as a distributed pattern of activity across the L_{i+1} units (see Hinton, McClelland, & Rumelhart, 1986, for a discussion of the advantages of distributed representations and coarse coding). In practice, I've found that the present architecture requires only on the order of $\alpha_i n^2 L_{i+1}$ units to do the job, a significant improvement over α_i^n.

What features are detected in L_2-L_5? The need for distributed representations precludes the existence of psychologically real features like "letters" and "letter pairs." In fact, BLIRNET goes to the opposite extreme: units in L_2-L_5 detect *random* conjunctions of features in the layer below. That is, the connection strengths between layers are actually chosen at random, under several constraints:

1. Connections are set such that all weights from L_i units of feature type u to L_{i+1} units of feature type v are identical. Thus, 5×45 different weights characterize the connections from L_1 to L_2. This constraint guarantees a uniform response across the spatial map: All units of a given feature type will respond identically to a given pattern appearing within their receptive field. Moreover, it guarantees a uniform response within a single unit's receptive field: a unit's response to a given pattern will not vary with location so long as the pattern lies entirely within the unit's receptive field. The group invariance theorem (Minsky & Papert, 1988) suggests that, given the present architecture and the desire to achieve translation invariance, there is no setting of the weights that will do better than to have the sort of uniform connectivity specified by this constraint.

2. The weights are either -1 (inhibitory connection), 0 (no connection), or $+1$ (excitatory connection).

3. At least one connection to each unit must be nonzero.

4. The density of nonzero (+1 or −1) connections between L_i and L_{i+1}, denoted ρ_i, is chosen to ensure that patterns of activity at higher layers do not become too distributed and that most information is preserved from one layer to the next. ρ_1 was .348, ρ_2 was .139, ρ_3 was .067, and ρ_4 was .065. These densities were arrived under the presupposition that information in the L_i representation is preserved to the extent that the conjunction of each pair of L_i features is detected by at least one L_{i+1} unit and that each L_{i+1} unit responds to as few such conjunctions as possible.[4] Thus, what one seeks is the *lowest* density of nonzero connections to ensure that nearly all L_i feature pairs are within the receptive field of at least one L_{i+1} unit.

If there are α_i L_i and α_{i+1} L_{i+1} feature types, then the probability that a given L_{i+1} unit contains a given pair of L_i units in its receptive field is

$$\frac{C^{\alpha_i-2}_{\alpha_i\rho_i-2}}{C^{\alpha_i}_{\alpha_i\rho_i}} = \frac{\alpha_i\rho_i(\alpha_i\rho_i-1)}{\alpha_i(\alpha_i-1)}.$$

The probability that no L_{i+1} unit contains a given pair is simply

$$\left[1 - \frac{\alpha_i\rho_i(\alpha_i\rho_i-1)}{\alpha_i(\alpha_i-1)}\right]^{\alpha_{i+1}}.$$

Setting this probability to an arbitrarily small desired value, say .05, one can solve for the minimum value of ρ_i and obtain the densities listed above.

Because of constraint 1, the mapping from one layer to the next is extremely "sloppy" or "blurry" in that a single L_{i+1} unit is unable to detect the relative arrangement of L_i features within its receptive

---

[4] Marr (1969) uses a similar criterion to determine the optimal size of the codon representation in his model of the cerebellum. Note that while this is a necessary condition for information to be preserved, it is not sufficient.

field; it is only able to detect the total number of tokens of a given feature type. Given this pattern of connectivity, L_2-L_5 units might respond when, for example, there are more tokens of type u within their receptive fields than tokens of type v, or when the total number of tokens of type u, v, and w exceeds a threshold.

The aim of the L_1-L_5 mapping is to construct a translation-invariant representation. However, the simple rules of connectivity stated above do not permit the network to achieve this goal exactly. The L_5 representation varies somewhat as a stimulus is moved across the retina because in different locations, different portions of the stimulus fall into different receptive fields. Due to constraint 1, however, the variation cannot be extremely large, and hence it is reasonable to suppose that some aspects of the L_5 representation—*cues* contained in the representation—ought to be translation invariant. The weights between L_5 and L_6 are adjusted with the aim of discovering these cues. The weight-training procedure will be discussed in section 2.4.1.

2.3.5 System Dynamics

L_1 units are turned on with an activation level of 1 if the corresponding feature is present on the retina, or 0 otherwise. L_2-L_6 units are set according to the activation rule

$$b_{vij}^{l} = f \left(\sum_{x \in X_{ij}^{l}} \sum_{y \in Y_{ij}^{l}} \sum_{u} w_{uv}^{l} b_{uxy}^{l-1} \right),$$

where b_{vij}^{l} is the activity level of the layer l unit in location (i, j) of feature type v (the b stands for BLIRNET), w_{uv}^{l} is the strength of connection from feature type u in layer $l-1$ to feature type v in layer l, and X_{ij}^{l} and Y_{ij}^{l} indicate the spatial extent of connectivity. The function f relates a unit's net input to its activation level:

$$f(net) = \frac{\dfrac{1}{1+e^{-\kappa_l net}} - \phi_l}{\Phi_l - \phi_l} .$$

This is an S-shaped sigmoid function whose range can be scaled by the constants Φ_l and ϕ_l. These constants were selected for each layer of BLIRNET so that the response of L_2-L_5 units ranged from approximately −1 to 1, and the response of L_6 units from 0 to 1. The steepness of the logistic function can be adjusted by the constant κ_l. Values of κ_l that are large relative to the domain of f result in highly nonlinear threshold-like behavior, whereas small values result in nearly linear behavior. Thus, for large κ_l, one obtains units that turn on if and only if the net input surpasses a threshold, and for small κ_l, units whose output is proportional to the net input. κ_l was selected for each layer so that units in L_2 behaved essentially as binary-threshold units, and successive layers yielded increasingly linear behavior. A key principle of BLIRNET is embodied in this choice of values: *Nonlinearities are important in the lowest layers of the network to encode local relationships among neighboring features, but linearity is important in higher layers to allow the superposition of activations from different words* (cf. Cavanaugh, 1984). This principle is BLIRNET's solution to the linearity-nonlinearity dilemma raised in section 2.2.

Values of κ_l, Φ_l, and ϕ_l are presented in table 2.1. Let me note several points concerning these values.

- One might have expected κ_l to decrease monotonically with l. However, the effect of this constant depends not only on its magnitude but also on the range of values spanned by the net input (*net*) which in turn is dependent on the unit's receptive field size.

- κ_5 was set such that all *net* inputs to L_5 fell within the linear range of the sigmoid function. Due to the linearity of L_5 units, there would have been no advantage to increasing the number of feature types from L_4 to L_5, because no additional information could have been preserved by doing so. Consequently, the number of L_5 feature types was 720, the same as L_4.

Table 2.1 Activation Function Parameters

layer	κ_l	Φ_l	ϕ_l
2	3.890	0.980	0.500
3	0.244	0.900	0.500
4	0.347	0.800	0.500
5	0.085	0.600	0.500
6	1.000	1.000	0.000

- Using the back propagation algorithm (Rumelhart, Hinton, & Williams, 1986), it is possible to derive a rule for adjusting κ_l in order to optimize performance ($\Delta\kappa_l \sim -\partial E/\partial\kappa_l$). It would be interesting to see whether such a rule would indeed select values of κ_l that yield increasingly linear behavior at successive layers of the network. I have not conducted this simulation.

2.3.6 Comments on the Architecture

Before settling upon the architecture and parameters described above, I explored a variety of alternatives (subject to computational constraints that limited the exploration). These alternatives included: different receptive field sizes; weights that decreased as a function of distance from the receptive field center; weights that were normalized to equate excitatory and inhibitory potentials, as well as to equate potentials across units; continuous as opposed to integer weights; and activation levels that ranged from 0 to 1 instead of -1 to 1. These alternatives were optimized according to the criteria that L_5 yielded: (1) as nearly as possible the same activity pattern when a given letter string was presented in various positions, and (2) as distinct as possible patterns when different strings were presented. This was measured by presenting a single string in various positions (*position varying* or *PV* trials) and presenting various strings in a single position (*identity varying* or *IV* trials). The resulting L_5 activity vector for each was recorded. Averaging the PV vectors, a *prototype* vector was obtained, and the angle between the prototype and each PV and IV vector was found. A z-statistic was then computed on the difference of the mean PV and IV angles (Winer, 1962, p. 36). The larger this statistic was, the more similar the PV vectors were to the prototype and the more distinct the IV vectors were from the prototype, a good indication of how easy it would be for a network to learn to discriminate PV trials (all having the same identity) from IV trials (all having other identities). Thus, in considering two alternative architectures, the one yielding the largest z-statistic was selected. The point of this digression is simply to state that the design of BLIRNET was not happenstance but involved an empirical study of the alternatives.

Nonetheless, the precise architecture of BLIRNET is not critical and surely does not affect the qualitative behavior of the model. One extreme constraint on the architecture comes from the fact that translation-invariant pattern recognition cannot be realized in a two-layer network of binary-threshold units (Minsky & Papert, 1988); thus, all solutions to the problem require at least one hidden layer. However, the exact number of layers used is not a critical parameter of the architecture. I've chosen six to allow for a smooth collapsing of the retinal map. Similarly, the exact number of feature types per layer and the particular connectivity pattern used are fairly arbitrary decisions.

It is interesting and suggestive that BLIRNET's hierarchical layered architecture and localized receptive fields are consistent with the qualitative neurophysiology and neuroanatomy of visual cortex (Crick & Asanuma, 1986; Van Essen & Maunsell, 1983). Other connectionist approaches to transformation-invariant visual recognition have also made use of essentially the same architecture (Fukushima & Miyake, 1982; Le Cun, et al., 1990; Sandon & Uhr, 1988; Uhr, 1987; Zemel, Mozer, & Hinton, 1989, 1990). A comparison of Fukushima & Miyake's *neocognitron* and BLIRNET is particularly illuminating, although the neocognitron was designed primarily for achieving invariance under pattern distortion, not for the recognition of multiple objects. The neocognitron is also a layered architecture, but each layer consists of two sets of units, *simple* and *complex* cells. The simple cells recognize location-specific patterns and the complex cells generalize across location. Such an architecture can yield fully translation-invariant representations, in contrast to the only approximate representation yielded by L_1-L_5 of BLIRNET, but requires extreme specificity in its connectivity as well as a far greater number of units and connections. Similar statements can be made for the other hierarchical connectionist architectures.

One important dimension along which the various hierarchical architectures differ is whether the lower layers are hardwired or whether their connections are adjusted via learning. This was not a decision I faced at the time with BLIRNET, primarily because connectionist learning algorithms for multi-layered nets had not come into practical use. However, there are good reasons for hardwiring the lower layers of BLIRNET. First, because the network is not specifically programmed for letter and word recognition, it promises to generalize well to the recognition of other two-dimensional shapes (see section 7.2.2). Second, allowing adaptable connections only in the last layer of BLIRNET greatly improves the convergence rate of learning; learning in deeply layered networks with back propagation can be very slow. Third, to achieve translation invariance, it is important for the network to detect the same features uniformly across the retina. If the connections in the lower layers are adaptable, there must be some means of enforcing this uniformity. In the neocognitron, for instance, connections are modified during training using a highly non-local weight updating scheme: the changes to one set of weights are broadcast to all other units of the same type. This sort of an updating scheme violates the connectionist spirit and is neurally implausible. In contrast, while the present architecture does require the replication of weights across each retinotopic map, these weights are hardwired and are based on simple rules of connectivity. It is not difficult to imagine genetic instructions to wire cells of one type to cells of another type. Alternatively, simple wiring patterns of the sort required here can be given developmental rather than genetic explanation (e.g., Linsker, 1988).

Despite the advantages of prewiring the lower layers of BLIRNET, I would suggest to others interested in implementing a similar model that they opt for back propagation learning in the lower layers, with additional weight constraints to ensure the uniformity of feature detection across the retina. Allowing learning should not affect the qualitative behavior of the system, but it should improve its quantitative performance: It is highly unlikely that the network designer will be as clever as back propagation in selecting intermediate features.

2.4 Training Methodology

2.4.1 Word Simulation

A full-scale implementation of BLIRNET is a costly proposition. While the total number of units in the network is only 12,660, the computational cost of a simulation is related to the number of *connections*, of which there are approximately 218,000 between L_1 and L_5 and 4,320,000 between L_5 and L_6. Consequently, it was necessary to scale down the simulation in some fashion. The method I chose was to reduce the number of letter-cluster (L_6) units. Instead of the 6,000 letter-cluster units I had assumed previously, only 540 were used—the 540 most frequently occurring clusters in English weighted by relative word frequency (as determined from the Kučera & Francis, 1967, corpus). This reduced the number of L_5-L_6 connections tenfold, and the total number of connections in BLIRNET to approximately 606,800.

What words can be formed from these clusters? Nine hundred and nine words were found which had the property that at least 70% of their clusters were among this set. The words ranged in length from 2 to 10 letters, with a mean of 6.2. The number of letter clusters per word ranged from 6 to 26, with a mean of 15.3. Each cluster appeared in at least one word, and the most frequent cluster in 295 words; the mean number of words per cluster was 24.8.

Using these words as stimuli, BLIRNET was trained to activate the appropriate clusters in response to a word appearing on its retina. Due to a slight decrease in sensitivity around the edges of L_1, words were not allowed to lie in the top or bottom row or in the three leftmost or rightmost columns. For an n-letter word, these constraints still permitted $62-6n$ possible locations.[5] There were a total of 22,626 word-location combinations.

On each training trial, a word was selected at random from the stimulus set and presented in a random location on L_1; activations were allowed to flow through BLIRNET to L_6; and the L_5 activity pattern was then associated with the word's letter clusters in L_6 by adjusting the weights w_{uv}^6 using a slightly modified form of the LMS rule (Widrow & Hoff, 1960):

$$\Delta w_{uv}^6 = \eta b_v^{6*} (1-b_v^{6*})(d_v^6-b_v^6)b_u^5,$$

where d_v^6 is the desired activation level of letter-cluster unit v—1 or 0, η is the learning rate, and

$$b_v^{6*} = \begin{cases} .1 & \text{if } b_v^6 < .1 \\ b_v^6 & \text{if } .1 \leq b_v^6 \leq .9 \\ .9 & \text{if } b_v^6 > .9. \end{cases}$$

---

[5] There are two legal vertical positions: rows 2-4 and rows 3-5. The number of legal horizontal positions depends on the length of the word. The word must begin to the right of column 3 and to the left of column $34-3n$, for a total of $31-3n$ legal positions. Taking the product of legal vertical and horizontal positions, one obtains $62-6n$.

This rule results in increased activity of the appropriate clusters and decreased activity of the inappropriate clusters on future presentations of the word. With appropriate choice of η, it is guaranteed to converge eventually on a set of weights that will perform the desired L_5-L_6 mapping with minimum squared error (Widrow & Hoff, 1960; Widrow & Stearns, 1985).

Initially, η was fixed at .0002 and was increased to .001 following 100 training passes. The initial values of w_{uv}^6 were chosen from a normal distribution with a mean of zero, and were normalized so that the sum of the positive weights equaled 1 and the sum of the negative weights -1. This led to an expected output of .5 for untrained letter-cluster units.

The training procedure was repeated for each of the 909 words in the corpus for approximately 300 passes through the corpus. Mean square error decreased steadily and in fact had not reached an asymptotic level after 300 passes (272,700 training trials). While it does not appear that the error will ever fall to zero, performance of the system is presently stable and should show few qualitative effects with further training.

2.4.2 Letter Simulation

In a separate simulation, BLIRNET was trained to recognize individual letters. BLIRNET's output consisted of 26 units of the form *X*. On each training trial, between one and three letters were selected at random and placed in random locations on the retina, with the constraint that letters were not allowed to overlap. Letters were presented in the same range of horizontal positions as the words but in only one vertical position (the top of the letter being in row two). This permitted over thirty million possible stimulus patterns. Nonetheless, the network was able to learn quite rapidly; the results to be presented were obtained after only 25,000 training trials.

This simulation could just as well have been part of the larger one. That is, a single network could have been constructed with 540 letter-cluster units plus the 26 individual letter units, instead of two distinct networks. Due to software considerations, however, it was easier to separate the two. Combining the two networks might slightly increase the difficulty of the learning task, because BLIRNET must learn not to activate the letter units when words are presented, and vice versa.

However, because the output units are not directly connected to each other and the lower level weights are fixed, the letter and word learning tasks are basically independent.

In the remainder of this chapter, I discuss the results of the word simulation; I will refer to the letter simulation in following chapters.

2.5 Simulation Results

2.5.1 Response to Single Words

Figure 2.4 shows a sample output of the system: the response to **BORED** presented on the retina with upper-left corner in location (17,3). The clusters of **BORED** (the *target activations*) are printed in upper case, all others (the *spurious activations*) in lower case. Spurious activations with activation levels below .05 have been omitted. The height of a cluster on the graph indicates its activity level, a value from zero to one. The clusters are spread out along the x-axis to

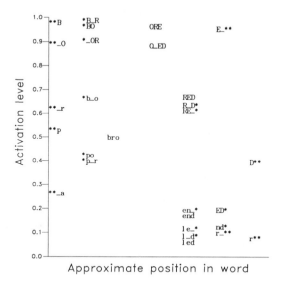

Figure 2.4 Letter-cluster activations in response to BORED with upper-left corner in location (17,3). (Reprinted with permission from "Early parallel processing in reading: A connectionist approach" by M. C. Mozer, in M. Coltheart, Ed., *Attention and performance XII: The psychology of reading*, p. 94. Copyright 1987 by Erlbaum Associates.)

represent the approximate position of a cluster within the word. Note that this dimension is not intrinsic to the letter-cluster representation; values along this dimension were manually selected for this particular example to simplify viewing of the clusters.

Figure 2.4 is typical of the letter-cluster activity pattern produced in response to a word. Most target clusters are highly active, at least relative to the spurious activations. The types of spurious activations are also typical. Generally, spurious activations fall into four categories:

1. *substitution errors*— clusters that would be appropriate if *one* letter of the word were substituted for another visually similar letter, such as **P** in position 1 (**P, *PO, *P_R) or **L** in position 3 (LED, L_D*, LE_*);

2. *insertion errors*—clusters that would be appropriate if a letter or two were inserted into the word, such as sticking an **N** between the **E** and the **D** (END, EN_*, ND*);

3. *deletion errors*—clusters that would be appropriate if a letter or two were deleted from the word, such as dropping the **ED** (R**) or just the **D** (R_**); and

4. *transposition errors*—clusters that would be appropriate if two adjacent letters of a word were transposed, such as the **O** and **R** (BRO, *B_O, **_R).

The response to **BORED** in other locations is quite similar; BLIRNET has clearly learned to recognize words independent of their retinal position. In fact, BLIRNET has even *generalized* to novel positions. This could be tested by presenting words near the edges of the retina, such that the word fell in the top row, bottom row, or leftmost or rightmost three columns. During training words were never presented in these exact positions, yet BLIRNET still produced reasonable responses.

The response to longer words is as accurate as to shorter words, indicating that the number of simultaneously presented letters is not a limiting factor. Figure 2.5 presents an example of a longer word, **NOMINATION**.

A more formal analysis of BLIRNET's performance was conducted by presenting each of the 909 words in five random locations and then

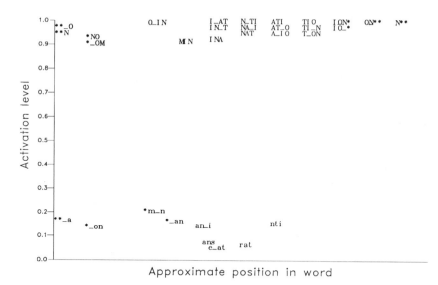

Figure 2.5 Letter-cluster activations in response to **NOMINATION** with upper-left corner in location (4,2).

collecting statistics on BLIRNET's responses. Starting with the simplest measure of performance, the mean activation level of target clusters was .64, whereas the mean activation of nontarget clusters was only .01. The summed activity of all target clusters was on average 9.95 per word, compared to only 4.25 for (the nearly 540) nontargets. Further, only 1.5 nontarget clusters per word had activation levels larger than the mean activation level of target clusters for that word.

To verify the breakdown of spurious activations suggested above, spurious activations in the 909 × 5 trial sample were analyzed. Only clusters whose activity level rose above .05 were considered; there were 101,399 such clusters in the sample. Each spurious activation was classified into one of the four error categories listed above in addition to a category for errors that could be interpreted as a combination of two primitive error types (e.g., both a deletion and a substitution error, such as activation of ER* in response to **FASTENS**), and finally, a catch-all category for other errors. The distribution of errors is shown in table 2.2. Although one cannot verify that the "combination" errors are indeed a combination of several primitive errors, as opposed to spurious noise, the distribution of errors nonetheless

Table 2.2 Distribution of Spurious Cluster Activations

Error Type	% of Errors
Substitution Errors	32.09
Insertion Errors	7.36
Deletion Errors	19.80
Transposition Errors	12.44
Combination Errors	14.31
Other Errors	14.00

strongly supports the classification in terms of four primitive error types.[6]

Shifting the focus from words to letter clusters, an important question concerns how good a letter-cluster unit is at discriminating words that contain the cluster from words that do not. At best, the cluster will always be active when a word containing it is presented and inactive otherwise; at worst, the cluster's activity level will have no relation to the word that was presented. A measure of discriminability was obtained in the following manner. The mean activity of each cluster was computed over trials in which it was a target and trials in which it was a nontarget. Taking these means to represent the probability of the unit being active when the cluster is contained in a word and the probability of being active when not contained in a word, respectively, an index of detectability of the cluster, d', was computed (Green & Swets, 1966). Over all clusters, the average d' was 2.83. Individual d' values are presented in appendix B along with the number of words in which each cluster appears. Because d' is measured in standard deviation units, d' values above 2 indicate a high degree of discriminability.

Admittedly, these statistics do not give the whole story because even a few spurious activations might allow an alternative interpretation of the letter-cluster activity pattern. Chapter 3 deals with the issue of interpreting the letter-cluster outputs.

---

[6] The psychological plausibility of this error distribution cannot be ascertained directly. Spurious activations do not strictly correspond to errors produced by human observers. However, spurious activations such as these allow BLIRNET to account for a variety of human error data (see chapter 6), and thus are validated indirectly.

2.5.2 Response to Unfamiliar Strings

Is BLIRNET able to generalize from the set of words on which it was trained to unfamiliar strings? Figure 2.6 shows the response to one unfamiliar string, the pseudoword **LING**. BLIRNET has successfully transferred its experience with strings like **LINE** and **RING** to **LING**.

To quantify the extent to which generalization of this sort occurred, 250 words not in the training set were found that had at least 65% of their letter clusters among the 540 known to BLIRNET. Presenting each of these words in a random location on the retina, performance statistics were computed. The mean activation level of target clusters was .47, whereas the mean activation of nontarget clusters was only .01. The mean d' for all clusters contained in the test set was 1.87. Although performance on this novel set of words is respectable, it is not as good as performance obtained on the training set. Fortunately, this decrement in performance is not a basic failing of the model; one can attribute a large part of the difficulty with unfamiliar strings to the training regimen. For BLIRNET to learn to recognize a string in terms

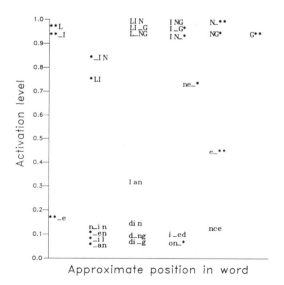

Figure 2.6 The response to LING in location (13,2). (Reprinted with permission from "Early parallel processing in reading: A connectionist approach" by M. C. Mozer, in M. Coltheart, Ed., *Attention and performance XII: The psychology of reading*, p. 94. Copyright 1987 by Erlbaum Associates.)

of its letter clusters, it must learn to recognize each letter cluster independent of the context in which it is embedded. This is relatively easy if, during training, each cluster is presented in a variety of contexts. If, however, a cluster appears in only a small number of contexts, it may be logically impossible to separate the cluster from the context. Consider an example. Suppose BLIRNET was instructed to associate the three words **HELLO**, **YELLOW**, and **ELLIPSE** with cluster unit number 423. (Remember, there is nothing intrinsic to the cluster unit itself to indicate what conjunction of letters is to be detected.) That the cluster to be detected is ELL can readily be induced. If given only the first two words, however, there is no way for BLIRNET to know whether the target cluster is ELL or LLO or even E_LO. Consequently, the letter-cluster unit that has been *labeled* ELL may actually be detecting some strange combination of the letters **E**, **L**, **L**, and **O**, and would respond inappropriately to unfamiliar strings. Suggestions are presented in section 2.5.3 for overcoming training deficits that result in such behavior.

To the extent that BLIRNET does learn to identify letter clusters independent of their context, it is able to recognize arbitrary strings, even ones containing few familiar clusters, e.g., **CTNR**. In cases like this, letter-cluster units denoting the starting and ending letters of the string become activated, **C, **_T, N_**, R**, and in this particular example, also *C_N and T_R*, which were clusters known to BLIRNET. Thus, strings with unfamiliar orthographic structure can be recognized. Because the letter-cluster representation supports position-specific encodings of only the outermost four letters, orthographically irregular strings of length five or more can not be faithfully represented or recognized in their entirety.

2.5.3 Response to Pairs of Words

BLIRNET was designed with the computational goal of being able to process single words, as well as unfamiliar letter strings, in arbitrary locations. The preceding results indicate that BLIRNET achieves this goal. Another goal—again, from a purely computational perspective—was for BLIRNET to be able to process several words simultaneously. (The direct psychological evidence that people can do this is described in section 6.1.1; additionally, chapter 6 provides indirect evidence by virtue of the fact that MORSEL, which assumes that parallel processing is possible, is able to parsimoniously explain a vast body of psychological data.)

BLIRNET does a reasonable job of analyzing several words at once. Figure 2.7 shows the response when two words, ANT and DEN, are simultaneously presented. To be honest, BLIRNET's performance on this example is somewhat better than average. As with unfamiliar strings, the difficulty with multiple words lies partly in the nature of the training regimen: Because BLIRNET was trained on single words, it has no experience in recognizing clusters of one word in the context of other words. Consequently, multiple-word presentations give rise to novel contexts and are troublesome.

There are several potential solutions to this problem. One is simply to increase the size of BLIRNET's training set in the hope that each cluster will then be seen in a greater number of contexts. A second solution is to include some training trials in which multiple words are presented. Perhaps the best solution, however, is to train BLIRNET with noise added to the background. That is, lay each stimulus word

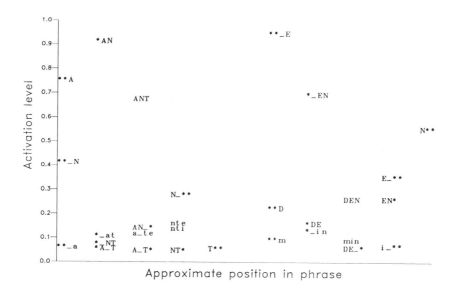

Figure 2.7 The response to ANT in location (8,3) and DEN in location (20,3). (Reprinted with permission from "Early parallel processing in reading: A connectionist approach" by M. C. Mozer, in M. Coltheart, Ed., *Attention and performance XII: The psychology of reading*, p. 95. Copyright 1987 by Erlbaum Associates.)

down on BLIRNET's retina, and then randomly turn on a small number of L_1 units in the outlying region. BLIRNET will then have to recognize each cluster in the face of noise. Given this situation, performance will be enhanced if BLIRNET learns to ignore all information in the outlying region—the region in which other words might appear. Thus, noise can actually focus training on the relevant information and thereby assist in the recognition of multiple words.

Due to computational limitations, it was impossible to fully implement any of these solutions. I did, however, carry out a small-scale investigation of the second solution—namely, to train BLIRNET on *pairs* of words. I selected 44 three- and four-letter words from the original training set and presented pairs of words drawn randomly from this sample. The words were adjacent to one another on a line, separated by a three-column gap, with the position chosen at random. There are 1,892 possible ordered word pairs, and taking the various retinal positions into account, 28,036 possible visual patterns.

The previously trained network was used, and three thousand additional training trials were then run using the word pairs. This is a small number of trials considering the many combinations of words and positions. In fact, each pair was presented on average only 1.6 times, and only 10.7% of the possible visual patterns were ever viewed. Further, it was a small enough number of trials that performance on single words was nearly unaffected.

There was, however, a dramatic effect on pairs of words. Performance was evaluated both before and after word-pair training in the following manner. One thousand word pairs were randomly generated and presented to BLIRNET. The measure of performance computed was the sum squared error—the same measure used to adjust the weights. Before training, error was 16.8 with a standard deviation of 4.37; after training, it was cut nearly in half, to 9.87 with a standard deviation of 4.31. (Unfortunately, the weight matrix was deleted before other, more informative, performance statistics could be computed.) Figure 2.8 shows an example of the outcome of this training regimen.

2.5.4 Discussion of Simulation Results

Does BLIRNET have the potential of recognizing letter clusters, independent of their absolute location on the retina and of the context

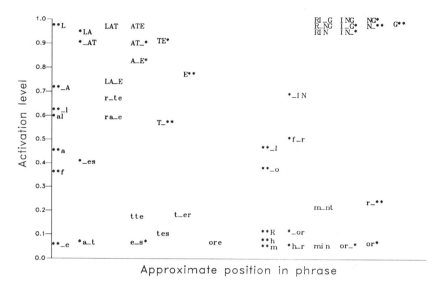

Figure 2.8 The response to LATE in location (7,2) and RING in location (21,2) following word-pair training. Prior to word-pair training, performance on LATE RING was no better than on ANT DEN (figure 2.7).

in which they are embedded? The simulation experiments reported above answer this critical question with a definitive "yes." Thus, the L_5 activity pattern appears to contain invariant cues for particular letter clusters, and the learning procedure is able to discover these cues. Because the activation of one letter-cluster unit does not directly interact with the activation of another, BLIRNET is likely to scale well to a larger training set and a more complete set of letter clusters. The current implementation with only 540 letter-cluster units should not be seen as restricting the generality of the results.

Nonetheless, in principle there are limitations on the number of simultaneous words that can be accurately processed. BLIRNET contains nonlinearities that, as discussed in section 2.2, cause interactions among simultaneously presented words. One clear case of such interactions can be seen when, for instance, ANT is moved very close to DEN. The words start to run together: the T_EN unit becomes active and T** and **D less so. Other effects of the nonlinearities are not nearly as obvious; two words may be presented and clusters appropriate for an altogether different word may become active. Reducing nonlinearities will not solve the problem because doing so decreases accuracy of letter localization within a word, and hence increases transposition errors such as **_A or TAN in response to ANT. Thus, the conflicting demands for linear and nonlinear behavior in the system place bounds both on how much information may pass through the system accurately at any time and the localization of individual letters. I show in chapter 6 that these limitations result in errors that the human perceptual system also makes.

3 The Pull-Out Network

The output of BLIRNET is difficult to interpret. As a typical example in figure 3.1a shows, letter-cluster activations are quite noisy. Clusters of the presented word are often not highly active; other clusters are often activated spuriously. What one would hope for is an activity pattern such as that depicted in figure 3.1b in which all target clusters of the presented word have activation levels of 1.0, all nontarget clusters 0.0. Although the clusters in figure 3.1a may have several interpretations, figure 3.1b affords only one.

Interpretation of BLIRNET's output is also made difficult by the fact that when several words are presented simultaneously, activations from one word mask activations from other words. Consider figure 3.2a, which shows the response to a pair of words, CON and MAN. In the figure, clusters of CON have been superimposed on clusters of MAN, unlike the figures showing the response to word pairs in chapter 2 in which clusters of the two words were spatially separated. Figure 3.2a is a more realistic depiction of the available information at the output of BLIRNET, in that letter-cluster units do not explicitly code to which word they belong and all positional information which might be used to straighten matters out has been discarded. To see MAN in this pattern of activity, one must disregard not only spurious clusters but also the clusters of CON. Interpretation of such outputs would be considerably simplified if the pattern in figure 3.2a could be reduced to that in figure 3.2b, and perhaps an analogous pattern focusing on CON.

To summarize, when single words are presented it is essential to clean up the noise—i.e., suppress inconsistent activations and enhance the consistent; and when multiple words are presented, it is essential to disentangle activations of one word from another. The process of cleaning up and disentangling the hodgepodge of activations is achieved by the pull-out network (henceforth, *PO net*). Figures 3.1b and 3.2b are examples of the desired behavior of the PO net.

(a)

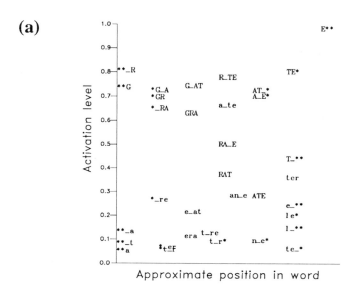

(b)

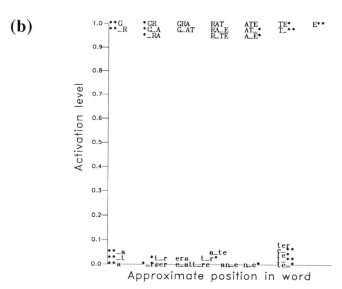

Figure 3.1 (a) The response to **GRATE** in location (10,2); (b) The response one might have hoped for.

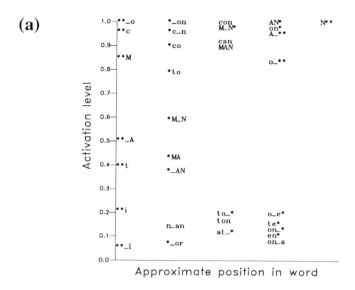

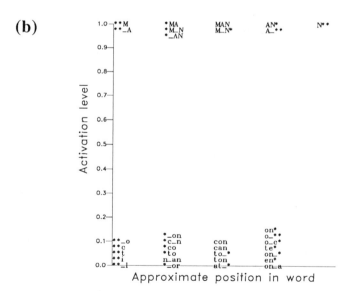

Figure 3.2 (a) The response to CON in location (4,3) and MAN in location (16,3). Clusters of MAN are printed in upper case. (b) The response one might have hoped for, if MAN were the item of interest.

To frame the job of the PO net more generally, think of the letter-cluster representation as a memory capable of holding on to several words at once. The PO net is a mechanism that allows retrieval of words one at a time from the memory. The fact that the original representation of each word is noisy poses no additional problem for the network because retrieval of one word in the presence of others can be likened to retrieval of one word in the presence of noise. Thus, the noise-suppression aspect of the PO net is intrinsic to the task, whether the activations produced by BLIRNET are noisy or not. Touretzky and Hinton (1985, 1988; Touretzky, 1986) have independently developed the notion of a PO net for the purpose of retrieval from short-term memory, and Hinton and Shallice (1989) have used a similar clean-up mechanism in their model of deep dyslexia for recovering information in a noisy signal.

3.1 PO Net Design

The PO net is composed of two sets of units (figure 3.3). The *PO net letter-cluster units* (hereafter, *PLC units*) are in one-to-one correspondence with the letter-cluster units of BLIRNET (hereafter, *BLC units*) and represent the orthography or spelling pattern of a word. The *semantic units* represent the semantics or meaning of a word. Each BLC unit excites its corresponding PLC unit, causing the pattern of letter-cluster activity in BLIRNET to be copied to the PO net. Interactions then take place among the PLC and semantic units to select a set of letter clusters that together form an internally consistent spelling pattern, and, if the spelling pattern corresponds to an English word, a set of semantic features that indicate the meaning of the word.[1] In the next two sections, I describe the role that orthographic and semantic knowledge play in the pull-out process.

3.1.1 The Role of Orthographic Knowledge

A pattern of activity over the PLC units is said to be *consistent* if the active units exactly correspond to a letter string—that is, if all letter

---

[1] In its present form, the PO net has been designed to recover single words and letter strings, but it would not be difficult to modify the network to pull out overlearned phrases as unitary entities. More on this in section 3.1.4.

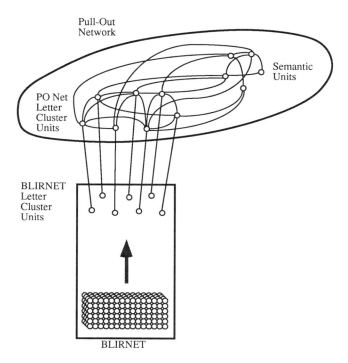

Figure 3.3 The PO net and its relation to BLIRNET. The PO net is composed of two sets of units: letter-cluster units and semantic units.

clusters of the string are active and no others are. The activity patterns in figures 3.1b and 3.2b satisfy this definition of consistency. The key to the PO net's operation is specifying what makes a set consistent, which is done in terms of pairwise relations among the letter clusters. Some pairs are likely to fit together within a single word (e.g., GRA and RAT), while others are relatively unlikely (e.g., G_AT and E_AT). Generally, one cannot state in absolute terms that a given pair will either fit or not. For instance, GRA and RAT do not go together in the word **GRADE**; and although it happens that no word contains both G_AT and E_AT, it is conceivable that such a word might exist, e.g., **GRATEWATER**. Thus, there are many weak constraints on how the letter clusters might be assembled to form words. A consistent set of letter clusters is one that best satisfies these weak constraints. That is, a set is consistent to the extent that each cluster within the set fits well with the rest and no cluster outside the set fits well.

The PO net attempts to discover sets of letter clusters that, roughly speaking, maximize consistency. It performs this computation through simple excitatory and inhibitory interactions among the units. I now describe the specifics of these interactions.

Two letter clusters are said to be *neighbors* if they can be aligned so as to overlap on two letters or delimiters ("*"), not necessarily adjacent. Some examples of neighbors are: GRA and RAT (overlap on **R** and **A**), G_AT and E_AT (**A** and **T**), RA_E and R_TE (**R** and **E**), **G and *GR (* and **G**), and T_** and L_** (* and *). Two clusters that both contain delimiters are neighbors only if the matching delimiters correspond in terms of the relative string position: E** and A** are neighbors, whereas E** and **A are not (delimiters in E** specify the end of the word, delimiters in **A the beginning); T_** and TE* are neighbors, whereas T_** and T_R* are not (if the two Ts are aligned, the matching delimiters specify different positions relative to the end of the word). The don't care symbol ("_") is not counted in determining overlap; thus, *_RA and T_RE are not neighbors, even though they do share _ and **R**.

Two neighbors are said to be *compatible* if, when aligned, they do not conflict in any letter position. Some examples of compatible neighbors are: G_AT and RAT, RAT and ATE, **G and **_R, AT_* and TE*. Other neighbors are *incompatible*, such as G_AT and E_AT, GRA and ERA, **G and **A, T_** and L_**, and TE* and TE_* (remember, "_" implies a nondelimiter).

Based on this classification of compatible and incompatible neighbors, four connection types were allowed:

1. *excitatory*—between compatible neighbors.

2. *inhibitory*—between incompatible neighbors.

3. **-excitatory*—a special case of excitatory connection where both letter clusters contain delimiters and the presence of one cluster necessitates the presence of another, e.g., *GR implies **G and **_R. Note that these connections are not symmetric: neither **G nor **_R alone implies *GR. Thus, while the units are mutually supportive, the connection from *GR to **G is *-excitatory but the connection in the other direction is merely excitatory.

4. **-inhibitory*—a special case of inhibitory connection where both letter clusters contain delimiters, in which case the

presence of one cluster precludes the presence of the other, e.g., *GR and **_E, E** and R**. These connections are symmetric.

The *-excitatory and *-inhibitory connections treat clusters representing the outermost letters of words apart from clusters representing inner letters. This is justified on the logical grounds that the outermost letters of words are unique. That is, it can be stated unequivocally that a word whose first two letters are **GR** must have **G** as its first letter, or that a word ending in **E** cannot also end in **R**. No such assertions can be made concerning inner letters: a word containing the string **RAT** may or may not also contain **ATE**. Some of the connections involving the clusters of **GRATE** are shown in table 3.1.

Each connection type has a different weight associated with it. The excitatory connections must have positive weights, inhibitory negative. The *-connections should have weights of a greater magnitude. I determined the magnitudes of the weights, as well as other parameters of the PO net, by informal experimentation. My objective was to find values that yielded fairly stable behavior regardless of the length of the word being processed. Fortunately, the qualitative behavior of the PO net is relatively insensitive to the precise weight values. The weights for the connections between PLC units are listed in the first four lines of table 3.2. In rare circumstances, multiple connections are possible between clusters. For example, LEE and LLE can be viewed as inhibitory if the **L** of LEE is aligned with the first **L** of LLE but excitatory if aligned with the second **L**. The net connection strength used in such cases was simply the sum of the individual connection strengths.

Table 3.2 PO Net Connection Strengths

Connection Type	Value
PLC-to-PLC excitatory	.06
PLC-to-PLC inhibitory	−.18
PLC-to-PLC *-excitatory	.24
PLC-to-PLC *-inhibitory	−.24
PLC-to-semlex excitatory	.10
semlex-to-PLC excitatory	.10
semlex-to-PLC inhibitory	−.001
semlex-to-semlex inhibitory	−.05
feedforward (ω_F)	.0005
global suppression (ω_G)	−.14

Table 3.1 Connections to Selected Units for GRATE Example

Unit	Connection Type			
	excitatory	**inhibitory**	***-excitatory**	***-inhibitory**
**G	**_R **_A **_T		*GR *G_A	**A *T_R
**_R	**G **A		*GR *_RA *_RE	**_A **_T *_ER
*G_A	**G *GR *_RA GRA G_AT			**A *_RE *_ER *T_R
GRA	*GR *G_A *_RA G_AT RAT RA_E	ERA		
G_AT	*G_A GRA RAT ATE AT_*	E_AT		
RAT	*_RA GRA G_AT RA_E R_TE ATE AT_* ERA E_AT			
R_TE	RAT RA_E ATE TE* TE_* TER	A_TE		
AT_*	G_AT RAT ATE A_E* TE* T_** E_AT			E_** L_** TE_* LE* T_R* N_E*
A_E*	RA_E ATE AT_* TE* E** LE*			TE_* T_R* N_E*
TE*	R_TE ATE AT_* A_E* T_** E** A_TE N_E*	TER		E_** L_** TE_* LE* T_R*
T_**	E**		AT_* TE*	E_** L_** TE_* LE*
E**	T_** E_** L_**		A_E* TE* LE* N_E*	T_R*
E_**	E**		TE_*	AT_* TE* T_** L_** LE*
**_A	**G **A			**_R *GR *_RA **_T *_RE *_ER
**A	**_R **_A **_T			**G *GR *G_A *T_R
TE_*	R_TE ATE E_** TER T_R* A_TE			AT_* A_E* TE* T_** L_** LE* N_E*
*_RE	**_R *GR	T_RE		*G_A *_RA **_A **_T *_ER *T_R
AN_E	A_TE N_E*			
T_R*	TE_* TER	T_RE		AT_* A_E* TE* E** LE* N_E*
A_TE	ATE TE* TE_* TER AN_E	R_TE		
N_E*	TE* E** LE* AN_E			AT_* A_E* TE_* T_R*
T_RE	TER *T_R	*_RE T_R*		
E_AT	RAT ATE AT_* ERA	G_AT		
*T_R	TER *_ER T_RE			**G *GR *G_A *_RA **A *_RE

3.1.2 The Role of Semantic Knowledge

The connections among PLC units embody knowledge about which pairs of clusters can appear together in a well-formed letter string. An additional source of information can assist the PO net selection process: higher-order knowledge about valid English words. Some form of lexical or semantic knowledge certainly plays a role in reading, as abundant evidence suggests that lexical status has a significant effect on performance (e.g., Carr, Davidson, & Hawkins, 1978; McClelland & Johnston, 1977).

As shown in figure 3.3, the PLC and semantic units are interconnected. Activation flows from the BLC units to the PLC units to the semantic units. The semantic units then feed back upon the PLC units and help to support sets of PLC units that form meaningful entities. The role of semantic units is easiest to envision if word meanings are represented locally, that is, by a single semantic unit. For instance, suppose a particular semantic unit represented the "to annoy or irritate" sense of **GRATE**. It would be connected to all clusters of **GRATE**. Activation of some clusters of **GRATE** would result in activation of the "annoy/irritate" semantic unit, which in turn would reinforce these clusters and help activate the remaining ones. Inhibitory interactions among the semantic units are also necessary to prevent multiple meanings from remaining simultaneously active.

For obvious reasons, a localist representation of meaning is undesirable, but because the mapping between words and meanings is arbitrary (any letter string can be assigned any meaning), it is not clear that a distributed representation of meaning will work. It seems difficult to conceive of a systematic mapping between a distributed representation of orthography—the letter clusters—and a distributed representation of meaning—a set of semantic features. Why should, say, a word starting with the letters **BR** be associated with particular semantic features? One argument in favor of such relationships can be made based on Lewis Carroll's *Jabberwocky*, which contains nonsense words such as **BRILLIG** that nonetheless have semantic connotations: **BRILLIG** is reminiscent of other words that begin with **BR** such as **BRIGHT, BRILLIANT**, and **BREEZY**. Simulation studies have also demonstrated that arbitrary associations can be formed between distributed orthographic and semantic representations (Hinton, McClelland, & Rumelhart, 1986; Hinton & Shallice, 1989; Miikkulainen, 1990).

The semantic units perform two critical computational functions. First, because all PLC-unit interactions are pairwise, the semantic units are necessary to provide a higher-order linking of the letter clusters. This linking helps clusters of a word to cohere. Indeed, although the PO net works fairly well without semantic units, it has the tendency to blend together clusters of different words. Second, the semantic units allow semantic access to be performed within the PO net. Semantic representations are clearly needed by higher-order processes.

On grounds of parsimony, I suggest that an explicit lexical representation is not necessary: the semantic representation obviates the need for a lexicon in the pull-out process; direct association between orthographic and semantic knowledge is possible without mediation by a lexicon; and the semantic representation is required in any case to represent word meanings. A lexicon is useful in that it affords a simple means of determining the lexical status of a letter string—an ability required in many psychological studies. However, lexical status can in principle be ascertained by examining the activity pattern over the semantic units: What really makes a word a word, as opposed to an orthographically regular string, is that it has a meaning associated with its spelling pattern.

Having spoken to the virtues of a true semantic representation, I must admit to the difficulty of devising a complete semantic feature set. To do so by hand would be unwieldy. I am presently engaged in a project, in collaboration with Phillip Wong, aimed at discovering a rich set of semantic features using unsupervised connectionist learning procedures and an electronic thesaurus. [2] However, in the current implementation of MORSEL, I have resorted to a bit of a cheat in the semantic representation: Associated with each word is a distinct pool of units that collectively represents all meanings of the word. These units are not shared by different words. While one might generously view this as a *semi-distributed* semantic representation (Smolensky,

---

[2] Fodor and Pylyshyn (1988), among others, have argued that connectionist models cannot adequately represent meaning because the full range of semantic possibilities cannot be expressed by a linear set of semantic features. Whether or not this argument applies at the level of individual word meanings, Pollack (1988) and Smolensky (1990) have conclusively demonstrated that distributed connectionist representations can encode complex hierarchical structures of the sort that Fodor and Pylyshyn demand.

1990), it is essentially a distributed lexical representation because the semantic features are not shared by different words with similar meanings. While it would be dishonest to continue calling this a semantic representation, the term "lexical" violates the spirit of the theoretical model. I therefore take the liberty of referring to these units as *semlex* units, because they have both semantic properties (in theory) and lexical properties (in the implementation). I emphasize that this semlex representation is used only as an implementational convenience; in principle, I see no reason why a fully distributed semantic representation would not work just as well.

The number of semlex units associated with each word in MORSEL's lexicon was twice the number of letters in the word. Each of these units was connected to five randomly selected letter clusters of the word, with the restriction that all letter clusters had approximately the same number of semlex connections. Because the number of letter clusters in an l-letter word is $3l+2$ and the total number of semlex-PLC unit connections is $10l$ ($2l$ units/word times 5 connections/unit) each PLC unit associated with a word is connected on average to slightly over three of the word's semlex units. This particular scheme was selected because it made the PO net fairly neutral with regard to word length; there was no bias toward either shorter or longer words.

As summarized in table 3.2, the connections between PLC and semlex units are symmetric and excitatory. In addition, each semlex unit slightly inhibits all PLC units to which it is not connected. Semlex units also inhibit all semlex units that are associated with different words. It is this inhibition that forces the PO net to select a pattern of activity in the semlex units corresponding to a single word.

The semlex units are crucial to the pull-out process because they impose a higher-order organization on the letter clusters. Without semlex units, all interactions among letter clusters are pairwise and local; that is, a letter cluster such as GRA can support only with its neighbors, e.g., *GR and G_AT. Semlex units allow higher-order interactions—between sets of 5 letter clusters—and interactions between nonadjacent clusters. Via the semlex units, GRA can support clusters at the other end of the word, e.g., E**. Without semlex units, the PO net occasionally produces *blend errors* in which the first part of one word is blended together with the second part of another (Mozer, 1987).

3.1.3 System Dynamics

Initially, the PLC units receive feedforward excitation from the BLC units. Interactions then take place within the PO net, which gradually iterates toward a stable state. PO net units (both PLC and semlex units) have the same dynamical properties as units in McClelland and Rumelhart's (1981) interactive-activation model. Units are continuous-valued in the range [−0.2,1.0]. Information coming in to each unit is summed algebraically, weighted by the connection strengths, to yield a net input:

$$net_i = \sum_{\substack{j \in \\ ACTIVE}} w_{ij} p_j + \omega_F b_i^6 + \omega_G \bar{p} \ ,$$

where *ACTIVE* is the set of all PO net units with positive activity at the current time, w_{ij} is the strength of connection to PO unit i from PO unit j, p_j is the activity of PO unit j, b_i^6—following the notation of chapter 2—is the activity of BLC unit i (if i is a semlex unit, then b_i^6 is zero), and ω_F is the strength of feedforward connections from BLIR-NET to the PO net. The final term, $\omega_G \bar{p}$, applies only to the PLC units and is explained below.

The activation value of each PO unit is updated by the net input according to the rule:

$$\Delta p_i = \begin{cases} net_i [1.0 - p_i] & \text{if } net_i > 0 \\ net_i [p_i - (-0.2)] & \text{otherwise.} \end{cases}$$

If the net input is positive, activation is pushed toward the maximum value of 1.0; if negative, activation is pushed toward the minimum value of −0.2. The effect of the net input is scaled down as the unit approaches its maximum or minimum activation level.

The dynamics as described thus far are inadequate, for the following reason. Many letter clusters compete and cooperate directly with one another, in particular, the clusters representing ends of words and the clusters sharing letters. Often, however, these interactions are not enough. For instance, suppose two words are presented, **LINE** and **FACT**, and that clusters of **LINE** are more active initially. Clusters like **F and CT* of **FACT** experience direct competition from the corresponding clusters of **LINE**, and are therefore suppressed, but the inner clusters of **FACT** such as FAC and F_CT do not. The pull-out process thus yields **LINE** along with the inner clusters of **FACT**. To get around this problem, some type of global inhibition is useful.

Two possibilities are immediately apparent. The first, which I'll call the *decay scheme*, is that the activity level of each PLC unit could decay over time without external input. The second possibility, the *total inhibition scheme*, is that each unit could be inhibited in proportion to the total activity in the network; this type of global inhibition can be implemented by small-weighted inhibitory connections between every pair of units. Neither scheme is appropriate, however. With the decay scheme, a unit reaches equilibrium when its net input exactly compensates for the decay. Generally, this stable state is not at the limits of the activity range, −.2 or 1, but can be at any intermediate value. Such intermediate values are not acceptable because the PO net's task is to reach a binary yes or no decision concerning each letter cluster. The total inhibition scheme does reach a binary decision, but the total size of the final activity pattern is predetermined by the magnitude of the inhibition. Increasing the inhibition decreases the number of active units that the network can support, and vice versa. This is undesirable because the PO net must allow patterns of arbitrary size. That is, a single stable coalition should win out, independent of the number of units in the coalition: **BLACK** and **BLACKBOARD** are both plausible pull-out candidates.

I opted for a different global-inhibition mechanism, which I call the *average inhibition scheme*. The idea is to inhibit each PLC unit in proportion to the average activity of all clusters above threshold, which can be computed as follows:

$$\bar{p} = \frac{1}{|ACTIVE_L|} \sum_{\substack{i \in \\ ACTIVE_L}} p_i \, ,$$

where $ACTIVE_L$ is the set of all PLC units with positive activity at the current time. The equation for net_i incorporates this term, weighted by the parameter ω_G. This scheme allows the set of PLC units whose activity grows the fastest to shut off the other units. Activity grows fastest for units that have many active compatible neighbors. In the **LINE FACT** example, clusters like FAC and F_CT have relatively few such neighbors (because neighbors like *FA and CT* have been suppressed through direct competition with **LINE**), and as a result will ultimately lose out. The average inhibition scheme does have the drawback that although the formal specification of the computation is simple it requires somewhat sophisticated connectionist hardware, specifically, a unit that can count the number of inputs above threshold and rescale the sum of the inputs by this count.

3.1.4 Comments on the Design

It is useful to examine how the PO net is related to other relaxation networks. Consider first a *winner-take-all (WTA) network* (Feldman & Ballard, 1982; Grossberg, 1976). A WTA network has the property that only the unit with highest initial activity level among a set of contenders has a final activity level above zero. For instance, the word level of the interactive-activation model is such a network. Every word competes with every other word, so that in the final state, only one word remains active. The PO net can be viewed as a *distributed* WTA network. It performs a function exactly equivalent to the word level of the interactive-activation model but operating on distributed instead of local representations: the pattern of activity representing one word suppresses the pattern of activity representing another, instead of the single unit representing one word suppressing the unit representing another. Although building a localist WTA network is trivial, a distributed WTA is quite complex because of potential overlap among patterns and variation in pattern size.[3]

The PO net is related to another type of relaxation network, a *completion network* (Smolensky, 1986), so named because it completes or fills in missing information from a pattern. Completion networks, once trained on a set of patterns, are able to reconstruct a known pattern given a partial or inaccurate description. In a sense, this is what the PO net does in finding the word closest to the jumble of letter-cluster activations. The PO net differs from the standard conception of a completion network in one important respect, however: it performs general, not specific, completions. The PO net operates based on the formal properties of the class of allowed patterns—which clusters are compatible and incompatible neighbors—not on knowledge of particular patterns.

---

[3] For other issues related to distributed WTA networks, see Touretzky (1989).

Like other completion networks, the PO net could have its connections trained through experience. One might note that the handcrafted connections I've constructed represent essentially second order statistics of letter cluster co-occurrence in words, and this is exactly the sort of information that Hebbian learning can pick up. Thus, there is little doubt that training the PO net would be at least as successful as handcrafted connections.

3.2 Simulation Results

Simulating a PO net with even a relatively modest number of letter-cluster units is an expensive proposition due to $O(n^2)$ connections in the network. To reduce the computational burden, simulations were run on only a subset of the letter-cluster units, the units that could plausibly play a role in a given situation. In other words, a mini PO net was constructed for each example that will be presented. Generally, these nets consisted of all target clusters as well as any spurious clusters whose BLC unit activity was above .05 (i.e., all clusters that appear in figures 3.1 and 3.2). It seems unlikely that other clusters could become sufficiently active to influence the results.

3.2.1 Cleaning up Noise in a Single Word

The operation of the pull-out net can be seen in figure 3.4. The top frame indicates the activity of the BLC units. The shading of a unit's name is proportional to its activity, black corresponding to a high level of activity and the light stippled pattern to a low level. The top frame is an alternative presentation of the information in figure 3.1a. The frames below indicate the activity of the PLC units after every ten iterations.

Initially, activity levels of the PLC units are reset to zero. Over time, activation trickles from the BLC units to the PLC units and interactions take place within the PO net. To demonstrate the power of letter-cluster competition and cooperation in the PO net, semlex units were not used in this example. Further, BLC unit G_AT was turned off (see fourth row, sixth column of top frame) and in its place E_AT was fully activated (third row, fourth column of top frame). The PO net is able to correct for these faulty activations: by iteration 40, E_AT and all spurious activations have been extinguished and G_AT

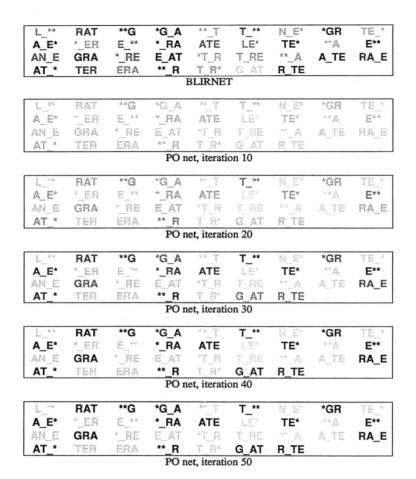

Figure 3.4 Pull out of **GRATE**. Note the activity of BLC units G_AT and E_AT.

and all target activations reinstated. Examination of neighborhood relations sheds light on the net's success. G_AT has five compatible neighbors—G_AT, GRA, RAT, ATE, and AT_*—while E_AT has only four—RAT, ATE, AT_*, and ERA—one of which is a spurious activation itself. G_AT's gang is larger than E_AT's, allowing G_AT to win out.

Figure 3.5 illustrates the PO net's operation for another example, **LINE**. To simulate a case of severe noise, all BLC units having two letters in common with **LINE** were activated with value 0.5, and all BLC units of **LINE** with value 1.0. Gaussian noise with mean zero and

L_NC	ON_*	IE*	*L_G	L_NG	*SI	*KI	*H_N	INI	SE*	A_E*	*K_N	LIV
IP_*	UI_E	PIN	*_EN	DN_*	L_ZE	UNE	LD_E	*L_V	L_WE	LIG	IG_*	*_IN
G_E*	*L_B	*_IR	WE*	L_TE	NA*	*AI	*_JE	L_NE	INO	I_A*	*S_N	SI_E
P_E*	INV	M_NE	LIN	LIB	*M_N	F_NE	FE*	*LI	SN_*	*_NN	LI_G	*NI
NN_*	AI_E	TIN	*L_N	EE*	I_T*	IVE	*LI	**L	YIN	LIP	LA_E	I_H*
*GI	WI_E	P_NE	NG*	*_IF	I_F*	BI_E	LI_S	FIN	LIO	IBE	LUN	MI_E
R_NE	*L_T	AN_*	L_RE	LI_I	NO*	*L_N	IND	GIN	IK_*	I_S*	L_CE	L_VE
*DI	S_NE	L_PE	IA_*	IZE	ME*	H_NE	GIN	*_IX	IKE	E_NE	LUN	*W_N
LO_E	*_UN	CI_E	PI_E	*LE	*C_N	LI_V	E**	*_IM	IE_*	I_S*	LUN	RN_*
KIN	*V_N	*_IK	LON	FI_E	E_E*	ENE	*IC	*IM	IZ_*	RI_E	T_E*	NK*
IT_*	TI_E	NY*	LU_E	*L_M	LI_R	RIN	I_R*	N_E*	*RI	INS	T_NE	NK*
UE*	VE*	ICE	LIA	*LO	*JL	LI_Y	*P_N	BIN	IO_*	L_NT	L_CE	OI_E
*L_K	INK	NIN	R_E*	D_E*	UIN	*TI	L_N*	IM_*	AIN	ISE	IS_*	SIN
RE*	L_KE	I_Y*	*J_N	*CI	*WI	KNE	IN_*	*L_W	*O_N	LE_E	*_IG	PE*
*B_N	*HI	*EI	LIE	*L_F	ITE	CE*	*A_N	A_NE	L_YE	CIN	EIN	TE*
Y_E*	ILE	*_IT	IU_*	I_M*	B_E*	LIS	L_ME	O_E*	ID_*	EN_*	IF_*	GNE
*_IS	WIN	*D_N	S_E*	*F_N	*L_D	*R_N	*MI	*_IP	LI_N	ZE*	INE	VIN
NE*	IR_*	LIM	I_L*	I_W*	VI_E	N_NE	IV_*	NT*	UN_*	I_D*	LI_M	LI_A
KE*	INF	LDN	*_ID	*_WN	D_NE	*LA	U_E*	INU	L_GE	L_E*	NNE	*_IB
DI_E	MIN	O_NE	I_NE	RNE	HE*	C_NE	DIN	GE*	IRE	I_D*	LI_E	LIK
*N_N	LAN	ANE	HI_E	GI_E	LI_T	*BI	L_DE	LIZ	BE*	L_FE	IDE	LEN
*_JA	IME	EI_E	N_**	*LU	LI_D	*G_N	OIN	B_NE	*_AN	U_NE	ONE	*L_S
*L_O	L_IE	INA	G_NE	NS*	*T_N	C_E*	LIT	INN	ZIN	IL_*	LIC	IFE
HIN	*PI	I_K*	INC	LID	LI_H	*FI	ND*	LE*	*VI	LIF	*L_C	L_BE
*_IV	DE*	L_SE	NI_E	INT	IC_*							

BLIRNET

L_NC	ON_*	IE*	*L_G	L_NG	*SI	*KI	*H_N	INI	SE*	A_E*	*K_N	LIV
IP_*	UI_E	PIN	*_EN	DN_*	L_ZE	UNE	LD_E	*L_V	L_WE	LIG	IG_*	**_IN**
G_E*	*L_B	*_IR	WE*	L_TE	NA*	*AI	*_JE	**L_NE**	INO	I_A*	*S_N	SI_E
P_E*	INV	M_NE	**LIN**	LIB	*M_N	F_NE	FE*	**_I**	SN_*	**_I**	LI_G	*NI
NN_*	AI_E	TIN	**L_N**	EE*	I_T*	IVE	**LI**		YIN	LIP	LA_E	ING
*GI	WI_E	P_NE	NG*	*_IF	I_F*	BI_E	LI_S	**L	LIO	IBE		MI_E
R_NE	*L_T	AN_*	L_RE	LI_I	NO*	*L_N	IND	FIN	IK_*	I_S*	LUN	L_VE
*DI	S_NE	L_PE	IA_*	IZE	ME*	H_NE	GIN	*_IX	IKE	E_NE	LUN	*W_N
LO_E	*_UN	CI_E	PI_E	*LE	*C_N	LI_V	**E**	*_IM	IE_*	I_S*	LUN	RN_*
KIN	*V_N	*_IK	LON	FI_E	E_E*	ENE	*IC	*IM	IZ_*	RI_E	T_E*	NK*
IT_*	TI_E	NY*	LU_E	*L_M	LI_R	RIN	I_R*	N_E*	*RI	INS	T_NE	NK*
UE*	VE*	ICE	LIA	*LO	*JL	LI_Y	*P_N	BIN	IO_*	L_NT	L_CE	OI_E
*L_K	INK	NIN	R_E*	D_E*	UIN	*TI	**IN_***	IM_*	AIN	ISE	IS_*	SIN
RE*	L_KE	I_Y*	*J_N	*CI	*WI	KNE	IN_*	*L_W	*O_N	LE_E	*_IG	PE*
*B_N	*HI	*EI	LIE	*L_F	ITE	CE*	*A_N	A_NE	L_YE	CIN	EIN	TE*
Y_E*	ILE	*_IT	IU_*	I_M*	B_E*	LIS	L_ME	O_E*	ID_*	EN_*	IF_*	GNE
*_IS	WIN	*D_N	S_E*	*F_N	*L_D	*R_N	*MI	*_IP	LI_N	ZE*	**INE**	VIN
NE*	IR_*	LIM	I_L*	I_W*	VI_E	N_NE	IV_*	NT*	UN_*	I_D*	LI_M	LI_A
KE*	INF	LDN	*_ID	*_WN	D_NE	*LA	U_E*	INU	L_GE	L_E*	NNE	*_IB
DI_E	MIN	O_NE	I_NE	RNE	HE*	C_NE	DIN	GE*	IRE	I_D*	**LI_E**	LIK
*N_N	LAN	ANE	HI_E	GI_E	LI_T	*BI	L_DE	LIZ	BE*	L_FE	IDE	LEN
*_JA	IME	EI_E	**N_****	*LU	LI_D	*G_N	OIN	B_NE	*_AN	U_NE	ONE	*L_S
*L_O	L_IE	INA	G_NE	NS*	*T_N	C_E*	LIT	INN	ZIN	IL_*	LIC	IFE
HIN	*PI	I_K*	INC	LID	LI_H	*FI	ND*	LE*	*VI	LIF	*L_C	L_BE
*_IV	DE*	L_SE	NI_E	INT	IC_*							

PO net, iteration 40

Figure 3.5 Pull out of LINE.

standard deviation 0.1 was then added to each activity level. Semlex units were not included in this simulation. Although the clusters of **LINE** are most active, they are masked by a large number of small gangs (e.g., *BI, *B_N, BIN, B_NE, BI_E). Nonetheless, the PO net is able to select every cluster of **LINE** to the exclusion of all others.

3.2.2 Disentangling Activations from Two Words

Figure 3.6 shows the pull out of CON from the set of clusters activated by BLIRNET in response to CON MAN. (These clusters are presented graphically in figure 3.2a.) The PO net must suppress not only spurious activations such as TE* but all clusters of MAN. Semlex units for the two stimulus words, CON and MAN, were included in the simulation, as well as several alternative responses that could be formed from the active letter clusters: TON, CAN, ATE, TEN, ONE, ION, and

N**	MAN	*MA	**C	N_AN	O_**	**M	CAN	**_O
*CO	ON_*	AN*	CON	**I	TE*	A_**	EN*	*_ON
**T	*M_N	**_A	TO_*	ON_A	O_E*	AT_*	TON	**_L
M_N*	*_AN	ON*	*_OR	*TO	*C_N			

BLIRNET

N**	MAN	*MA	**C	N_AN	O_**	**M	CAN	**_O
*CO	ON_*	AN*	CON	**I	TE*	A_**	EN*	*_ON
**T	*M_N	**_A	TO_*	ON_A	O_E*	AT_*	TON	**_L
M_N*	*_AN	ON*	*_OR	*TO	*C_N			

PO net, iteration 5

N**	MAN	*MA	**C	N_AN	O_**	**M	CAN	**_O
*CO	ON_*	AN*	CON	**I	TE*	A_**	EN*	*_ON
**T	*M_N	**_A	TO_*	ON_A	O_E*	AT_*	TON	**_L
M_N*	*_AN	ON*	*_OR	*TO	*C_N			

PO net, iteration 10

N**	MAN	*MA	**C	N_AN	O_**	**M	CAN	**_O
*CO	ON_*	AN*	CON	**I	TE*	A_**	EN*	*_ON
**T	*M_N	**_A	TO_*	ON_A	O_E*	AT_*	TON	**_L
M_N*	*_AN	ON*	*_OR	*TO	*C_N			

PO net, iteration 15

N**	MAN	*MA	**C	N_AN	O_**	**M	CAN	**_O
*CO	ON_*	AN*	CON	**I	TE*	A_**	EN*	*_ON
**T	*M_N	**_A	TO_*	ON_A	O_E*	AT_*	TON	**_L
M_N*	*_AN	ON*	*_OR	*TO	*C_N			

PO net, iteration 20

N**	MAN	*MA	**C	N_AN	O_**	**M	CAN	**_O
*CO	ON_*	AN*	CON	**I	TE*	A_**	EN*	*_ON
**T	*M_N	**_A	TO_*	ON_A	O_E*	AT_*	TON	**_L
M_N*	*_AN	ON*	*_OR	*TO	*C_N			

PO net, iteration 25

Figure 3.6 Pull out of CON from CON MAN. Only the letter-cluster units are depicted.

TOE. CON wins the competition in the semlex units as well as in the PLC units. This is shown in figure 3.7. Due to letter cluster overlap, several semlex units become active initially. In particular, note the **CAN** and **ION** units at iteration 15; they are nearly as active as the **CON** units. However, the PO net suppresses these activities and **CON** comes to dominate.

For this pattern of BLC activity, **CON** is selected. The PO net can select **MAN** if noise is added to the BLC activations, or if the semlex or PLC units of **MAN** are preactivated. In figure 3.8, I set the initial activity of PLC unit **M to .01; the effect of this slight boost can be seen over time as **M leads the activity in the PO net, resulting in the ultimate selection of the letter clusters of **MAN**. The semlex units of **MAN** also win their competition. I discuss further how selection among multiple stimuli can be biased in section 3.3.

Figure 3.9 presents a further example in which two longer words, **CHURCH** and **STATION** are disentangled. In this example, the input to the PO net was determined not by presenting **CHURCH STATION** to BLIRNET and observing the resulting pattern of BLC activity, but by bypassing BLIRNET altogether and directly activating all BLC units appropriate to either word, and then injecting Gaussian noise. This noise allowed the PO net to select **CHURCH** on some trials and **STA-TION** on others.

3.3 Influences on the Pull-Out Process

When multiple words are present in the BLC representation, the PO net must select one. In the **CHURCH STATION** simulation and others reported in chapter 6, I have simply injected noise into the system so that a word is chosen at random. I do not wish to suggest that this noise is intrinsic to the system. Rather, the noise substitutes for hitherto unspecified factors. In the following sections, I elaborate on several factors that can influence pull out. These factors are of three varieties: *representational biases*, *bottom-up biases*, and *top-down biases*.

3.3.1 Representational Biases

BLIRNET's output layer contains only a subset of the possible letter clusters. Consequently, some words are bound to have a greater

con-1	man-1	ton-1	can-1	ale-1	ion-1	one-1	ion-1	toe-1
con-2	man-2	ton-2	can-2	ale-2	ion-2	one-2	ion-2	toe-2
con-3	man-3	ton-3	can-3	ale-3	ion-3	one-3	ion-3	toe-3
con-4	man-4	ton-4	can-4	ale-4	ion-4	one-4	ion-4	toe-4
con-5	man-5	ton-5	can-5	ale-5	ion-5	one-5	ion-5	toe-5
con-6	man-6	ton-6	can-6	ale-6	ion-6	one-6	ion-6	toe-6

PO net, iteration 5

con-1	man-1	ton-1	can-1	ale-1	ton-1	one-1	ion-1	toe-1
con-2	man-2	ton-2	can-2	ale-2	ion-2	one-2	ion-2	toe-2
con-3	man-3	ton-3	can-3	ale-3	ion-3	one-3	ion-3	toe-3
con-4	man-4	ton-4	can-4	ale-4	ton-4	one-4	ion-4	toe-4
con-5	man-5	ton-5	can-5	ale-5	ton-5	one-5	ion-5	toe-5
con-6	man-6	ton-6	can-6	ale-6	ton-6	one-6	ion-6	toe-6

PO net, iteration 10

con-1	man-1	ton-1	can-1	ale-1	ion-1	one-1	ion-1	toe-1
con-2	man-2	ton-2	can-2	ale-2	ton-2	one-2	ion-2	toe-2
con-3	man-3	ton-3	con-3	ale-3	ton-3	one-3	ion-3	ton-3
con-4	man-4	ton-4	con-4	ale-4	ton-4	one-4	ton-4	toe-4
con-5	man-5	ton-5	can-5	ale-5	ion-5	one-5	ion-5	toe-5
con-6	man-6	ton-6	can-6	ale-6	ion-6	one-6	ion-6	toe-6

PO net, iteration 15

con-1	man-1	ton-1	can-1	ale-1	ton-1	one-1	ion-1	toe-1
con-2	man-2	ton-2	can-2	ale-2	ion-2	one-2	**ion-2**	toe-2
con-3	man-3	ton-3	can-3	ale-3	ion-3	one-3	**ion-3**	toe-3
con-4	man-4	ton-4	can-4	ale-4	ton-4	one-4	ion-4	toe-4
con-5	man-5	ton-5	can-5	ale-5	ton-5	one-5	ion-5	toe-5
con-6	man-6	ton-6	can-6	ale-6	ton-6	one-6	**ion-6**	toe-6

PO net, iteration 20

con-1	man-1	ton-1	can-1	ale-1	ion-1	one-1	ion-1	toe-1
con-2	man-2	ion-2	can-2	ale-2	ton-2	one-2	**ion-2**	toe-2
con-3	man-3	ion-3	can-3	ale-3	ton-3	one-3	**ion-3**	toe-3
con-4	man-4	ton-4	can-4	ale-4	ion-4	one-4	ion-4	toe-4
con-5	man-5	ton-5	can-5	ale-5	ion-5	one-5	ion-5	toe-5
con-6	man-6	ton-6	can-6	ale-6	ion-6	one-6	**ion-6**	toe-6

PO net, iteration 25

con-1	man-1	ion-1	can-1	ale-1	ton-1	one-1	ion-1	toe-1
con-2	man-2	ton-2	can-2	ale-2	ion-2	one-2	**ion-2**	toe-2
con-3	man-3	ton-3	can-3	ale-3	ion-3	one-3	**ion-3**	toe-3
con-4	man-4	ion-4	can-4	ale-4	ion-4	one-4	ion-4	toe-4
con-5	man-5	ion-5	can-5	ale-5	ton-5	one-5	ion-5	toe-5
con-6	man-6	ion-6	can-6	ale-6	ton-6	one-6	ion-6	toe-6

PO net, iteration 30

Figure 3.7 Pull out of CON from CON MAN. Only the semlex units are depicted. Each word included in the simulation is represented by six semlex units, numbered 1-6. The words are written in lower case to distinguish them from letter-cluster units.

N**	MAN	*MA	**C	N_AN	O_**	**M	CAN	**_O
*CO	ON_*	AN*	CON	**I	TE*	A_**	EN*	*_ON
**T	*M_N	**_A	TO_*	ON_A	O_E*	AT_*	TON	*_L
M_N*	*_AN	ON*	*_OR	*TO	*C_N			

BLIRNET

N**	MAN	*MA	**C	N_AN	O_**	**M	CAN	**_O
*CO	ON_*	AN*	CON	**I	TE*	A_**	EN*	*_ON
**T	*M_N	**_A	TO_*	ON_A	O_E*	AT_*	TON	*_L
M_N*	*_AN	ON*	*_OR	*TO	*C_N			

PO net, iteration 5

N**	MAN	*MA	**C	N_AN	O_**	**M	CAN	**_O
*CO	ON_*	AN*	CON	**I	TE*	A_**	EN*	*_ON
**T	*M_N	**_A	TO_*	ON_A	O_E*	AT_*	TON	*_L
M_N*	*_AN	ON*	*_OR	*TO	*C_N			

PO net, iteration 10

N**	MAN	*MA	**C	N_AN	O_**	**M	CAN	**_O
*CO	ON_*	AN*	CON	**I	TE*	A_**	EN*	*_ON
**T	*M_N	**_A	TO_*	ON_A	O_E*	AT_*	TON	*_L
M_N*	*_AN	ON*	*_OR	*TO	*C_N			

PO net, iteration 15

N**	MAN	*MA	**C	N_AN	O_**	**M	CAN	**_O
*CO	ON_*	AN*	CON	**I	TE*	A_**	EN*	*_ON
**T	*M_N	**_A	TO_*	ON_A	O_E*	AT_*	TON	*_L
M_N*	*_AN	ON*	*_OR	*TO	*C_N			

PO net, iteration 20

N**	MAN	*MA	**C	N_AN	O_**	**M	CAN	**_O
*CO	ON_*	AN*	CON	**I	TE*	A_**	EN*	*_ON
**T	*M_N	**_A	TO_*	ON_A	O_E*	AT_*	TON	*_L
M_N*	*_AN	ON*	*_OR	*TO	*C_N			

PO net, iteration 25

Figure 3.8 Pull out of MAN from CON MAN. In this example, PLC unit **M has been preactivated to a level of 0.01.

proportion of their clusters among the BLC units than others. The better a word is represented, the better it is expected to fare in the PO net competition. If a single cluster is missing, up to eight other clusters will lose a compatible neighbor, and the number of compatible neighbors is a critical factor in determining whether a given cluster will survive the competition. The G_AT/E_AT example (figure 3.4) attests to this point.

**_H	O_**	N**	**S	**C	**_T	C_**	ON*	H**
ION	T_ON	TI_N	TIO	I_N*	IO_*	ATI	*ST	A_IO
AT_O	CH*	*S_A	STA	*CH	*C_U	*_TA	TAT	ST_T
S_AT	C_UR	CH_R	TA_I	T_TI	R_H*	RCH	RC_*	*_HU
UR_H	U_CH	URC	HUR	CHU	H_RC	HU_C		

BLIRNET

**_H	O_**	N**	**S	**C	**_T	C_**	ON*	H**
ION	T_ON	TI_N	TIO	I_N*	IO_*	ATI	*ST	A_IO
AT_O	CH*	*S_A	STA	*CH	*C_U	*_TA	TAT	ST_T
S_AT	C_UR	CH_R	TA_I	T_TI	R_H*	RCH	RC_*	*_HU
UR_H	U_CH	URC	HUR	CHU	H_RC	HU_C		

PO net, iteration 10

**_H	O_**	N**	**S	**C	**_T	C_**	ON*	H**
ION	T_ON	TI_N	TIO	I_N*	IO_*	ATI	*ST	A_IO
AT_O	CH*	*S_A	STA	*CH	*C_U	*_TA	TAT	ST_T
S_AT	C_UR	CH_R	TA_I	T_TI	R_H*	RCH	RC_*	*_HU
UR_H	U_CH	URC	HUR	CHU	H_RC	HU_C		

PO net, iteration 15

**_H	O_**	N**	**S	**C	**_T	C_**	ON*	H**
ION	T_ON	TI_N	TIO	I_N*	IO_*	ATI	*ST	A_IO
AT_O	CH*	*S_A	STA	*CH	*C_U	*_TA	TAT	ST_T
S_AT	C_UR	CH_R	TA_I	T_TI	R_H*	RCH	RC_*	*_HU
UR_H	U_CH	URC	HUR	CHU	H_RC	HU_C		

PO net, iteration 20

**_H	O_**	N**	**S	**C	**_T	C_**	ON*	H**
ION	T_ON	TI_N	TIO	I_N*	IO_*	ATI	*ST	A_IO
AT_O	CH*	*S_A	STA	*CH	*C_U	*_TA	TAT	ST_T
S_AT	C_UR	CH_R	TA_I	T_TI	R_H*	RCH	RC_*	*_HU
UR_H	U_CH	URC	HUR	CHU	H_RC	HU_C		

PO net, iteration 30

**_H	O_**	N**	**S	**C	**_T	C_**	ON*	H**
ION	T_ON	TI_N	TIO	I_N*	IO_*	ATI	*ST	A_IO
AT_O	CH*	*S_A	STA	*CH	*C_U	*_TA	TAT	ST_T
S_AT	C_UR	CH_R	TA_I	T_TI	R_H*	RCH	RC_*	*_HU
UR_H	U_CH	URC	HUR	CHU	H_RC	HU_C		

PO net, iteration 40

Figure 3.9 Pull out of CHURCH from CHURCH STATION.

The significant effect of missing clusters is surprising because on first glance, the letter-cluster encoding appears highly redundant; it does not seem that clusters like G_AT add much to the representation of **GRATE** given a multitude of clusters like GRA, RAT, and GR_T. Nonetheless, such redundancy is observed to be clearly beneficial in the pull-out process. Words that will benefit the most are those having the highest proportion of their clusters present; as a general rule, these will be the most orthographically regular words.

Regularity of a different sort might be important too—letter-cluster frequency. If frequent activation caused units to have higher resting activation levels (McClelland & Rumelhart 1981) or lower thresholds, high-frequency clusters would respond the quickest and words containing these clusters would tend to be pulled out first. Further, if connections between units were strengthened based on frequency of use, the PO net would recognize highly familiar words faster and with greater ease.

3.3.2 Bottom-Up Biases

Pull out is strongly influenced by the activity levels of the BLC units, whose activity levels in turn are dependent on the operation of BLIR-NET. Because of inaccuracies in BLIRNET, some clusters will not receive the activation they deserve, and other spurious clusters will receive undue activation; both sorts of error interfere with the pull-out process. In general, if multiple words are presented, the PO net will select the word having the highest signal strength. This is illustrated in the **CHURCH STATION** example: In figure 3.9, several critical clusters of **STATION**—**S, *ST, *_TA—have degraded activity, causing **CHURCH** to be pulled out.

In chapter 4, I present an attentional mechanism that is capable of raising the relative signal strength of attended items. Basically, if attention is focused on a particular word, letter clusters of that word will have greater activations than letter clusters of other words, and the attended word will tend to win the PO net competition.

3.3.3 Top-Down Biases

In addition to assisting the pull-out process by imposing a higher-order structure on the letter clusters, the semlex units have further implications for the pull-out process. The highlights are as follows.

- The PO net is biased toward legitimate words over orthographically regular strings that do not have associated meanings (*pseudowords*) because the lexical or semantic information helps clusters of a legitimate word to cohere. Further, if the overall strength of the PLC-semlex unit pathway were externally modulated, the influence of word knowledge could be varied. With the pathway enhanced, the PO net would tend to turn pseudowords into words; with the pathway attenuated, the PO net would be indiscriminate as to the word status of a string. People appear to have such control over word-level knowledge: The tendency to misperceive briefly presented pseudowords as words containing similar letters (e.g., reading **LERE** as **LORE**) is strongly influenced by expectations as to the nature of the stimuli (McClelland & Mozer, 1986).

- By preactivating or *priming* semlex units prior to pull out, pull out could be biased in favor of words with certain meanings. In this respect, semlex units act as a top-down influence on pull out.

- The PO net as constructed reads out single words at a time, where a word is defined as a string of letters delimited by blank space. It seems desirable, however, for the PO net to operate on larger units of text if they form a semantically meaningful whole. This might happen if, through experience, a phrase took on a unitary meaning. This meaning, represented in the semlex units, could help to hold together words of the phrase and overcome the inhibition resulting from multiple words, thereby allowing all words in the phrase to be pulled out at once. In this sense, semlex units help to "chunk" letters on a page, and experience allows the construction of larger and larger chunks, as has been suggested for more abstract units of knowledge (Rosenbloom & Newell, 1987). This is a radical proposal in that it could give the PO net responsibility for parsing syntactic elements such as idioms and noun phrases, and suggests that such parsing may be facilitated by the system's ability to process multiple words in parallel.

4 The Attentional Mechanism

People deal with only a small fraction of the visual information in their midst at any instant. Consider the task of reading aloud: dozens of words strike the retina simultaneously, yet the reader can vocalize no more than one word at a time. To perform this task, the processing system requires the ability to access visual information selectively and sequentially. This is the primary function of an attentional mechanism: to control the amount and the temporal order of information passing through the system.

What might such a mechanism look like in the context of MORSEL? I propose a simple mechanism, one that directs a "spotlight" to a particular region of the retina (e.g., Eriksen & Hoffman, 1973; Koch & Ullman, 1985; Laberge & Brown, 1989; Posner, 1980; Posner, Snyder, & Davidson, 1980), enhancing the relative value of stimulus information falling within that region.[1] More concretely, the attentional spotlight serves to highlight low-level featural activations arising from the attended region. As these activations propagate through BLIRNET they maintain their relative status, so that BLIRNET units appropriate for the attended item(s) will tend to become most active as well. Consequently, these letter-cluster units will dominate the PO net competition, causing the attended item(s) to be pulled out. In this way, the attentional mechanism allows preferential processing of attended stimuli.

The attentional mechanism (AM) serves four distinct functions in MORSEL, suggesting the following roles of selective attention in visual information processing.

- *Controlling order of readout.* The AM allows MORSEL to selectively access information in the visual field by location.

---

[1] Crick (1984) has suggested that just such a mechanism resides in the reticular complex of the thalamus, although more recent neurophysiological data (Moran & Desimone, 1985) casts doubt on this theory.

- *Reducing crosstalk.* As discussed in chapter 2, when multiple words are analyzed simultaneously by BLIRNET, interactions within the network cause the processing of one word to interfere with another. Even if this form of crosstalk were not a serious problem, processing multiple words can be difficult because the resulting pattern of letter-cluster activity may be such a jumble that the PO net cannot unambiguously reconstruct the original stimuli. By focusing attention on one word at a time, crosstalk can be eliminated.

- *Recovering location information.* Remember that the output of BLIRNET—the letter-cluster representation—encodes the identity of a letter or word but not its retinal location; the operation of BLIRNET and the other modules factor out location information. However, because the current focus of attention reflects the spatial source of letter-cluster activations, the AM can convey the lost location information. This is discussed further in chapter 5.

- *Coordinating processing performed by independent modules.* Each processing subsystem operates independently of the others. Consequently, it is imperative to ensure that the results from the various modules are grouped appropriately. The AM allows this by guiding processing resources of all modules to the same spatial region. This function of attention seems analogous to that suggested by feature-integration theory (Treisman & Gelade, 1980; Treisman & Gormican, 1988). Chapter 5 elaborates on this point.

4.1 Implementation

4.1.1 The AM as a Filter

The AM, sketched in figure 4.1, is a set of units arranged in a retinotopic map in one-to-one correspondence with the L_1 units of BLIRNET. Activity in an AM unit indicates that attention is focused on the corresponding retinal location and serves to *gate the flow of activity* from L_1 to L_2. To be concrete,

$$\bar{b}_{fxy}^1 = \begin{cases} b_{fxy}^1 & \text{with probability } \xi + (1-\xi)a_{xy} \\ 0 & \text{otherwise,} \end{cases}$$

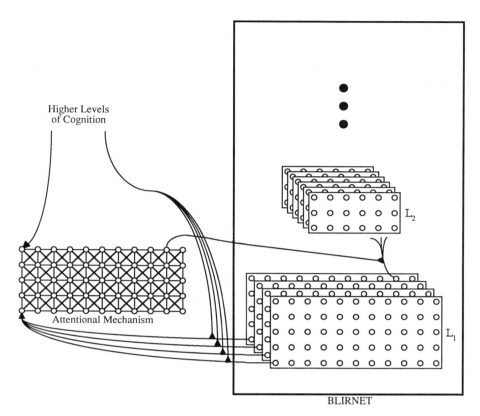

Figure 4.1 The AM and its relationship to BLIRNET. Layers 1 and 2 of BLIRNET (L_1 and L_2) are shown. The third array of units is the AM. As described in the text, AM units receive input from L_1 of BLIRNET and higher levels of cognition (the connections with arrowheads). The AM units gate the flow of activity from L_1 to L_2 (the triangle junction indicates such a gate). Finally, higher levels of cognition can gate the flow of activity from L_1 to the AM. (Reprinted with permission from "A connectionist model of selective attention in visual perception" by M. C. Mozer, in *Proceedings of the Tenth Annual Conference of the Cognitive Science Society*, p. 196. Copyright 1988 by Erlbaum Associates.)

where b^1_{fxy} is the actual activity level of the L_1 unit in location (x,y) of feature type f, $\tilde{b}^1_{fxy}$ is the level transmitted to L_2, a_{xy} is the activity level of AM unit in location (x,y) and has range $[0,1]$, and ξ is a scaling parameter with a value of approximately .25. As long as ξ is greater than zero, the AM serves only to *bias* processing; it does not absolutely inhibit activations from unattended regions (similar to the

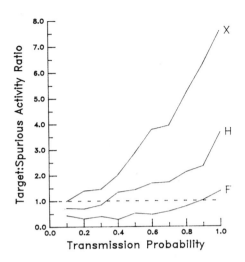

Figure 4.2 Mean ratio of target activation to the maximum spurious activation for X, H, and F presented in location (14,2) as a function of transmission probability. (Reprinted with permission from "A connectionist model of selective attention in visual perception" by M. C. Mozer, in *Proceedings of the Tenth Annual Conference of the Cognitive Science Society*, p. 197. Copyright 1988 by Erlbaum Associates.)

model of Norman and Shallice, 1985). I call $\xi+(1-\xi)a_{xy}$ the *transmission probability*.

As one might expect, highly familiar stimuli outside the focus of attention can work their way through the system better than other stimuli. To illustrate this point, the version of BLIRNET trained to recognize individual letters (section 2.4.2) was tested midway through training. Some letters were recognized better than others: X was detected in every location and in the context of virtually any other simultaneously presented letters, H was less consistently detected, and F even less so.[2] Taking stability of detection to be an indication of familiarity, one might predict that performance on X should suffer less than performance on H, and H less than F, when attention is removed. This prediction is borne out in figure 4.2. Performance here is

---

[2] The difference in performance is most likely a quirk of the initial random weights in BLIRNET. A replication of the simulation could confirm this, or it might indicate the alternative that some letters are intrinsically easier to recognize due to their physical distinctiveness.

measured as the ratio of the activation level of the target cluster (*X*, *H*, or *F*) to the activation level of the maximally active spurious cluster, averaged over thirty presentations of the target letter. When this ratio falls below 1.0, the target cannot be discriminated from the nontargets. X is discriminable as long as the transmission probability is greater than .1, H .3 and F .8. Thus, BLIRNET is able to recognize familiar stimuli based on fewer perceptual features than less familiar stimuli. If this result is typical, it would appear that focal attention is less critical for highly familiar stimuli. Although this property is unlikely to distinguish MORSEL from other theories of attention, it is reassuring to verify that the computational model does indeed behave as expected. The observed behavior is not logically necessary: The model might well have produced a nonmonotonic decline in performance as the transmission probability was decreased, or the performance on X might have dropped so rapidly that H or F fared better at low transmission probabilities.

To further illustrate the filtering properties of the AM, BLIRNET was tested on two letters—L and G—presented simultaneously. Figure 4.3 shows the strength of response to the two letters, relative to the strength of alternate responses, with the transmission probability of L fixed at 1.0 and the transmission probability of G varying from 0.0 to 1.0. At the right edge of the graph, when attention is fully divided, the L response is weak compared to the G response. The reason for this is some combination of factors, including the current level of training, the initial random weights in BLIRNET, and the particular presentation positions used. The exact reason is unimportant; what matters for this example is that by concentrating attention on L, its relatively weak response can be improved dramatically, although this improvement is matched by a corresponding decrement in the response to G. Thus, inter-item crosstalk is reduced by focusing attention on one item.[3]

4.1.2 System Dynamics

In the previous section, I described the way that a given AM state influences processing in MORSEL. In this section, I turn to the issue

---

[3] Unlike when single letters are presented, the target:spurious activity ratio is not an absolute measure of discriminability here. This is because there are two stimuli, so what matters for recognition are the *two* most active units. Even if a target has a ratio less than one, it may still be the second most active unit.

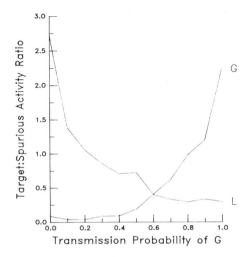

Figure 4.3 Mean ratio of target activation to the maximum spurious activation for L in location (11,2) and G in location (20,2) as a function of attention to the G, averaged over thirty trials. The transmission probability of the L was held constant at 1.0. (Reprinted with permission from "A connectionist model of selective attention in visual perception" by M. C. Mozer, in *Proceedings of the Tenth Annual Conference of the Cognitive Science Society*, p. 197. Copyright 1988 by Erlbaum Associates.)

of how this state is computed. I begin by assuming external sources of knowledge are available that offer suggestions about where to focus. Sometimes these suggestions will conflict with one another; the task of the AM is to resolve such conflicts and construct an attentional spotlight that highlights a single item appearing on MORSEL's retina. Defining an item to be a set of features in close proximity, the spotlight should form a *contiguous* region on the retina.

In connectionist modeling, the standard method of transforming this description of the target behavior of the AM into a network architecture is to view the AM's task as an *optimization* problem: to what activity value should each unit in the AM be set in order to best satisfy a number of possibly conflicting constraints? The two primary constraints here are that the AM should focus on locations suggested by the external knowledge sources, and the AM should focus on a single item.

The first step in tackling such an optimization problem is to define a *Harmony* function (Hopfield, 1982; Smolensky, 1986) that computes the goodness of a particular AM *state*, i.e., a pattern of activity over the AM units. This goodness is a scalar quantity indicating how well the AM state satisfies the optimization problem. The maxima of the Harmony function correspond to desired states of the AM. Given a Harmony function, H, one can ask how the activity of the AM unit at a retinal location (x,y), denoted a_{xy}, should be updated over time to increase Harmony and eventually reach states of maximal Harmony. The simplest rule, called *steepest ascent*, is to update a_{xy} in proportion to the derivative $\partial H / \partial a_{xy}$. If $\partial H / \partial a_{xy}$ is positive, then increasing a_{xy} will increase H; thus a_{xy} should be increased. If $\partial H / \partial a_{xy}$ is negative, then decreasing a_{xy} will increase H; thus a_{xy} should be decreased.

Returning to the problem faced by the AM, devising a Harmony function that computes whether the pattern of activity is contiguous is quite difficult. Instead of constructing a function that explicitly rewards contiguity, I have combined several heuristics that together generally achieve convex, contiguous patterns of activity. The Harmony function incorporating these heuristics is:

$$
H = \sum_{\substack{(x,y) \\ \in ALL}} ext_{xy} a_{xy} - \frac{\mu}{4} \sum_{\substack{(x,y) \\ \in ALL}} \sum_{\substack{(i,j)\in \\ NEIGH_{xy}}} (a_{ij} - a_{xy})^2
$$

$$
+ \frac{\theta}{2} \sum_{\substack{(x,y)\in \\ ACTIVE}} (\gamma \bar{a} - a_{xy})^2 ,
$$

where *ALL* is the set of all retinal locations, ext_{xy} is the net external input to the AM at location (x,y), $NEIGH_{xy}$ is the set of 8 locations immediately adjacent to (x,y)—the *neighbors*, *ACTIVE* is the set of locations of all units with positive activity, $\bar{a}$ is the mean activity of all units with positive activity—

$$
\bar{a} = \frac{1}{|ACTIVE|} \sum_{\substack{(x,y)\in \\ ACTIVE}} a_{xy} ,
$$

and μ, θ, and γ are constants.

The first term encourages each unit to be consistent with the external bias. The second term encourages each unit to be as close as possible to its neighbors; if a unit is off and the neighbors are on, the unit will tend to turn on, and vice versa. The third term encourages units below the mean activity in the network to shut off, and units above the mean activity to turn on. The constant γ serves as a discounting factor: with γ less than 1, units need not be quite as active as the mean in order to be supported. Instead of using the average activity over *all* units, it is necessary to compute the average over the *active* units. Otherwise, the effect of the third term is to limit the total activity in the network, i.e., the number of units that can turn on at once. This is not suitable because small or large spotlights should be allowed, depending on the nature of the external input. The same scheme was used to limit activity in the PO net, as described in chapter 3.

The update rule for a_{xy} is:

$$\Delta a_{xy} = \frac{\partial H}{\partial a_{xy}} = ext_{xy} + \mu \sum_{\substack{(i,j)\in \\ NEIGH_{xy}}} (a_{ij} - a_{xy}) - \theta (\gamma \bar{a} - a_{xy}).$$

Further, a_{xy} is prevented from going outside the range [0,1] by thresholding activity at these limits. [4] A neighbor is assumed to have activity level zero if it is outside the 36×6 retinotopic map.

To explain the activation function intuitively, consider the time course of activation. Initially, the activity of all AM units is reset to zero. Activation then feeds into each unit in proportion to its external bias (first term in the activation function). Units with active neighbors will grow the fastest because of neighborhood support (second term). As activity progresses, high-support neighborhoods will have activity above the mean; they will therefore be pushed even higher, while low-support neighborhoods will experience the opposite tendency (third term).

In all simulations, μ was fixed at .125, θ at .5, and γ at .11 times the total external input with minimum and maximum values of .75 and 1.0, respectively. These constants were selected on the basis of informal experimentation. Other parameter settings and Harmony functions would suffice equally well as, if not better than, the ones chosen. In fact, I tested several variations of the Harmony function, and the qualitative system behavior was unaffected. Nonetheless, the

---

[4] To follow the objective function exactly, the third term should actually be zero if a_{xy} is currently inactive. However, including this term at all times prevents oscillation in the network and does not otherwise appear to affect the quality of the solution.

dynamics of the AM are somewhat brittle in that appropriate parameter settings are dependent on the nature of the external input. I would recommend a more serious computational analysis of the problem to others interested in building attentional mechanisms.

4.1.3 Guiding the Spotlight

Having addressed the question of how to implement an attentional spotlight given knowledge of where to focus, I now take a stab at the deeper question of how MORSEL knows where to focus. Sources of knowledge guiding attention can be dichotomized into two classes: *data driven* and *conceptually driven*. This dichotomy has a long history in the psychological literature. Milner (1974) distinguishes *extrinsic* and *intrinsic* control of attention; Butter (1987) distinguishes *reflexive* and *voluntary* control; LaBerge and Brown (1989) use the terms *bottom-up* and *top-down* control.

Attention is often data driven. To consider a simple case, attention is drawn to objects but not empty regions in the visual field. This property is incorporated into the AM by having every L_1 unit project to its corresponding AM unit (as depicted in figure 4.1). Similar connections to the AM should be made from other elementary feature maps, e.g., maps detecting color and motion. Perhaps most importantly, input to the AM should include feature *gradient* maps—an explicit representation of inhomogeneities in the various feature maps (LaBerge & Brown, 1989; Sandon, 1990); this serves as a primitive form of texture boundary information. Through such inputs, attention can be captured by such varied stimuli as an intense or flashing light, object motion, or an odd element against a uniform background.

Further control is required, however. The mere presence of any feature should not cause an attentional shift willy nilly: attention is dependent on higher-level expectations and task demands. For example, in the task of detecting a "−" in a display of vertical line segments, one would like for only the "−" to trigger attention to allow for parallel search. (This "pop-out" effect, in which the target is detected equally fast, independent of the number of distractors, has been documented by Egeth, Jonides, & Wall, 1972, Neisser, 1964, and Treisman, Sykes, & Gelade, 1977.) I thus propose that higher levels of cognition can modulate the effect of each feature type on the AM, allowing only the features of interest to capture attention (see LaBerge &

Brown, 1989, for a similar proposal). Mechanistically, this is not difficult to implement: higher levels of cognition simply need to gate the connections from each feature type in L_1 (and other such feature maps) to the AM. These higher levels of cognition are beyond the scope of MORSEL. Nonetheless, it is interesting to speculate on what forms of control higher levels have over the AM.

Koch and Ullman (1985) discuss two further heuristics for the data-driven guidance of attention based on Gestalt grouping principles: *proximity* and *similarity*. Building a proximity preference into the AM would bias shifts to locations in the neighborhood of the presently selected location. Building a similarity preference would bias shifts to locations with the same or similar elementary features as the presently selected location.

Besides data-driven guidance, conceptually driven guidance— direct control by higher levels of cognition—is required in many situations, from reading, where text must be scanned from left to right, to a variety of experimental tasks where selection is based on location. For example, in the work of Jonides (1981) and Posner (1980), a centrally presented arrow cue is used to indicate that attention should be shifted to the peripheral location specified by the arrow. I have shown the requisite input in figure 4.1 to symbolize top-down influences on attention. The sort of control mechanism I envision might operate based on principles similar to those of Thibadeau, Just, & Carpenter's (1982) model of eye movement control. Although attentional focus can perhaps be dissociated from eye fixation (Eriksen & Hoffman, 1972; Posner, 1980), the two are surely related. From a more general computational perspective, Chapman (1990a, 1990b) and Wiesmeyer and Laird (1990) have discussed attentional strategies and control primitives for visually-guided behavior. This important work is a major step toward transforming the unspecified top-down AM inputs into a concrete model of top-down attentional control.

If items of interest in the visual field vary in size, so must the spotlight. Empirical evidence confirms this intuition (Eriksen & Yeh, 1985; Laberge, 1983). Thus, it seems critical that higher levels of cognition be able to influence not only the locus of the spotlight but also its radius. In the simulation experiments reported below, I show that the size of the spotlight is dependent on the nature of the inputs. The spotlight size can be further modulated by the parameter θ. Consequently, I assume that θ can be regulated dynamically by higher levels of cognition as a function of time and task, although this was not necessary in the reported simulations.

4.2 Simulation Results

In the AM simulations reported below, external inputs are determined from the activations in one or more feature maps of BLIRNET's L_1, or they may be specified by hand. An input to the AM at location (x, y) contributes a value of .1 to ext_{xy}, as well as a value of .002 to the neighboring positions. The purpose of this blurring to neighboring positions was to give the input a more continuous spread of activity, and presumably, a closer approximation to early representations in the human brain.

Figure 4.4 presents a simple example in which I have specified three blobs of external input. The output of the network is shown after iterations 1, 5, 10, 15, and 20. Initially, activity levels of all AM units are reset to zero. After iteration 1, the external inputs have been copied into the corresponding AM units. After iteration 5, spotlights are forming around all three stimulated locations, but by iteration 10, activity in the two outer regions is beginning to be suppressed. This is due to the fact that only one spotlight can be supported and the external input to the center region is the strongest (four external inputs, versus two for the left region and three for the right). By iteration 20, the network has reached equilibrium.

Figure 4.5 shows an example with two input blobs. Once again, the AM selects the blob having largest external input. In this example, however, the resulting spotlight is wider than in the first example. The ultimate size of the spotlight depends on the base of external support a region receives; the support for the selected region is much greater in the second example.

The next example is intended to simulate the presentation of two letter strings, **WIX** and **MUJ**. Figure 4.6 shows the pattern of elementary feature activity in L_1 of BLIRNET in response to presentation of the two strings. Assuming the sort of connections from L_1 of BLIRNET to the AM discussed in section 4.1.3, the input to the AM will be based on the total number of active features in each location, as depicted in the top frame of figure 4.7. It is extremely difficult for the AM to select one word because the total feature activations produced by **WIX** and **MUJ** are quite similar—35 versus 38—as is the

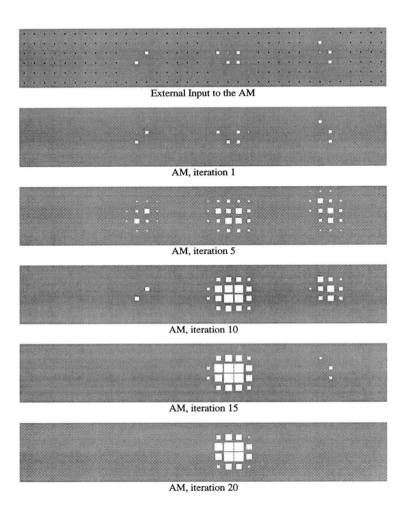

Figure 4.4 Activations in the AM resulting from three input blobs. Each frame consists of 36×6 array of activations, with the area of a white square corresponding to the activity level; the largest squares represent an activity level of 1.0. The top frame shows the external input to the AM. Small black dots are drawn in the locations where the external input is zero, simply to indicate the extent of the array. The frames below show activity in the AM over time as the network settles. By iteration 20, the network has reached a stable state.

distribution of features within the strings. Nonetheless, after 100 iterations, the AM selects **MUJ**, as shown in the bottom frame of figure 4.7. Note that for the first 20 iterations or so, activity in the AM

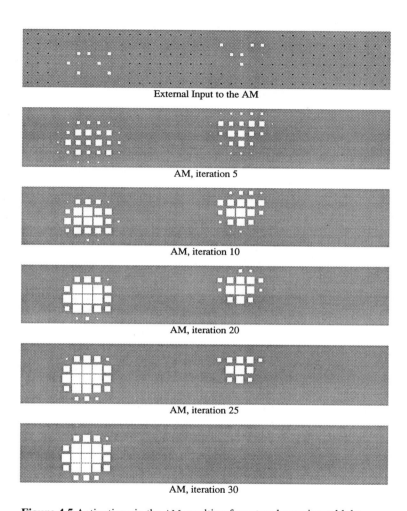

External Input to the AM

AM, iteration 5

AM, iteration 10

AM, iteration 20

AM, iteration 25

AM, iteration 30

Figure 4.5 Activations in the AM resulting from two larger input blobs.

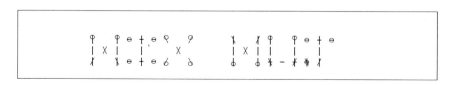

Figure 4.6 The pattern of elementary feature activity in L_1 of BLIRNET in response to the two strings **WIX** and **MUJ**.

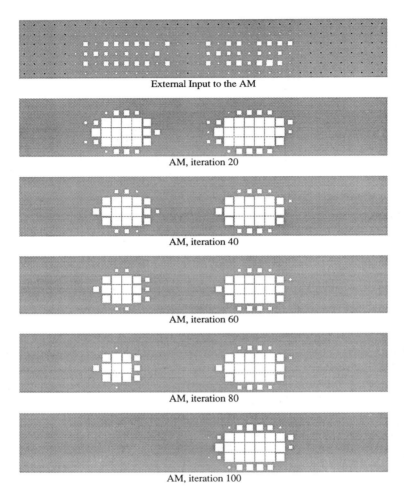

Figure 4.7 Activations in the AM resulting from the pattern of external input produced by the strings **WIX** and **MUJ**.

reflects all external sources of input: attention is broadly tuned to include all items in the visual field. Over time, however, attention narrows on a single region.

Ordinarily, English readers have a strong left-to-right bias. This bias can be provided by the conceptually driven inputs to the AM. Figure 4.8 shows the consequences of combining the bottom-up input from presentation of **WIX** and **MUJ** and a top-down input biasing the

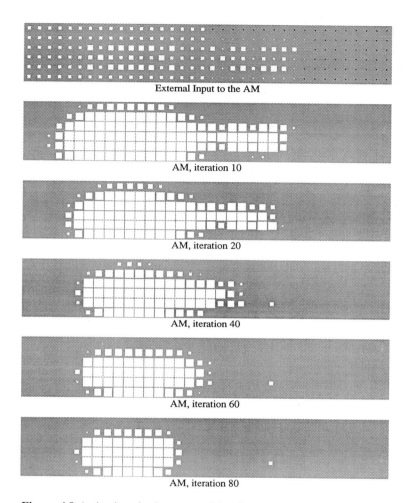

Figure 4.8 Activations in the AM resulting from bottom-up external input from **WIX** and **MUJ**, and a top-down input biasing the entire left field.

entire left portion of the field. After 60-80 iterations, the region corresponding to **WIX** is selected.

A final example of the operation of the AM is presented in figure 4.9. I have simulated the situation in which higher levels of cognition gate the L_1-AM connections so that only the \ and / feature maps trigger the AM. Consequently, when the features of **WIX MUJ** are activated in L_1, the letter **X** is selected. In this manner, higher levels

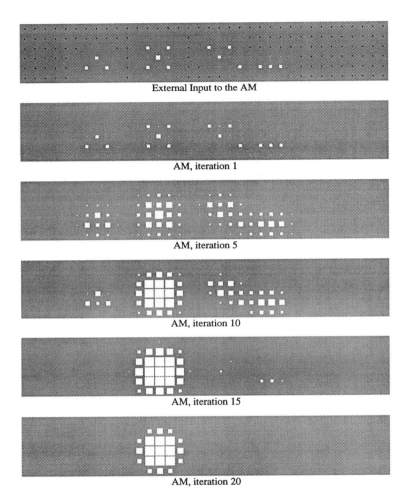

Figure 4.9 Activations in the AM resulting from external inputs based on the \ and / features of the stimulus WIX MUJ. The location of the X is selected.

of cognition can control which item will be selected, but only if the item has distinctive elementary features: in MORSEL's encoding, letters like W and M cannot be differentiated on the basis of elementary features.

In each simulation, note that during the initial phase of processing, the locations of all stimuli become active. It isn't until competitive mechanisms take reign that a winning location emerges. Thus, the

AM is unfocused initially, but over the course of processing it narrows in on a single item. Because BLIRNET begins processing a display as soon as it is presented—and before the AM has settled to equilibrium—initially BLIRNET attempts to handle all information in the display simultaneously. If one were to observe the activity of units in BLIRNET, it would appear as if the units responded to unattended stimuli at first, but this activity was eventually suppressed. In single cell studies of monkey visual cortex, Desimone (1989) has observed this type of behavior: 60 msec after stimulus onset a response is triggered in the extrastriate cortex, but not until 90 msec does attention kick in and suppress unattended stimuli.

The AM was not designed with these data in mind, but it does appear a natural consequence of such a filtering mechanism. There are two basic designs one can envision: (1) a system that does not allow the processing of any information until selection is complete; and (2) a system that allows the processing of all information until selection is complete. The AM, and apparently the mammalian brain, is of type 2. This is sensible because it seems likely that the cost of a cautious type 1 system is greater than that of a more cavalier type 2 system. A type 2 system allows meaningful information to be extracted from the visual input before the attentional system settles, the only drawback being that attention may not be finely focused on the item of interest and that items may interfere with the processing of each other. One might object to the operation of the AM on the grounds that it takes too long to converge on a stable state. Attention shifts must be fairly brief: Treisman and Gelade (1980) estimate the scanning rate to be 50 msec per item, although other estimates of the time to focus on an item are larger, on the order of 200 msec (e.g., Colegate, Hoffman, & Eriksen 1973). Note, however, that these estimates are at best an indirect measure of attention shifts; they are based on the rate at which stimuli can be processed. Given that stimulus processing commences before the AM converges, it is difficult to know how these estimates relate to the operation of the AM. Further, the speed of convergence of the AM is highly dependent on the parameters θ and μ and the strength of the external input. One can double these values and greatly increase the speed of the AM, at the expense of some instability. And finally, note that at the start of the simulations presented here, AM activity levels were reset to zero. During ongoing processing, however, the AM must pass from one nonzero state to another. This turns out to help matters. To push the AM out of its current state, it is necessary to suppress the active units, either endogenously—via habituation that builds up over time (Posner & Cohen, 1984)—or exogenously—via biases from high-level processes. Such suppression should facilitate shifts to nearby locations, allowing a rapid and smooth flow of attention.

4.3 Early Versus Late Selection: Where Does the Attentional Mechanism Fit?

A central issue in perceptual psychology over the past three decades has been the level at which attentional selection operates. Theories of attention can be dichotomized into two opposing views: *early* and *late selection*. Early-selection theories (Broadbent, 1958; Treisman, 1969) derive their name from the assertion that selection occurs early in the sequence of processing stages, prior to stimulus identification. In contrast, late-selection theories (e.g., Deutsch & Deutsch, 1963; Norman, 1968; Posner, 1978; Shiffrin & Schneider, 1977) posit that selection occurs late in processing, following stimulus identification. Additional properties go hand in hand with the central assumption of each theory (Pashler & Badgio, 1987). Early selection generally implies that (a) selection is based on low-level features such as stimulus location or color, (b) the processing system is of quite limited capacity, and (c) stimulus identification is necessarily serial. In contrast, late selection generally implies that (a) selection is based on high-level features such as stimulus identity, (b) the processing system is without capacity limitations, and (c) stimulus identification proceeds in parallel.

The early- versus late-selection dichotomy has been proven inadequate to account for the immense body of attentional data (Johnston & Dark, 1986) and current theorizing toward hybrid views that include aspects of both early and late selection (Mozer, 1988; Navon, 1989; Pashler & Badgio, 1985; van der Heijden, Hagenaar, Bloem, 1984). The view of attention presented by MORSEL is perhaps the most explicit of such theories. It agrees with late-selection theories in suggesting that multiple display items can be processed in parallel to a high level of representation, even to the point of making simultaneous contact with semantic knowledge. Further, selection via the PO net can be based on high-level (semantic or orthographic) features; this is accomplished by priming semlex units or PO net units, respectively, to bias the pull out process, as discussed in chapter 3.[5] In other respects, however, MORSEL embodies an early-selection theory. First, the AM is an early selection device. It operates on a low-level representation, much in the spirit of filtering and attenuation operations proposed by early-selection theories. Second, the processing capacity of MORSEL is limited. If multiple items are analyzed simultaneously, interactions among the items can lead to damaging crosstalk; and there is the further problem that information about the absolute location of each item is lost. Thus, MORSEL shows characteristics of both early- and late-selection theories.

Pashler and Badgio (1985, 1987) have proposed a similar hybrid view of attentional selection based on a large body of empirical work. They summarize their view with a list of six properties required of an attentional mechanism:

1. Visual attention can be optionally allocated to the locations of one or many visual stimuli, by their location.

2. Objects in locations that are *not* attended are subject to attenuation early in processing, prior to object identification.

3. All the objects present in locations that *are* attended are identified in parallel.

4. This parallel identification makes only limited information available centrally (i.e., for response selection or conscious awareness): specifically, the *identities* of the attended objects...

5. The system has an important additional capability: to redirect visual attention to the location where a token of an active identity is present...

6. Finally, it is hypothesized that...the only way one attribute of a stimulus (e.g., color, identity) is tied to another

---

[5] Note that pull out implies serial access, not serial identification: all processing for the identification of an item takes place before the pull out stage. Many late-selection models, which allow a great deal of parallel processing, have similar readout bottlenecks (e.g., Allport, 1977; Duncan, 1980; Johnston & McClelland, 1980; Posner, 1978).

attribute of that stimulus is that detection of any attribute permits narrowing of visual attention onto its location... (Pashler & Badgio, 1987, pp. 78–79)

These properties are entirely compatible with MORSEL. Properties 1–4 describe MORSEL directly. Property 5 is not intrinsic to MORSEL but can easily be incorporated, as I suggest in more detail in section 7.1.4. Finally, property 6 is possible via the gated connections from L_1 to the AM (see section 4.1.3), which can be used to guide attention to the location(s) in which a particular elementary feature appears. I find it both surprising and exciting that MORSEL is in such close accord with the conclusions of Pashler and Badgio. MORSEL was not designed specifically to address attentional issues, yet it makes strong predictions concerning the nature of attentional selection. Furthermore, the hybrid view of attentional selection presented here seems like a possible resolution to the longstanding debate between proponents of early and of late selection.

4.4 Related Work

Koch and Ullman (1985) have developed a related neurally inspired model of the attentional spotlight. Their model is similar to the AM in that it consists of a topographic map in which units are activated to indicate the allocation of attention. Additionally, it operates by gating the flow of activity from a low-level input representation composed of elementary features. In Koch and Ullman's model, however, selection is performed by a simple winner-take-all network. This results in a single point of activity, as compared to the distributed activity pattern produced by the AM. Their model is thus unable to adjust the radius of the attentional spotlight.

LaBerge and Brown (1989) have described an attentional control mechanism which also has many properties in common with the AM. Their model is intended as an alternative to a *moving-spotlight model* of attention, the key feature of which is that shifts in the spotlight take time monotonically related to the distance of the shift. LaBerge and Brown present data arguing against such a model. Although I have described the AM as forming a spotlight, it is not a moving-spotlight model in that the time required for the AM to focus on a location is not necessarily related to the previous location of focus. The emphasis of

LaBerge and Brown's work is different from that reported in this chapter. LaBerge and Brown have emphasized attention shifts—movements from one attentional focus to another—while my simulation studies of the AM have been based on the assumption of no prior attentional bias. Nonetheless, the two approaches seem compatible and complementary. To handle the effects of expectation, LaBerge and Brown have included a *location expectation* input to the attention system that biases attention shifts to task-relevant locations. It would be straightforward to incorporate this into the AM.

A drawback of both the Koch and Ullman and the LaBerge and Brown models is that they are embedded in a serial processing system, capable of recognizing only one item at a time. Without a system like BLIRNET, these models serve merely as an early selection device. This brings up the point that it is not the attentional mechanism itself that determines whether the system as a whole is best characterized in terms of early or late selection, but rather how the attentional mechanism is integrated into the rest of the system. This is where MORSEL makes a distinct contribution to theories of attention.

5 The Visual Short-Term Memory

In this chapter, I gather together the components of MORSEL described in chapters 2–4 and discuss the final stage of perception: the formation of a visual short-term memory. I begin with a short digression to recap MORSEL's overall processing structure.

5.1 Meanwhile, Back in the Color Detection Module

MORSEL was designed to perform more than just letter and word recognition. The original sketch of MORSEL (figure 1.2) contains a number of processing modules, of which BLIRNET is but one. Each module is responsible for extracting information about a particular attribute dimension of the visual stimuli appearing on the retina. BLIRNET detects information about the identities of letters and words. [1] One might imagine other modules that detect information about arbitrary 2D geometric forms, faces, colors, motion, etc. To be concrete, consider two additional modules: a *color detection module* that produces a description of the colors that appear in the attended region and a *case detection module* that produces a description of the case in which letters in the attended region are printed. With these additional modules, MORSEL would be capable of recognizing colored letters of various cases.

Each module is presumed to operate similarly to BLIRNET in that it maps a collection of low-level position-specific features into a collection of high-level position-independent features. In fact, to be consistent, "BLIRNET" should really have been the generic name for the

---

[1] In the current implementation, BLIRNET is sensitive to the size and case of letters as well as their identities. This is simply because BLIRNET was trained on letters of only one size and case. With suitable training, BLIRNET could in principle learn to respond only on the basis of letter identity and to ignore letter form, just as it has learned to ignore absolute letter location.

architecture of each module, rather than the name of the module deal-ing specifically with word recognition: By replacing the inputs to BLIRNET with, say, elementary color features and the outputs with units representing color names and perhaps color patterns (e.g., blue and yellow stripes, black and red checkerboard), BLIRNET is transformed into a color detection module. I shall not attempt to specify the representations further. Clearly a great deal of work would be involved, but it is not germane at present. The important point here is that when an object is presented to MORSEL, it is characterized along a number of attribute dimensions.[2]

Just as BLIRNET can process several items simultaneously, so can the other modules. Just as BLIRNET yields noisy patterns of activity, so do the other modules. Thus, just as BLIRNET requires a PO net to disentangle and clean up activity patterns, so do the other modules. For BLIRNET, the PO net serves to select a single word description from the assortment of letter-cluster activations. Similarly, for the other modules, a single color-description, letter-case description, motion description, etc., is pulled out. It is unimportant whether one envisions individual PO nets for each module or a single PO net that encompasses all modules. Because the modules are functionally dis-tinct, there should be few, if any, interactions among the units of dif-ferent modules. It is necessary, however, for the semlex units, which interact with the pull-out process, to be shared among modules. For instance, semlex units representing the abstract notion of redness should play a role both in the pull out of the word **RED** and the color red.

5.2 Integrating the Attributes of an Object

The next problem is how to bind together the attributes belonging to a single object which have been independently registered by various modules. For instance, if MORSEL is shown a display consisting of a red **X** and a blue **O**, the output of BLIRNET will indicate the presence

---

[2] I distinguish between the terms "attribute" and "feature." An attribute corresponds to a pattern of activity arising in a processing module, a feature to the information represented by a single unit. Thus, word identity is an attribute, a particular letter cluster is a feature; the color red is an attribute, but it may be represented in the color detection module by the collective activation of a number of more primitive features.

of an X and an O, and the output of the color detection module will indicate some red and some blue, but how does MORSEL recognize and represent the red as being an attribute of X, and the blue an attribute of O? Further, how does MORSEL tie an object to a location in the visual field? What follows is my interpretation of feature-integration theory (Treisman & Gelade, 1980; Treisman, Sykes, & Gelade, 1977) within the framework of MORSEL.

In agreement with feature-integration theory, MORSEL requires that the binding of attributes be performed serially. In contrast to feature-integration theory, however, the attributes can be of a relatively high order. To bind attributes, attention must first be focused on the object of interest. This causes the object's attributes to become most active in the top layer of each module, allowing the attributes to win their respective competition in the PO net. Moreover, since attention is currently focused on the object, the state of the AM represents the object's retinal location and size; the location and size of the object can therefore be considered as additional attributes. [3] LaBerge and Brown (1989) have also noted that location can be derived from the operation of the attentional system and is therefore a somewhat special attribute (cf. Nissen, 1985). At this point, one could say that the object's attributes—identity, color, location, and size—are bound by their simultaneous activation. That is, we know what attribute goes with what because all relevant attributes are simultaneously active. This method of binding, first suggested by Hinton (1981b), takes advantage of temporal coherence and contrasts with Feldman's (1980) use of spatial coincidence.

As in feature-integration theory, attention in MORSEL provides the glue necessary to tie together attributes of an object. Specifically, the AM coordinates processing so that each module concentrates its resources on the same retinal region, hopefully on the same object. This role of attention is distinct from the role suggested in chapter 4—that of preventing crosstalk among objects. It is interesting that a single mechanism subserves both the function of enhancing performance in a spatially restricted region and of feature integration (cf. Briand & Klein, 1987, for a contrasting view).

---

[3] At some point in processing, the description of the object's location and size in a retinal coordinate frame must be converted to a viewer- or scene-based frame. MORSEL currently has little to say about where and how this critical transformation occurs.

5.3 Recoding the Representation: A Visual Short-Term Memory

Binding attributes of an object using the method of simultaneous activation works only when no more than one object needs to be represented. If MORSEL is shown, say, a red X to the left of a blue O, however, two sets of bindings—{red, X, left} and {blue, O, right}— must be generated. As long as iconic information (L_1 feature activations) remains available, MORSEL can simply switch attention back and forth from one object to the other. But people do not require iconic information to access the attributes and location of an object. Thus, a visual short-term memory (STM) is required to hold the sets of bindings.

An STM is a structure in which some relatively small number of items can be stored and later retrieved. In common terminology, short term memories are ones that reside in the activity of a set of units, as contrasted with long term memories, which are held in the connection strengths between units (Grossberg, 1982). We have already encountered an STM of sorts in MORSEL: the letter-cluster representation. A particular word is stored in this memory by turning on units for each of its letter clusters; several words can be held simultaneously by superimposing their activity patterns.

More formally, an STM consists of a set of processing units in which an item is represented by a sparsely distributed pattern of activity. As depicted in figure 5.1, the activity pattern of one item may overlap with that of another. To store an item in the memory, its subset of units are turned on by an external source. Recurrent connections from each unit to itself sustain activity, perhaps with gradual decay over time. The activation function for an STM unit might look like:

$$s_i(t+1) = f\left[\delta s_i(t) + ext_i(t)\right],$$

where $s_i(t)$ is the activity level of STM unit i at time t, δ is a decay rate, $ext_i(t)$ is the external source, and

$$f(x) = \begin{cases} 0 & x < 0 \\ x & 0 \le x \le 1 \\ 1 & x > 1. \end{cases}$$

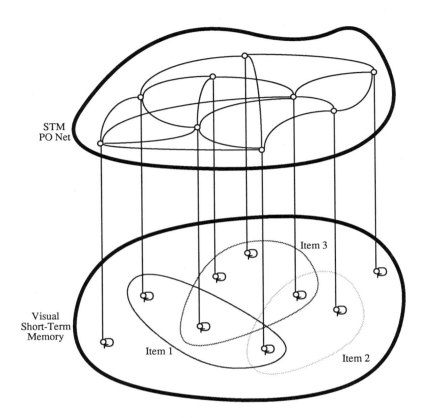

Figure 5.1 A generic short-term memory.

Each item in MORSEL's STM is a visual object—i.e., a conjunction of attributes from the various modules that jointly characterize an object. In order to permanently bind the attributes together, the independent attribute representations are recoded into a multi-dimensional representation (Hinton, 1981b; Smolensky, 1990). The basic idea is that each STM unit is activated by the presence of a particular combination of features across the modules. One implementation might be:

$$ext_i(t) = \prod_{m \in M_i} \sum_{j \in J_i^m} p_j^m(t),$$

where $p_j^m(t)$ is the activity of PO net unit j in module m at time t, M_i is the subset of modules to which STM unit i is connected, and J_i^m is the subset of PO net units within module m to which STM unit i is connected. In the equilibrium state of the PO net, where all p_j^m are 0 or 1, an STM unit will be turned on by a conjunction across modules of a disjunction of features within a module. Intermediate states of the PO net will tend to reinforce these values; ones that do not will decay away if $\delta < 1$.

Consider a simple example that demonstrates how colored letters in various locations might be represented. Figure 5.2 shows two PO nets, one representing the outputs of BLIRNET and the other of a color detection module. Units for the letters **X** and **O** and the colors **red** and

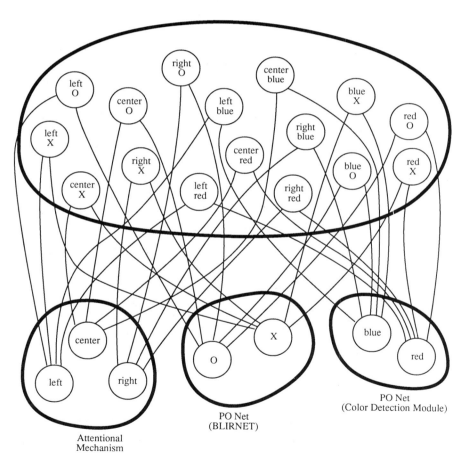

Figure 5.2 A short-term memory that permits the representation of colored letters.

blue are depicted. In addition, the attentional system activates units indicating the focus of attention, coded here as **left**, **center**, and **right**. The STM has a unit for every inter-dimensional pair of features. Thus, if the pattern {**red**, X, **left**} appears, STM units **red-**X, **red-left**, and X-**left** become active. If the pattern in the PO net switches to {**blue**,O,**right**}, then STM units **blue-**O, **blue-right**, O-**right** are also activated. Using this coding scheme, several conjunctions of features can be represented simultaneously in the STM.

This example trivializes the problem in assuming that each attribute is encoded locally at the PO net level. In general, attribute representations will be distributed, e.g., word identity is encoded by a set of letter-cluster units. This does not change the nature of the binding computation; the STM must simply bind together the features that compose an attribute rather than binding the attributes themselves. Smolensky's (1990) tensor-product notation allows the binding of both localist and distributed representations to be described by the same formalism.

One cause for concern with this proposal is the number of units required for the STM. With each attribute dimension represented by a reasonably small number of features, say 5,000, a STM that binds triples of features would require as many units as there are neurons in the brain! The hardware requirements can be eased in three ways. First, it may not be necessary to represent *all* possible conjunctions. Some form of unsupervised regularity detection (e.g., Rumelhart & Zipser, 1985) could be used to determine the conjunctions that occur in the stimulus environment. Second, it is known that with a statistical sample of the possible conjunctions, any combination of attributes can be reconstructed with high probability due to the inherent redundancy of the conjunctive encoding. This is the principle underlying Marr's (1969) codon representation. Third, by increasing the set size of J_i^m to several elements, rather than just one as in the example, the receptive field of each STM unit becomes coarse coded. As a result, the STM units are used more efficiently, allowing the number of STM units to be reduced, but at the expense of the number of items that can be represented simultaneously in the STM. This principle has been the basis of other connectionist STMs (St. John & McClelland, 1986; Touretzky, 1986; Touretzky & Hinton, 1985, 1988; see Rosenfeld & Touretzky, 1988, for a mathematical analysis of the capacity of coarse-coded STMs).

5.4 A Short-Term Memory Pull-Out Net

Once information has been stored in the short-term memory, how is it retrieved? A PO net can be used to pull individual items out of the STM, just as one was used to recover single words from BLIRNET's letter-cluster representation. This network is drawn above the STM in figure 5.1.

The STM PO net must be capable of retrieving an item given a partial description of the item. This is readily achieved by priming units of the STM PO net. For instance, if higher-level processes wish to retrieve a blue item, all PO units representing the attribute **blue** can be given a slight amount of initial activation, which will bias the selection process in favor of blue items. This same trick was used to pull out a word with a particular initial letter from BLIRNET's letter-cluster representation. Because the STM is a visual memory, each item is indexed by its location. Thus, even if higher level processes have no expectations as to what is contained in the STM, the location index allows a convenient means of accessing items: the memory can be scanned by priming each location sequentially.

Unfortunately, nonvisual STMs do not have this convenient location "hook" from which retrieval can be guided. It would therefore seem necessary to have a more general mechanism for enumerating the items in memory. I propose the following two-step scheme. First, a random set of units in the STM PO net are primed and the network is allowed to settle, resulting in one item being selected. Second, activity levels of the selected units are reset to zero *and* their thresholds are raised slightly. The stochastic priming procedure is then repeated. Previously retrieved items will have a lower probability of being selected again because of their raised thresholds.[4] Eventually, all items should be read out of the memory.

The nature of STM representations and the pull out process place limitations on memory capacity. Readout from STM will be difficult if stored items are highly similar or if too many items are stored. While limitations are seldom desirable, these limitations are in accord with human data: The degree of similarity and number of items are

---

[4] This method of implementing a serial search by raising the thresholds of previously retrieved items is similar to that used in Adaptive Resonance Theory (Carpenter & Grossberg, 1987, 1988).

well-known factors affecting the accuracy of auditory short-term memory (Baddeley, 1986; Wickelgren, 1966).

6 Psychological Phenomena Explained by MORSEL

Visual perception and attention have been central concerns of experimental psychology during the past century. As such, the body of relevant data has grown so vast that no single model of visual processes can hope to account for the data in all its intricacy. By necessity, a model's domain must be limited, either by restricting its scope to the quantitative results of a small collection of data, or by allowing a considerably broader scope but at the expense of detail. I have taken the latter approach with MORSEL, having tried to account for a wide range of psychological phenomena. As this introduction is intended to forewarn, the accounts are sometimes qualitative in nature and are justified in terms of single examples rather than extensive simulation experiments. It was, however, necessary to sacrifice some depth of analysis to attain the breadth.

In each of the sections to follow, I describe a phenomenon, cite relevant experimental and/or anecdotal data, and then argue that MORSEL behaves in accord with the data. In most cases, rather than simulating the behavior of the complete model, I focus on the component of MORSEL responsible for the phenomenon in question. The purpose of doing so is to avoid losing sight of the model's key properties in a sea of details.

6.1 Basic Phenomena

Here, I present evidence in support of three basic properties of MORSEL: parallel recognition of multiple objects, capacity limitations, and translation invariant recognition.

6.1.1 Parallel Recognition of Multiple Objects

There is an assortment of evidence suggesting that the visual system can process more than one object at a time. Beginning with anecdotal reports, I've recorded a number of my own perceptual errors in reading that make a case for parallel processing. Here are three such errors, all of which, coincidentally, come from newspaper headlines:

1. **PHILLIPINE FORCES ON RED ALERT**
   ROADBLOCKS RISE AFTER REPORTS THAT AQUINO FOES JOIN

2. **COUNTY ACTS TO BAR SINGLETON HERE**

3. **TOLL RISES IN BRIDGE COLLAPSE**

In the first example, I misread **FOES JOIN** as **JOINS FOES**; in the second, **BAR SINGLETON** turned into **SINGLES BAR**. Both examples indicate some confusion in the linear order of text, difficult to imagine if words were analyzed left-to-right serially. In the third example, I had the immediate sense that **TOLL** referred to a monetary toll, not a cost in lives. It seems quite surprising that the "monetary toll" meaning came to mind initially, given that in newspaper headlines **TOLL** generally refers to a "cost in lives"; had the headline read **TOLL RISES IN BUILDING COLLAPSE**, a misinterpretation seems unlikely. One explanation for this error is that several words of the headline were analyzed in parallel, allowing semantic features of **BRIDGE** to prime the "monetary toll" meaning of **TOLL**. (Admittedly, other interpretations of these errors are possible.)

Although there is no conclusive experimental evidence stating that several different words can be processed in parallel, there is a reasonable amount of data suggesting that, at very least, irrelevant and unattended words are often processed (Allport, 1977; Bradshaw, 1974; Willows & MacKinnon, 1973). Further, the fact that more than one word is processed on a fixation in reading (McConkie & Rayner, 1975; Rayner, 1975) might argue that information is extracted from several retinal locations simultaneously. Direct experimental evidence suggesting facilitation from redundant words is found by Mullin and Egeth (1989). In their study, observers were faster to make a lexical decision when two copies of a four-letter string were presented than when a single instance was presented.

The evidence for parallel detection of single letters and digits is much stronger. Four sets of results are relevant. First, redundant single-letter targets have also been shown to facilitate perception, in proportion to the number of such targets (van der Heijden, 1975). Second, relatively flat slopes can be found in visual search tasks with an increasing number of items in the display (Egeth, Jonides, & Wall,

1972; Schneider & Shiffrin, 1977). Third, Pashler and Badgio (1985) established that degrading a visual display slows reaction times in a search task by the same amount regardless of display size. They argue that the degradation interferes with character recognition and that if recognition were serial, the slowing would have increased with display size. Fourth, the most compelling evidence of all comes from studies comparing the accuracy of target detection when an array of four characters is exposed in successive pairs, each for a fixed duration, to when all four characters are exposed simultaneously for the same duration. The simultaneous condition does not reduce the level of performance (Duncan, 1980; Eriksen & Spencer, 1969; Pashler & Badgio, 1987; Shiffrin & Gardner, 1972). All of these results speak directly against the involvement of serial visual processes.

BLIRNET was, of course, designed to permit the parallel recognition of multiple objects. In chapter 2, I presented examples of two words being recognized simultaneously. BLIRNET has not been tested on more than two words, primarily due to the limited size of its retina. I have, however, trained BLIRNET to recognize individual letters (see section 2.4.2) using a regimen that included up to three simultaneous letters, and this posed no significant problem for the model.

6.1.2 Capacity Limitations

Many investigators have noted that the ability to identify familiar stimuli in parallel does not necessarily imply a freedom from capacity limitations (e.g., Kleiss & Lane, 1986; Pashler & Badgio, 1987; Rumelhart, 1970); the efficiency with which any item is processed might be reduced by the number of other items being processed. Using the simultaneous-successive paradigm described above, an advantage for successive displays can be found if the items are highly confusable (Kleiss & Lane, 1986; Pashler & Badgio, 1987) and if the number of display items is increased from four to nine (Prinzmetal & Banks, 1983), indicating a limit on parallel processing. Even with small displays of nonconfusable items, a conclusion of strict parallelism must be tempered by experiments showing that stimuli separated by less than approximately one degree of visual angle interact (Collins & Eriksen, 1967; Eriksen & Hoffman, 1972; Estes, 1972).

BLIRNET, although designed to process multiple items, is by no means free of capacity limitations. Interactions among items are common and escalate when items are similar and closely spaced (both of which become more likely as the number of items is increased). Examples of these interactions are presented in section 6.2. BLIRNET concurs with earlier theoretical work that has stressed crosstalk as the basis for the degradation of performance with multiple display items (Kinsbourne, 1981; McClelland, 1985, 1986a; Milner, 1974, Schneider, 1985).

BLIRNET shows an additional limitation on parallel processing: when multiple items are analyzed simultaneously, identity codes are activated but location information is lost. To respond based on location, attention must be directed to the location of interest, restricting encoding to the item at that location; this sort of processing is necessarily serial. Kahneman and Treisman (1984) have noted that experimental tasks requiring selection by location generally find in favor of sequential processing, whereas those requiring selection by higher-level stimulus properties such as identity find in favor of parallelism. More to the point, Pashler (1984) presents experimental support for the notion that the locations of multiple items cannot be ascertained in parallel.

Even in circumstances where BLIRNET has the capacity to process multiple items, the PO net presents a bottleneck. Only one coherent pattern can be read out from the PO net at a time. Because the semlex units are tied to the pull-out process, there is a limit on semantic and lexical access. This behavior is consistent with results of Mullin and Egeth (1989) indicating a capacity limitation on the ability to semantically categorize words and analyze the lexical status of two different words in parallel.

6.1.3 Translation Invariant Recognition

Objects can be recognized regardless of their exact location on the retina. This is trivially demonstrated by fixating on a point and bringing an object of interest into view. Whether the object is left or right of center, it can be identified.

BLIRNET endeavors to perform translation invariant recognition. Translation invariance comes about partly from the architecture of BLIRNET (see section 2.3.4), and partly from the fact that objects are presented in a variety of retinal locations during training. In other words, BLIRNET's design facilitates translation invariant recognition, but the complete solution is not hardwired into the network. This fact suggests the unintuitive prediction that learning involving stimuli presented in one retinal position may not transfer perfectly to stimuli presented in another position. Walter Schneider (personal communication, 1990) has preliminary experimental results supporting this prediction.[1]

While BLIRNET's task is the detection of identity information, factoring out any effects of location, location information is preserved along a different pathway—running from the input maps to the AM to the STM. This is consistent with the impressive collection of neuroanatomical and neurophysiological evidence for the separation of processing of "what" and "where" in the primate cortex (Ungerleider & Mishkin, 1982).

6.2 Perceptual Errors

People produce a variety of perceptual errors when several objects are simultaneously present in the visual field. In the following sections, I describe some of these errors and the conditions giving rise to them, and then show how they can be accounted for by MORSEL. As it turns out, MORSEL offers a uniform interpretation of all the errors in terms of locational uncertainty at various levels of processing.

6.2.1 Feature Perturbation Errors

Studies suggest that features of an object can be incorrectly perceived as belonging to neighboring objects (Treisman & Gelade, 1980; Wolford & Shum, 1980; cf. Duncan, 1987, for a dissenting opinion). For example, when an **F** and **L** are briefly presented side by side, observers might report seeing an **E** if the underbar of the **L** is perceived as part of the **F**.

Such *feature perturbation errors* occur in MORSEL due to large receptive fields of BLIRNET's units and the fact that these units do not encode the relative locations of features within their receptive fields.

---

[1] In Schneider's task, subjects are instructed to look at a fixation point and then the stimulus is briefly presented. The presentation is sufficiently brief that subjects do not have time to make eye movements, hence the retinal location of the stimulus is controlled.

For example, a BLIRNET L_2 unit cannot distinguish a stimulus like F_ from E if all features fall within the unit's receptive field. Information about relative location of features is not completely lost, however, because units have overlapping receptive fields; even if the F_ falls entirely within one unit's receptive field, there will be another in which only the F or _ or their parts lie. Although the information needed to distinguish F_ and E is preserved in BLIRNET, it is represented only implicitly: the two stimuli produce extremely similar patterns of activity and accurate recovery of the information requires careful analysis of activity patterns. Thus, the information is sufficiently delicate that recovery may be impossible if noise is present in the system. Such noise can be conquered only by increasing processing time (because the effects of noise average out over time) or by focusing attention on single items.

To simulate feature perturbation errors in BLIRNET, I performed an experiment with the version of BLIRNET trained to recognize individual letters. The letters T, F, O, and P were presented as input in three different contexts: adjacent to a horizontal *underbar* ("_"), adjacent to a *diagonal bar* oriented at 135 degrees ("\"), and in isolation. When the T and F are combined with the underbar, I and E are formed, respectively; when the O and P are combined with the diagonal bar, Q and R are formed. The letters were presented in seven randomly selected locations, with the additional segment immediately on the right. The ratio of activation of the target letter (T, F, O, or P) to the conjunction letter (I, E, Q, or R) was measured for each trial. The mean ratio was 5.66 when the target was presented in isolation, 1.63 when presented with a control context (diagonal bar for T and F, underbar for O and P), but only .43 when presented with the conjunctive context (underbar for T and F, diagonal bar for O and P). When this ratio is less than one, the conjunction letter is liable to be chosen over the target letter.

This effect seems related to the phenomenon of *lateral interference*, in which the perceptibility of an item depends on its distance from other items (Estes, 1982; Townsend, Taylor, & Brown, 1971; Wolford & Hollingsworth, 1974). As such, the target letter should become more discriminable as the spacing between it and the adjoining context is increased. In figure 6.1, BLIRNET shows this property both for control and conjunction contexts. Separation between the target and the context is measured in letter widths (three cells on BLIRNET's

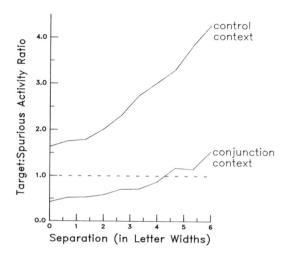

Figure 6.1 Demonstration of lateral interference in BLIRNET. A target letter is more readily detected as the distance between it and other information in the visual field is increased.

retina); zero separation means that the target is immediately adjacent to the context—the data reported above. Note that for conjunction contexts, more than four intervening spaces are required before the target becomes clearly discriminable. Although these results cannot be compared quantitatively to human data, they appear qualitatively similar.

6.2.2 Letter Transposition Errors

When observers are presented with brief displays containing random letter strings, they have great difficulty localizing letters; in particular, adjacent letters are often transposed (Estes, Allmeyer, & Reder, 1976; Mewhort & Campbell, 1978). For instance, CVNR might be perceived as CNVR. Such errors, known as *transposition errors*, are far less frequent within words, even when the transposition would result in another word, e.g., CALM to CLAM (Duncan, 1987; Johnston, Hale, & van Santen, 1983).

In BLIRNET, letter position uncertainty is attributable to the same source as feature position uncertainty—broadly tuned receptive fields—but at a higher level of the system. Evidence of letter position uncertainty in BLIRNET can readily be seen in the spurious letter-cluster activations: one common type of spurious activation involves clusters whose letters are contained in the display but in a slightly rearranged order (see section 2.5.1). For instance, when CALM is presented, not only are the appropriate clusters **C, **_A, *CA, CAL, AL_*, etc. activated, but so are spurious clusters like CLA and **_L, which suggest L in the second position. The PO net, however, is effective in suppressing spurious clusters, and hence, in suppressing the alternative interpretation CLAM. The PO net succeeds because clusters supporting CALM form a *gang* (McClelland & Rumelhart, 1981) and overcome the spurious activations. To be concrete, consider the spurious activation **_L. This cluster competes directly with **_A. Additionally, the neighboring clusters *CA and *_AL excite **_A but inhibit

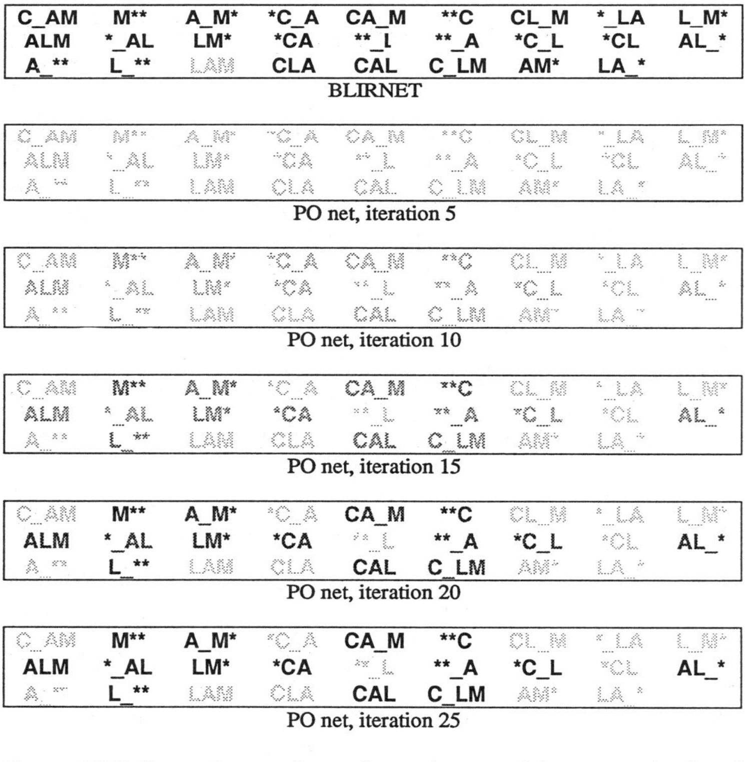

C_AM	M**	A_M*	*C_A	CA_M	**C	CL_M	*_LA	L_M*
ALM	*_AL	LM*	*CA	**_I	**_A	*C_L	*CL	AL_*
A_**	L_**	LAM	CLA	CAL	C_LM	AM*	LA_*	

BLIRNET

PO net, iteration 5

PO net, iteration 10

PO net, iteration 15

PO net, iteration 20

PO net, iteration 25

Figure 6.2 Pull out of CALM from a letter cluster activity pattern that is only slightly more consistent with CALM than CLAM.

**_L. Because **_L is not consistent with most of the other active units, it is eventually suppressed.

Supposing that **_L had sufficient support from other spurious activations, perhaps CLAM could win out. To test this notion, I ran a simulation and obtained a surprisingly powerful result. The simulation involved activating all clusters of CALM and all but *one* of CLAM, the LAM unit. This is just about the worst signal to noise ratio imaginable. Still, the PO net selects CALM, as figure 6.2 shows. This result is obtained whether or not semlex units are included in the simulation. Thus, the mutual support of neighboring clusters suppresses an amazing amount of noise.

Now what happens with an orthographically irregular string like CVNR? When CVNR is presented, not only are the appropriate clusters **C, **_V, N_**, and R** activated, but so are spurious clusters like **_N and V_**. Unlike CALM, CVNR does not benefit from the pull out process because its clusters do not encode combinations of letters and thus cannot form mutually supportive coalitions to suppress the spurious clusters, and further, there is no top-down support from semlex units. Consequently, the relative ordering of V and N in CVNR remains ambiguous. To summarize, MORSEL proposes that letter transposition errors result when: (1) the positions of individual letters are registered with slight inaccuracy, and (2) there is no higher-level knowledge to encode relationships among the letters.

6.2.3 Letter Migration Errors

In brief presentations of multi-word displays, letters of one word are sometimes perceived as belonging to another word (Allport, 1977; McClelland & Mozer, 1986; Mozer, 1983; Shallice & McGill, 1978). For instance, when SAND and LANE are presented, observers might report seeing LAND or SANE instead of SAND. These responses are indeed due to the migration of the L or E of LANE: when SAND is presented in the context of, say, BANK, which contains no L or E, the probability of reporting LAND or SANE instead of SAND is considerably reduced. *Letter migration errors* are far less frequent when the two words share no letters in common, say SAND and LOVE, even though the same letter migration responses are possible. This result is termed the *surround-similarity effect*.

MORSEL can produce letter migration errors, in the following manner. When attention is not focused, letter clusters of both words in the display are activated simultaneously to some degree. In addition, clusters sharing letters with either of the presented words are often activated (see section 2.5.1); clusters sharing letters with *both* of the presented words become particularly active, e.g., S_NE, SA_E, L_ND, and LA_D. The amalgam of letter-cluster activations is consistent not only with the two presented words, but is also reasonably consistent with the two potential migrations. For instance, the migration response **SANE** can be formed by combining clusters from the beginning of **SAND** (e.g., **S, *SA, SAN) and from the end of **LANE** (e.g., ANE, NE*, E**), along with the partially activated clusters S_NE and SA_E. Consequently, the migration words are plausible candidates for selection by the PO net.

Why are migrations infrequent when **SAND** is presented in the context of **LOVE** instead of **LAND**? Examination of letter-cluster activity resulting from **SAND** and **LOVE** reveals that the migration words are unlikely candidates for pull out. **SANE**, for instance, is missing its ending clusters—A_E*, ANE, and NE*—as well as clusters linking its two halves—SA_E and S_NE. Another way of looking at the situation is that the fewer letters two words share in common, the less overlap is found in their patterns of activity; and the less overlap, the easier it is for the PO net to disentangle one word from the other. To the extent that the PO net succeeds in disentangling words, migration errors are unlikely. Thus, MORSEL predicts that **SAND** and **LOVE** should produce fewer migration errors than **SAND** and **LANE**.

To simulate the production of migration errors during pull out, the PO net was run on a set of letter clusters that might be activated by presentation of **SAND** and **LANE**. This set consisted of all clusters belonging to either word, which were assigned activation levels of 1.0, and all clusters matching both words on two letters or delimiters (e.g., S_NE, *_AG), which were assigned activation levels of 0.6. Gaussian noise, $N(0,0.1)$, was added to each activity level; this noise represents perceptual error due to brief exposures and lack of focused attention. In 100 replications of the pull-out process, the migration responses **SANE** or **LAND** were obtained on 43 of the runs. Figure 6.3 presents one run that yielded **SANE**. The pull out process was also tested on **SAND** and **LOVE**. With this pair, only 6 of the 100 runs yielded migration responses **SANE** or **LAND**. The exact proportion of

A_R*	A_K*	AK_*	ANY	*_AN	LA_E	**L	AD_*	*V_N	*VA	IAN	*WA	*_EN
AR_*	**S	*_IN	*JA	AF_*	*C_N	*A_N	*_AR	A_T*	MAN	AT_*	CAN	VAN
RN_*	AY_*	A_D*	*_AB	ANS	*_AG	NK*	*CA	NG*	*MA	*K_N	*_AW	*R_N
NT*	A_O*	*_AK	*O_N	EN_*	*L_N	NN_*	*S_N	AS_*	*G_N	DN_*	*F_N	SN_*
*RA	*_UN	*_AC	*D_N	AP_*	L_NE	NO*	N_**	S_NE	*_AM	LA_D	*NA	*PA
*_AU	NE*	ANI	ON_*	*_AP	RAN	BAN	*_WN	ANE	*T_N	*HA	AM_*	AI_*
AW_*	*_AY	EAN	SAN	PAN	AN_*	L_ND	*J_N	D**	AC_*	*FA	*W_N	*_AS
*_AJ	*LA	NS*	AL_*	A_F*	NY*	ANN	*EA	S_ND	*_AD	*BA	*H_N	*M_N
NA*	*N_N	*_NN	HAN	AND	ANT	A_H*	*_AZ	A_M*	ND*	*P_N	*B_N	AG_*
ANG	*GA	*I_N	*_ON	A_Y*	*_AL	IN_*	AV_*	*_AX	*SA	DAN	ANC	NAN
ANO	A_S*	*_AT	SA_E	A_L*	*_AI	SA_D	A_N*	*_AV	UN_*	ANK	E**	**_A
LAN	GAN	*DA	A_A*	*TA	A_E*	WAN	ANA	*YA	TAN	*KA		

BLIRNET

A_R*	A_K*	AK_*	ANY	*_AN	LA_E	**L	AD_*	*V_N	*VA	IAN	*WA	*_EN
AR_*	**S	*_IN	*JA	AF_*	*C_N	*A_N	*_AR	A_T*	MAN	AT_*	CAN	VAN
RN_*	AY_*	A_O*	*_AB	ANS	*_AG	NK*	*CA	NG*	*MA	*K_N	*_AW	*R_N
NT*	A_O*	*_AK	*O_N	EN_*	*L_N	NN_*	*S_N	AS_*	*G_N	DN_*	*F_N	SN_*
*RA	*_UN	*_AC	*D_N	AP_*	L_NE	NO*	N_**	S_NE	*_AM	LA_D	*NA	*PA
*_AU	NE*	ANI	ON_*	*_AP	RAN	BAN	*_WN	ANE	*T_N	*HA	AM_*	AI_*
AW_*	*_AY	EAN	SAN	PAN	AN_*	L_ND	*J_N	D**	AC_*	*FA	*W_N	*_AS
*_AJ	*LA	NS*	AL_*	A_F*	NY*	ANN	*EA	S_ND	*_AD	*BA	*H_N	*M_N
NA*	*N_N	*_NN	HAN	AND	ANT	A_H*	*_AZ	A_M*	ND*	*P_N	*B_N	AG_*
ANG	*GA	*I_N	*_ON	A_Y*	*_AL	IN_*	AV_*	*_AX	*SA	DAN	ANC	NAN
ANO	A_S*	*_AT	SA_E	A_L*	*_AI	SA_D	A_N*	*_AV	UN_*	ANK	E**	**_A
LAN	GAN	*DA	A_A*	*TA	A_E*	WAN	ANA	*YA	TAN	*KA		

PO net, iteration 50

Figure 6.3 The PO net operating on clusters of SAND and LANE, yielding the migration response SANE.

migration responses of course depends on the noise level; when noise is turned down, correspondingly fewer migration responses are obtained. The qualitative behavior of the PO net, however, does not depend on the exact rules of letter cluster activation. I tried a number of schemes for activating letter clusters, and all yielded a strong surround-similarity effect.

6.2.3.1 Migrations Involving Orthographically Irregular Strings

Migrations occur when letters are embedded in orthographically irregular strings. Treisman and Souther (1986) have studied triconsonantal (*CCC*) strings such as SXT and PRN. McClelland and Mozer (1986) have studied strings composed of a letter and three identical digits (*letter-in-digit* or *LID* strings) such as S666 and L777. No surround-similarity effect is obtained for LID strings, however: S666 and L777 yield as many migrations as S666 and L666.

Consider what happens in MORSEL when an LID string is presented. The pattern of activation at the letter-cluster level is fairly sparse. There may be units that detect single digits, small clusters of digits, and single letters, but there would be few, if any, that directly detect combinations of letters and digits; for example, the string S666 will be encoded by units such as **S, **_6, and 66*, but there are no units such as S66 or *S_6. When two LID strings are presented, say S666 and L777, and attention is unfocused, the units **S and **L will both become active, but it will be impossible to correctly determine which letter appeared in which location, or for that matter, which letter appeared with which surround. Consequently, migrations will result. Similarity of the digit surrounds is irrelevant because the letters are not encoded with respect to their surrounds. Thus, no surround similarity effect should be obtained; S666 and L777 will yield as many migrations as S666 and L666.

On this account, migrations of letters in digits should be at least as frequent as migrations of letters in words, yet the results of McClelland and Mozer indicate otherwise. However, McClelland and Mozer used longer stimulus exposure durations on LID trials, affording greater opportunity to focus attention on one or both LID strings. McClelland and Mozer mention a pilot study in which exposure durations were matched for LID and word stimuli, and the results there indicated at least as many migrations in LID strings as in words. Also, Treisman and Souther's experiments indicate that migrations among orthographically irregular CCC strings are as frequent as among orthographically regular consonant-vowel-consonant strings.

6.2.3.2 Effects of Lexical Status

McClelland and Mozer have observed effects of lexical status. Migrations are more likely when the target string is an orthographically regular nonword (a *pseudoword*) than when it is a word, and when the potential migration responses are words than when they are pseudowords. In contrast, Treisman and Souther found less impact of the lexical status of strings.

MORSEL provides an explanation of these lexical effects in terms of the PO net's semlex units. Semlex units help the clusters of a word to cohere and form a mutually supportive coalition, but semlex units do not help clusters of a pseudoword. Consequently, when presented with a pattern of letter-cluster activity that is equally consistent with a word and a pseudoword, the PO net will select the word. Due to this preference, migrations forming words are relatively more likely, especially when the target is a pseudoword.

Assuming that the influence of the semlex units can be modulated by higher level processes (see section 3.3.3), their effect on pull out is adjustable. With the semlex units suppressed entirely, MORSEL's behavior is identical on words and pseudowords. This allows MORSEL to account for the smaller impact of lexical status found by Treisman and Souther, although it is necessary to understand why observers in Treisman and Souther's experiments "shut off" their lexical knowledge. My suspicion is that the answer lies in the particular stimuli used by Treisman and Souther—three-letter words, all of which had the same center letter. Given the predictability of these strings (i.e., observers knew that only the two outer letters differed from one string to the next), observers may have treated words and pseudowords alike—as strings of letters rather than as meaningful units—thereby minimizing the role of lexical knowledge.

6.2.4 Letter-Cluster Migration Errors

Joint migrations of several letters also occur. Consider the following phrases from Wilkins (cited in Woodworth, 1938, p. 744):

PSYCHMENT	**WOODSON**	**TALDER**
DEPARTOLOGY	**WILROW**	**POWCUM**

In brief presentations, observers often misread these phrases in their more familiar form. Apparently, letter clusters belonging to one word provide perceptual evidence for the neighboring word. I have also collected a number of similar errors from my everyday experience. Though anecdotal, these errors are somewhat more convincing because, unlike the above examples, there were no apparent semantic constraints that might have biased the interpretation. For instance, in reading the text

UNFORTUNATELY, HELMHOLTZ WAS UNABLE TO ...
THEORETICALLY REPRESENT THE NONSTATIONARY ...

I misread UNABLE as UNSTABLE; presumably the ST came from STA-TIONARY. The illusion was quite convincing and can hardly be attributed to semantic constraints. Interestingly, and perhaps not mere coincidence, the context in which the ST is embedded—an N to the left and an A to the right—is identical in NONSTATIONARY and UNSTABLE. Other cases from my collection are similar in this regard:

> **DEAR ANN LANDERS: FOR THREE YEARS**
> **I HAVE BEEN EMPLOYED IN A LARGE OFF-**
> **ICE. I ENJOY MY JOB AND THE PEOPLE I**
> **WORK WITH...**

EMPLOYED was misread as **ENJOYED**, as if the **NJ** migrated to replace **MPL**. (Of course, this could also be regarded as a migration of the entire word **ENJOY**.)

Although letter-cluster migrations seem quite different in nature than single-letter migrations, MORSEL produces both sorts of error by the same mechanism: the PO net acting to recombine letter clusters from several simultaneously active words. To illustrate this phenomenon, a simulation was conducted using only the PO net. All clusters of the strings **PSYCHMENT, DEPARTOLOGY, PSYCHOLOGY,** and **DEPARTMENT** were included, but semlex units existed only for the latter two words. The BLIRNET letter-cluster units were manually assigned activation levels: the clusters of **PSYCHMENT DEPARTOL-OGY** were set to 1.0, all other clusters 0.0. Gaussian noise was then added to the activity of each BLIRNET letter-cluster unit. Figure 6.4 shows one run of the PO net on this configuration in which **DEPART-MENT** is read out.

Even without the semlex units, MORSEL may have a strong bias toward recombining morphemes based on the set of letter-cluster units included in the model. In the simulation above, all relevant clusters were included. However, if the simulation were based on only the most frequent letter clusters of English, say the top 6,000, the representation of **DEPARTMENT** is more complete than that of **DEPAR-TOLOGY**. Eight clusters in the top 6,000 code the junction between **DEPART** and **MENT** (R_ME, RT_E, RTM, T_EN, TM_N, TME, A_TM, AR_M), whereas only four code the junction between **DEPART** and **OLOGY** (A_TO, AR_O, TO_O, TOL). Thus, based on English orthography, there is more glue to tie **DEPART** to **MENT** than to **OLOGY**. Simulation studies with only the most frequent letter clusters and excluding semlex units support this conclusion. It remains an experimentally untested prediction, however, whether orthographic regularity influences recombinations in human observers.

6.2.5 Word Migration Errors

In brief multiword displays, observers may identify a word correctly without being able to localize it (Allport, 1977; Mozer, 1983). This

P_YC	OG_*	OLO	R_ME	P_RT	*PS	MEN	L_GY	T**	YC_O	E_AR
GY*	HME	**P	SYC	RT_E	C_ME	N_**	A_TO	TM_N	CH_L	HM_N
ART	PS_C	LO_Y	HO_O	DE_A	OGY	H_LO	O_Y*	**_E	PAR	S_CH
*_EP	*D_P	**D	Y_HO	**_S	H_EN	T_LO	PA_T	DEP	EPA	R_OL
G_**	YCH	LOG	TME	D_PA	O_OG	*DE	TO_O	TOL	Y**	*_SY
AR_O	NT*	YC_M	CH_E	RTO	AR_M	O_OL	EN_*	SY_H	E_T*	T_EN
CHM	RT_L	CHO	EP_R	M_NT	HOL	ENT	RTM	Y_HM	PSY	OL_G
ME_T	A_TM	*P_Y								

BLIRNET

P_YC	OG_*	OLO	R_ME	P_RT	*PS	MEN	L_GY	T**	YC_O	E_AR
GY*	HME	**P	SYC	RT_E	C_ME	N_**	A_TO	TM_N	CH_L	HM_N
ART	PS_C	LO_Y	HO_O	DE_A	OGY	H_LO	O_Y*	**_E	PAR	S_CH
*_EP	*D_P	**D	Y_HO	**_S	H_EN	T_LO	PA_T	DEP	EPA	R_OL
G_**	YCH	LOG	TME	D_PA	O_OG	*DE	TO_O	TOL	Y**	*_SY
AR_O	NT*	YC_M	CH_E	RTO	AR_M	O_OL	EN_*	SY_H	E_T*	T_EN
CHM	RT_L	CHO	EP_R	M_NT	HOL	ENT	RTM	Y_HM	PSY	OL_G
ME_T	A_TM	*P_Y								

PO net, iteration 10

P_YC	OG_*	OLO	R_ME	P_RT	*PS	MEN	L_GY	T**	YC_O	E_AR
GY*	HME	**P	SYC	RT_E	C_ME	N_**	A_TO	TM_N	CH_L	HM_N
ART	PS_C	LO_Y	HO_O	DE_A	OGY	H_LO	O_Y*	**_E	PAR	S_CH
*_EP	*D_P	**D	Y_HO	**_S	H_EN	T_LO	PA_T	DEP	EPA	R_OL
G_**	YCH	LOG	TME	D_PA	O_OG	*DE	TO_O	TOL	Y**	*_SY
AR_O	NT*	YC_M	CH_E	RTO	AR_M	O_OL	EN_*	SY_H	E_T*	T_EN
CHM	RT_L	CHO	EP_R	M_NT	HOL	ENT	RTM	Y_HM	PSY	OL_G
ME_T	A_TM	*P_Y								

PO net, iteration 20

P_YC	OG_*	OLO	R_ME	P_RT	*PS	MEN	L_GY	T**	YC_O	E_AR
GY*	HME	**P	SYC	RT_E	C_ME	N_**	A_TO	TM_N	CH_L	HM_N
ART	PS_C	LO_Y	HO_O	DE_A	OGY	H_LO	O_Y*	**_E	PAR	S_CH
*_EP	*D_P	**D	Y_HO	**_S	H_EN	T_LO	PA_T	DEP	EPA	R_OL
G_**	YCH	LOG	TME	D_PA	O_OG	*DE	TO_O	TOL	Y**	*_SY
AR_O	NT*	YC_M	CH_E	RTO	AR_M	O_OL	EN_*	SY_H	E_T*	T_EN
CHM	RT_L	CHO	EP_R	M_NT	HOL	ENT	RTM	Y_HM	PSY	OL_G
ME_T	A_TM	*P_Y								

PO net, iteration 30

P_YC	OG_*	OLO	R_ME	P_RT	*PS	MEN	L_GY	T**	YC_O	E_AR
GY*	HME	**P	SYC	RT_E	C_ME	N_**	A_TO	TM_N	CH_L	HM_N
ART	PS_C	LO_Y	HO_O	DE_A	OGY	H_LO	O_Y*	**_E	PAR	S_CH
*_EP	*D_P	**D	Y_HO	**_S	H_EN	T_LO	PA_T	DEP	EPA	R_OL
G_**	YCH	LOG	TME	D_PA	O_OG	*DE	TO_O	TOL	Y**	*_SY
AR_O	NT*	YC_M	CH_E	RTO	AR_M	O_OL	EN_*	SY_H	E_T*	T_EN
CHM	RT_L	CHO	EP_R	M_NT	HOL	ENT	RTM	Y_HM	PSY	OL_G
ME_T	A_TM	*P_Y								

PO net, iteration 40

Figure 6.4 Pull out of DEPARTMENT from PSYCHMENT DEPARTOLOGY.

corresponds to the subjective experience of glancing at a page of text and seeing a word, but being unsure where the word appeared; or of substituting a word from elsewhere on the page into a line being read. (Several examples of this phenomenon were given in section 6.1.1.) Such *word migration errors* arise in MORSEL because BLIRNET registers the identity of a word, but not its location. Unless attention is focused, the spatial source of the letter cluster activity may be apprehended incorrectly.

6.2.6 Illusory Conjunction Errors

Treisman and Schmidt (1982) have shown that when attention is overloaded or diverted, attributes of several items in a display may be wrongly combined, giving rise to *illusory conjunctions* of the attributes. For example, if observers are shown a display containing a blue O on the left, a red X in the center, and a green T on the right, they may incorrectly report having seen a green O in the center.

The general framework of MORSEL, which can be viewed as an elaboration of Treisman's feature-integration theory (see section 5.2), allows the possibility of illusory conjunctions in the following manner. If attention is unfocused, objects everywhere in the visual field will be analyzed automatically and in parallel by each processing module. The modules compute what feature-integration theory might call "features" of the display (which I call "attributes," to distinguish them from the entities represented by individual processing units). At the top layer of each module, many attributes are active. If the attributes are about equally active, the PO net will pull out an attribute at random from each module. Thus, random conjunctions of attributes may arise; the PO net may select the color green from the color detection module, the letter O from BLIRNET, and the center location from information provided by the attentional system. These attributes will then be bound together and transferred to the STM, yielding an illusory conjunction.

6.2.6.1 MORSEL and Feature-Integration Theory

As a possible elaboration of feature-integration theory, MORSEL helps to specify several details of the theory. First, MORSEL establishes a mechanistic account of how attention is used to bind features to spatial locations, and what the binding consists of. Second, feature-integration theory claims only that features are registered automatically and in parallel; MORSEL proposes that there are capacity limitations as well. Third, feature-integration theory makes no prediction as to how much spatial information is maintained by a processing module. MORSEL suggests that each module factors out *all* spatial information except for local relations among features, e.g., that an **I** appeared beside an **N**.

MORSEL goes against the grain of feature-integration theory in other respects, however. First, the features of feature-integration theory are assumed to be primitive, yet MORSEL's modules are able to compute abstract, experience-dependent attributes of a visual stimulus. Second, the features of feature-integration theory are registered preattentively whereas MORSEL's attributes are registered beyond the point of attentional filtering. (See Hillyard, Munte, & Neville, 1985, for a summary of evidence from event-related potential studies favoring the claims of MORSEL in this regard.) Third, MORSEL suggests that illusory conjunctions between dimensions, such as the color of one stimulus coupled with the shape of another, must be distinguished from illusory conjunctions within a dimension, such as the underbar of an **L** merging with an **F** to form an **E**. In MORSEL, between-dimension conjunctions arise at the level of pull out, as described above for colored letters; within-dimension conjunctions, examples of which are feature-perturbation and letter-transposition errors, occur inside a processing module. It may thus be a mistake to try accounting for within-dimension conjunctions in the framework of feature-integration theory (e.g., Treisman & Gelade, 1980, Experiment 4).[2]

---

[2] Experimental evidence supports the notion that within- and between-dimension conjunctions are different in nature. Between-dimension conjunctions are insensitive to the distance among items and do not produce "ghost" images (Treisman & Schmidt, 1982), whereas within-dimension conjunctions are more frequent when items are close together (Wolford & Shum, 1980) and often leave copies of an attribute behind when the attribute migrates (Prinzmetal, 1981). MORSEL is consistent with this dichotomy. The insensitivity to distance of between-dimension conjunctions is due to the fact that all spatial information is factored out by BLIRNET and other processing modules; thus, the activity pattern at the output of each module does not depend on whether items are adjacent or far apart. Within-dimension conjunctions, however, are sensitive to distance: interactions take place within a module only when two items lie

6.2.6.2   *Illusory Conjunctions Involving High-Level Attributes*

MORSEL predicts illusory conjunctions beyond those studied by Treisman and Schmidt (1982), involving not just letters but words. If a display contains several colored words printed in different cases, MORSEL may incorrectly combine the outputs of BLIRNET, the color detection module, and the letter-case detection module. Lawrence (1971) has reported such a recombination involving the identity and case of visual words presented successively in the same location. Although I know of no direct evidence for simultaneously presented words, there is the suggestive finding that letters of a word tend to cohere in the formation of illusory conjunctions of identity and color, but letters of a nonword do not (Prinzmetal & Millis-Wright, 1984). Anecdotally, I have a pertinent story in this regard. I was editing a typed draft of a paper containing the sequence **ONE CONTEXT WITH RESPONSES**. I crossed out **WITH** and wrote in **AGAINST** by hand in red ink. A moment later I glanced back at the page and saw, quite positively and to my great surprise, **AGAINST** printed in black type and in the location where **CONTEXT** should have been.

Another sort of illusory conjunction involving high-level attributes has been reported by Virzi and Egeth (1984). They asked observers to report the identity and the color of adjectives displayed in different colors of ink, say, the word **BROWN** in red ink and **HEAVY** in green ink. Observers sometimes saw the word **RED** in green ink or **HEAVY** in brown ink. MORSEL has the potential of producing such cross-dimensional confusions via the semlex units of the PO net. Semlex units representing a meaning like "redness" could be interconnected with units for the word **RED** and the color red. Activation from the word **RED** flows to the semlex units, and in turn flows back down to the units for the color red, and vice versa, allowing a word identity to transform into a color and a color into a word identity.

---

in a single unit's spatially restricted receptive field. The absence of "ghost" images in the formation of between-dimension conjunctions could be due to the PO net suppressing the activity of attributes as they are selected to prevent them from being pulled out a second time (see section 5.4). Within-dimension conjunctions, however, allow for features of one item being copied to another item: Activation of one unit by a given feature does not preclude the activation of another unit by the same feature.

6.2.7 Similarity-Based Interference Effects

Studies have shown that interference among display items in a recognition task is a function of the similarity of the items (Estes, 1982; Gardner, 1973; Krumhansl & Thomas, 1977). Estes, for example, presented triads of letters in an unpredictable location, and instructed observers to report the center letter (the *target*). When the target was visually similar to the outer letters (the *distractors*), accuracy of target identification was significantly reduced. Estes concludes that the effect of similarity on discriminability can be attributed to a poorer encoding of target and distractor locations when target and distractors are similar and the target is imperfectly identified.

MORSEL shows similarity effects for precisely this reason. Compare MORSEL's ability to recognize a target that is visually similar to the distractors, say, I with distractors L and T (forming the triad LIT), and one that is dissimilar, say, A with L and T (LAT). BLIRNET will produce certain letter-cluster activations that support the correct responses, e.g., with target I, *LI, **_I, I_**. Other activations support one of the distractors in the center position, e.g., **_L, T_**. These spurious activations are caused in part by the presence of L and T in the display and the fact that BLIRNET often transposes the ordering of letters (see section 2.5.1). Additionally, the target I will contribute to these spurious activations because of its similarity to the distractors and the fact that BLIRNET often activates clusters with visually similar letters (see section 2.5.1). Due to this second source, spurious activity supporting L or T in the center position will be stronger for LIT than LAT. Simulations of BLIRNET have shown this to be the case: the ratio of activations supporting a distractor in the center position to those supporting the target was .80 for LIT but only .32 for LAT. Assuming that the probability of the PO net selecting a particular letter is related to these ratios (e.g., Luce, 1959), perception of L or T in the center position should be more likely with LIT, and veridical perception of the target less likely.

As a further demonstration, six pairs of words were selected from BLIRNET's training corpus: LINE-LANE, LISTING-LASTING, LITER-LATER, FIRES-FARES, FINS-FANS, and FIST-FASTER. The words all begin with L or F and the two words in each pair are pretty much identical except that one contains I in the second position (the *I words*) and the other A (the *A words*). If similarity indeed has a detrimental effect, perception of the first letter in each word should be impaired for I-words relative to A-words because L and F are similar to I but not to A. The impairment should take the form of the L or F being confused with visually similar letters (which I will call the *alternatives*). For words beginning with L, the alternatives considered were E, F, and T; for F, the alternatives were E, L, and T. Each word was presented in three random locations; the total activity of clusters supporting the alternatives was computed on each presentation. On average, this activity was .828 for an I word but only .412 for an A word, a reliable difference ($F(1,17)=9.29$, $p<.01$), indicating that the first letters of I-words should be confused more often than A-words. This result reinforces the LIT-LAT demonstration, and seems to be in accord with experimental reports of similarity-based interference effects.

6.2.7.1 Between-String Similarity

The human and simulation experiments discussed hitherto involve similarity of letters *within* a string. Similarity-based interference also arises *between* two strings. In an unpublished experiment by Jay McClelland and myself, we presented pairs of four-letter words and postcued observers to report one of the words. Two conditions were run: *similar surround* and *different surround*. Words in the similar-surround condition shared two letters in common, e.g., SOLE and SITE, and in the different-surround condition no letters in common, e.g., SOLE and WITH. Letters of the two words could not recombine to form another word; thus, migration errors were highly unlikely, and in fact occurred on fewer than 1% of the trials in either condition, contrasting with our earlier studies (McClelland & Mozer, 1986) in which surround similarity resulted in an increase in migration errors. Nonetheless, surround similarity did result in a significant increase in *intrusion errors*, i.e., errors containing letters from neither of the presented words (see also Mozer, 1983, and McClelland & Mozer, 1986, for supporting evidence). Although it seems perfectly natural that similar words are confusable, and that when words are confusable migration errors may occur because it is difficult to keep track of which letters appeared in which word, it is not obvious why confusability should lead to intrusion errors.

MORSEL offers a plausible explanation for these intrusion errors. Suppose that two words are presented to MORSEL, SOLE and SITE, and attention is unfocused. The PO net must select one of the two words, say that it chooses SITE. Once this word has been transferred to short-term memory, the other word must be recovered. What is to prevent the PO net from selecting SITE once again? If attention can be forcefully shifted to SOLE, there is no problem because activations from SITE will be relatively inhibited. However, if attention cannot be focused, as when the words are presented only briefly and the low-level feature information has vanished, some other mechanism is necessary to avoid repeated pull-out of the same item. I therefore suggested in section 5.4 that once a pattern of activation has been extracted by the PO net, activity of the selected PO units is slightly inhibited. Complete inhibition is unnecessary, and undesirable, but partial inhibition should be sufficient to allow activations from other items to come through. Returning to the example, because the pattern of activation produced by SITE overlaps with that produced by SOLE, suppression of SITE will also suppress SOLE. Consequently, the signal/noise ratio for SOLE decreases and intrusions become more probable. If the word pulled out first had little similarity to SOLE, e.g., WITH, SOLE would not have suffered as a result.

How does MORSEL avoid both within- and between-string similarity-based interference effects? The answer is simple: by focusing attention serially on letters in the within-string case, or on words in the between-string case. Human data shows that attentional involvement is required to veridically perceive similar items (e.g., Connor, 1972; Mozer, 1989).

6.2.8 Type-Token Errors

At an extreme degree of similarity, namely when several objects in a display are identical, perception appears to be further impaired: Observers have trouble detecting the repetitions (Frick, 1987; Kanwisher, 1990; Mozer, 1989; Schneider & Shiffrin, 1977, Experiment 3; for a related effect in successive presentations see Kanwisher, 1987, and Kanwisher & Potter, 1989, 1990). In my experiments, observers were shown brief multi-letter displays and were asked to count the number of items that are members of a target set. Estimates are lower when the display contains repetitions of a single target letter than when it contains several distinct target letters. This finding, called a *homogeneity effect*, indicates that observers have difficulty in distinguishing two instances (*tokens*) of the same category (*type*).

Two qualitatively different homogeneity effects were studied. A *form homogeneity effect* was obtained when displays contained between two and nine letters arranged in a row and observers were simply asked to report the total number of letters. Estimates were lower when a single letter was repeated than when all the letters were distinct. This effect occurred only when the repeated letters shared a common visual *form*, and depended on the spatial proximity and adjacency of the letters. Thus, an effect was observed for displays like *d d d d* or *D D D D*, but not *d D d D d D d D d*. In a second set of experiments, an *identity homogeneity effect* was obtained when observers were required to identify, not just count, stimulus items. Pairs of vowels were presented, one printed in uppercase and the other in lowercase, and observers were instructed to report the number of As and Es that appeared. On some trials, two instances of the same target letter were presented—*A* and *a*, or *E* and *e*; on other trials, one instance of each target letter was presented—*A* and *e*, or *E* and *a*. (The vowels were embedded in a context of consonant letters, but this context did not influence performance.) Estimates were lower when the target was repeated than when two distinct targets were shown. This effect occurred when repeated letters shared a common *identity*, despite the lack of visual similarity, and was not critically dependent on the adjacency of repeated letters. Thus, an effect was observed for the two Es in a display like *peb CER*.

As with the other errors reported in this section, the homogeneity effect appears to arise from the failure to accurately encode location information. If location information is lost, the residual representation is insufficient to distinguish one token from another. Difficulty in detecting repetitions of an object is an inevitable consequence. The critical question addressed by these experiments is at what stage of processing location information is lost. The form homogeneity effect appears to arise at an early stage where the stimulus display is encoded in terms of visual form, while the identity homogeneity effect appears to arise at a late stage where the display is encoded in terms of letter identities.

BLIRNET provides a framework in which these homogeneity effects can be interpreted (which is not surprising, given that the experiments were motivated by the model in the first place). The form homogeneity effect can arise via interactions in the early layers of BLIRNET. As BLIRNET transforms elementary features into more complex, higher-order features, features from nearby regions are combined. If two objects in close proximity have the same form, their features may be collapsed together and their distinct existence is thereby discarded. Another way of arguing this is to point to the results showing that BLIRNET exhibits local location uncertainty. For instance, when a word like **BORED** is presented, both the BRO and BOR clusters may become active (section 2.5.1), indicating that the **R** and the **O** were detected but there was some uncertainty as to their precise locations. (See sections 6.2.1 and 6.2.7 for further evidence.) If each letter can be localized only approximately, then the activations from two identical letters in close proximity could be interpreted as providing evidence for the existence of just a single letter.

The identity homogeneity effect arises at the output of BLIRNET. BLIRNET and other processing modules do not encode the absolute retinal location of the attributes that they detect. For example, letter-cluster units indicate the relative order of letters within a string but not the string's location in the visual field. Further, activity of a letter-cluster unit specifies only the presence of the cluster, not the number of tokens present. In the case of processing lowercase and uppercase As simultaneously, both contribute to the activation of a unit like *A*, but activity of *A* does not indicate whether one or two As was present. This difficulty will arise regardless of the locations of the two As, because evidence from the entire visual field converges on the letter-cluster units. Consequently, MORSEL accounts for the finding that proximity is irrelevant for the identity homogeneity effect.

How are repetitions of an item ever veridically perceived if the loss of location information is intrinsic to BLIRNET? Both form and identity homogeneity effects can be overcome through attentional processing. By focusing attention on each display item sequentially, MORSEL is able to create a unique token in STM for each item by binding its location to its identity. Further experiments by Mozer (1989) support the notion that the homogeneity effect is tied to limitations in attentional processing: The effect is obtained when performance is limited by attentional manipulations, but not when performance is limited by stimulus quality degradation.

6.3 Other Perceptual and Attentional Phenomena

I now describe other perceptual and attentional phenomena for which MORSEL can offer at least a qualitative explanation.

6.3.1 Visual Search

In visual search experiments, observers are asked to detect particular *target* stimuli in a display containing irrelevant *distractors*. The task may involve determining which of several targets is present, for example, a T or F among Os (Shiffrin & Gardner, 1972), or whether a target appears at all, for example, whether a red X is present in a display of colored letters (Treisman & Gelade, 1980). The fundamental empirical question in these experiments is how search efficiency—say, response time—is affected by the nature of the targets and distractors. Response time may be independent of the display size, suggesting a parallel search; or the time may be proportional to the display size, suggesting a serial search. Many other possibilities exist and are actually observed, including sublinear and supralinear relations between response time and display size (Pashler, 1987a; Wolfe, Cave, & Franzel, 1989).

To examine how MORSEL would respond in this paradigm, consider the task of searching for a T in a display of vertical and horizontal bars. Presenting the display causes a pattern of activity on MORSEL's retina. This activity propagates through BLIRNET, producing activities in the letter-cluster units. If the T is present, the *T* unit will become active. But the vertical and horizontal bars also may cause some activation of the *T* unit. Hence, the activity level of *T* may be insufficient to determine whether the T was actually present. This is a basic limitation of BLIRNET: if display items are similar and/or if items are closely spaced, interactions within BLIRNET will produce spurious activations (see sections 6.2.1 and 6.2.7 for illustrations). This prevents MORSEL from using a fully parallel search. The alternative is for MORSEL to direct attention to individual items or to small groups of items in order to limit crosstalk within BLIRNET.

This implicates the AM in performing visual search. How will the AM determine where to focus? Higher levels of cognition could dictate a systematic, sequential scan of the display through the direct top-down inputs to the AM. One might call this a *brute force* strategy. But a better strategy is available to the AM in some circumstances. Remember that higher levels of cognition can control the focus of attention not only with direct inputs to the AM, but also by modulating which elementary feature maps activate the AM. If the target possesses elementary features that make it highly discriminable from the distractors, higher levels of cognition can predicate selection on these critical features. An example of this *intelligent filtering* strategy was given in chapter 4: the AM was able to pick out an X from a set of distractors when higher levels of cognition selectively suppressed all but the 45° and 135° line-segment feature maps. Wolfe et al. (1989) and Treisman (1990) have recently sketched models based on a method much like the intelligent filtering strategy. This strategy does not allow for selection on the basis of relationships among features or on the distribution of features within an object, but only on the basis of whether a feature or combination of features is present in the object.

In the case of searching for a T among horizontal and vertical bars, the relevant elementary features are the 0° and 90° line segments. Basing selection on these features, high levels of cognition can achieve an input to the AM like that shown in the top frame of figure 6.5. This frame depicts an input consisting of six items, the T being in the fifth position. The AM selects the T because its input strength is greatest.[3] The AM requires 16 iterations to completely suppress the distractors. The selection time decreases slightly as the number of display items decreases: when four items are presented, the AM requires 14 iterations, and when two items are presented, the AM requires only 12 iterations. This behavior is robust to different target locations and inter- and intra-stimulus arrangements. It is a consequence of the AM activation rule: Inhibition in the AM is proportional to the average activity of all active units. The more distractor stimuli present in the display, the lower the average activity will be and hence the lower the inhibition and the slower the AM will be to select one item.[4]

The nature of the target and distractors dictates the type of processing that will be required in visual search. As indicated in the previous discussion, the task can be performed in one of three ways:

---

[3] In this example, the input strength of each item is confounded with the number of active units composing the item. When the two factors are teased apart, it does indeed turn out that the input strength is the critical variable: if the T is replaced by a vertical or horizontal bar with twice the input strength, performance of the AM is unaltered.

[4] The AM was not designed with this property in mind. The only design criterion was to construct a mechanism that worked reliably. On revaluation, however, it is not clear how one could build a mechanism that did not exhibit this property.

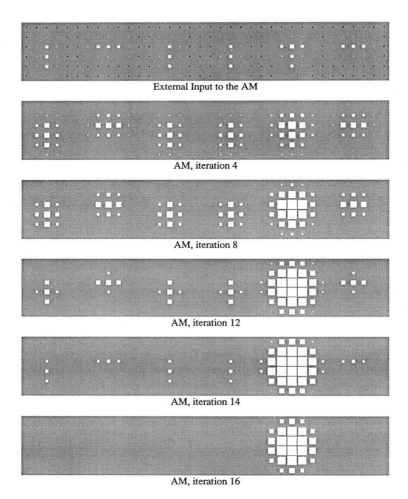

External Input to the AM

AM, iteration 4

AM, iteration 8

AM, iteration 12

AM, iteration 14

AM, iteration 16

Figure 6.5 The operation of the AM when a T is presented in a background of horizontal and vertical line segments.

1. If the items in the display are not densely packed and if the target is highly dissimilar from all distractors, then BLIRNET should be capable of detecting the target without involvement of the AM because interference from the distractors will be negligible. Call this strategy *parallel processing*.

2. Otherwise, if the target can be distinguished from distractors by the presence of some elementary feature or combination of

elementary features, higher levels of cognition can direct the AM to these features and thereby filter out the distractors. Call this strategy *pop out*.

3. Otherwise, serial attentional search is mandated. Call this strategy *serial search*.

If the parallel processing strategy applies, response time is independent of display size. If the pop-out strategy applies, response time is fairly independent of display size; the AM requires only one settling, no matter how many items are in the display, but the settling time is somewhat influenced by display size, as the example above illustrated. For the serial search strategy, response time is highly dependent on display size, because the AM must settle once for each item or cluster of items in the display.[5]

To account for human visual search data, it is first necessary to expand upon the conditions that allow the AM to select the target via the pop-out strategy. In figure 6.5, the target is highly distinctive in the sense that the net input to the AM supporting the target location is twice that of any of the distractor locations. This ratio of target:distractor strength is critical because it is a measure of the ease with which the AM can pick out the target. If the target is not sufficiently distinctive, the serial-search strategy will be required. A simulation experiment was conducted to validate this claim. The AM was given the same input as in figure 6.5, with Gaussian noise added. The noise value at each location had zero mean and a standard deviation equal to the input strength at that location multiplied by a scaling factor (the *noise level*). The noise level was varied from 0.0 to 1.0. The noise could correspond to intrinsic randomness in the system, or it might be viewed as a manipulation to moderate the target:distractor strength. The stronger the noise is, the more the data-driven inputs to the AM are masked. To vary the target:distractor strength more directly, simulations were run not only with the input of figure 6.5, which has a 6:3 strength ratio, but similar displays with 5:3 and 4:3 ratios.

---

[5] Even for serial search, processing need not be serial on an item-by-item basis. The AM might focus on clusters of items sufficiently small to allow for BLIRNET to process all items in a cluster in parallel.

Figure 6.6 shows the results of 100 replications of each condition. The AM was judged to have succeeded in selecting the target if, upon reaching equilibrium, the mean activity of the region around the target was above .9 and the mean activity of the region around each distractor was below .1. There are two ways of looking at this figure. First, for a fixed noise level, one can see that the AM is more likely to succeed if the target:distractor strength is higher. Second, for a particular target:distractor strength, the AM is more likely to succeed as the noise level decreases. The same pattern of results is observed for other display sizes and other target-distractor sets. The results strongly indicate that as the target becomes less distinctive, the AM becomes unable to reliably detect the target among distractors. The detection difficulty is a continuous function of the relative target strength. Thus, it is not the case that the model must respond *either* as if it were in pop-out mode *or* serial-search mode. As the target becomes less distinctive, serial search behavior becomes more likely, causing response time to become increasingly bound to display size.

This general picture is in agreement with psychological data. Duncan and Humphreys (1989) note that there is no clear dichotomy between serial and parallel search modes in the literature, as MORSEL

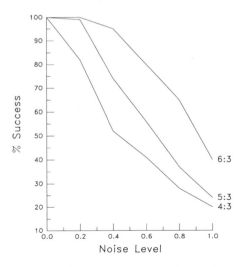

Figure 6.6 Percent of trials in which the AM successfully selects a target item among five distractors, as a function of the target:distractor strength (6:3, 5:3, and 4:3) and the noise level.

would predict from the gradual transition between situations where the AM can reliably select the target on the basis of elementary features (pop out) and where serial search is required. Even in experiments where behavior is interpreted as parallel search, response time does increase slightly with display size (say, 5 msec per item). In MOR-SEL, this corresponds to the pop-out mode, where the AM can success-fully pick out the target, but the settling time is influenced by display size. To elaborate this general picture, I now survey specific results in the literature and relate them to the framework provided by MORSEL.

If targets can be distinguished from distractors on the basis of an elementary feature, search is generally easy (Beck & Ambler, 1973; Bergen & Julesz, 1983; Treisman & Gelade, 1980). For instance, Beck and Ambler found a small effect of display size when searching for a tilted T among upright Ts. In this case, the target has strokes of a unique orientation, allowing attentional selection on the basis of these strokes. When searching for an L among upright Ts, however, a large effect of display size was observed. An L and a T contain the same elementary features—a horizontal and a vertical line segment—which makes them equivalent as far as attentional selection is concerned, because attention cannot be guided by information about the relation-ships among features of an object.

That targets contain a unique elementary feature is not *sufficient* for easy search (Treisman & Gormican, 1988). For instance, search for a vertical line among lines tilted 18° to the left is difficult, but search for a vertical line among horizontal lines is easy; search for a straight line among arcs of low curvature is difficult, but search for a straight line among semi-circles is easy. Thus, the *distinctiveness* of target features is as critical as their uniqueness. These results can be explained in MORSEL by postulating some inaccuracy in the registra-tion of elementary features. If 18° tilted line segments partially activate the vertical-line detectors, and the AM is asked to select on the basis of activity from the vertical-line feature map, the distractors each provide some input. Consequently, the relative target strength may be insufficient to achieve pop out.[6]

---

[6] Although I have described the broad tuning of feature detectors as an inaccuracy in feature registration, it is precisely what is required for the veridical representation of feature values with a limited number of detectors (Hinton, McClelland, & Rumelhart, 1986). Unfortunately for the AM, this type of coarse-coded representation is often in-compatible with the pop-out strategy.

Treisman and Souther (1985) and Treisman and Gormican (1988) have observed asymmetries in search that can also be accounted for in this framework. Search for the presence of a feature is easier than search for its absence, a direct implication of MORSEL. More interestingly, while search for a vertical line among tilted ones can be hard, search for a tilted line among verticals is easy. This is compatible with MORSEL by assuming an asymmetry in the feature registration process such that tilted lines produce some partial activity in the vertical detector, but not vice versa.

Treisman and Gelade (1980) have suggested a qualitative distinction between search for single features and search for conjunctions of feature. They found that search for an X among colored O is easy, as is search for a blue shape among red Xs and Os, but search for a blue X among red Xs and blue O is difficult. Although MORSEL suggests no qualitative difference between single feature and conjunction search per se, the model does predict that pop out should be more difficult for conjunction search. When searching for a blue shape among red shapes, higher levels of cognition should allow activity from the "blue" feature map to propagate to the AM. The location of the target will receive strong input, whereas the locations of the distractors will receive none. When searching for a blue X among red Xs and blue Os, however, higher levels of cognition should allow activity from, say, the 45° and 135° line-segment feature maps, as well as the "blue" feature map, to propagate to the AM. The location of the target will receive about twice the input as the locations of the distractors. Thus, the target:distractor strength is 1:0 for feature search but only 2:1 for conjunction search, a large quantitative difference. With some noise in the activation process, the relative target strength may be insufficient for pop out in conjunctive search (see figure 6.6), although feature search will be far more noise resistant.

This argument implies that in situations where the features are highly distinctive, pop out may be possible for conjunction search because highly distinctive features will increase the signal strength relative to the noise. Indeed, Wolfe et al. (1989) have demonstrated exactly this result: Search is easy for conjunctions of color and form, color and orientation, and color and size when stimulus salience is increased over the displays used by Treisman and Gelade (1980). Wolfe et al. conclude that the accumulation of results showing easy search for feature conjunctions (Egeth, Virzi, & Garbart, 1984; Humphreys, Quinlan, & Riddoch, 1989; Nakayama & Silverman, 1986; Pashler, 1987b; Steinman, 1987; Treisman, 1988) may indicate that easy search is the general rule not the exception. Sketching an attentional model that receives input much like the AM, Wolfe et al. proceed to test a further prediction: that search for a conjunction of *three* features can be easier than a conjunction of two features when the distractors share only one feature with the target. The target:distractor strength is 3:1 in the triple conjunction condition versus 2:1 for the double conjunction. The greater signal strength facilitates pop out.

The theoretical perspective offered by MORSEL is consistent with the conclusions reached by Wolfe et al. and Duncan and Humphreys (1989). Wolfe et al. point to stimulus salience as being a critical factor in determining ease of search; Duncan and Humphreys point to the similarity of targets to distractors. Increasing salience and decreasing similarity has the effect of amplifying the relative target strength, making the pop-out strategy more viable.[7] MORSEL goes beyond the statement that target-distractor similarity affects search efficiency in claiming that similarity can have an effect at several distinct loci in the system: in the initial registration of features on MORSEL's retina,

---

[7] Duncan and Humphreys also conclude that search efficiency improves with increased similarity of distractors, to the extent that target-distractor similarity is high. In MORSEL, there are two ways in which distractor similarity can influence performance. First, if the distractors are nearly identical, they form a homogeneous background, and preattentive texture segregation processes could distinguish the target from the background. As discussed in chapter 4, the results of texture segregation serve as another input to the AM, biasing selection to locations where inhomogeneities occur and allowing pop-out of the target. A second way in which distractor similarity can influence performance is via BLIRNET. According to MORSEL, when target-distractor similarity is high, the pop-out strategy is generally unsuitable and a serial-search strategy is necessary. When serial search is performed, response time depends on what size cluster of items can be processed at once. If BLIRNET can process many items in parallel, the clusters can be large and search will be fast. The number of items that BLIRNET can process simultaneously depends in turn on the similarity of the distractors. The more homogeneous the distractors are, the less spurious activity they will produce in BLIRNET, and the easier it will be to detect the presence of the target. Consequently, with homogeneous distractors, it will be possible to process larger clusters of items, and search efficiency is increased.

in the difficulty of attentional selection, in the amount of interference in BLIRNET, and possibly even in the difficulty of readout from the PO net. It appears that the visual search data depend on many components of the model, and worse yet, on interactions among components. If this view is correct, all hope of uncovering a simple account of the visual search data should be abandoned; instead, detailed simulations of computational models like MORSEL must be conducted.

6.3.2 Facilitatory Effect of Redundant Targets

Although the type-token experiments described in section 6.2.8 indicate that observers have difficulty detecting repetitions of a target, a facilitatory effect of repetition can be obtained nonetheless. When observers are required to detect a target letter in an array of letters, detection accuracy improves with the number of instances of the target presented (Bjork & Estes, 1971; Eriksen, 1966; Eriksen & Lappin, 1965; van der Heijden, 1975).

MORSEL also benefits from target redundancy. When multiple targets are processed simultaneously, each contributes to the activation of the units that signal the target's presence. Multiple sources of information help enhance the signal-to-noise ratio. To demonstrate this behavior, I ran a simulation experiment using the version of BLIR-NET trained to recognize individual letters. Either one, two, or three instances of a target letter were presented at a time. No distractors were present. The identity and location(s) of the target were selected at random, except that spatial overlap of letters was prohibited. Two hundred trials were run in each condition. Table 6.1 shows the outcome of this simulation. The second column contains the mean activity of the target letter. The third column contains the median ratio of target-letter activity to the largest of the other 25 letter

Table 6.1 Redundant Target Simulation Experiment

number of targets	mean activity of target	ratio of target to spurious cluster activity
1	.582	3.11
2	.683	4.00
3	.732	4.47

activities; this is an indication of the relative signal strength. By both measures, performance improves with the number of targets.[8]

6.3.3 Word Superiority Effect

Letters are better perceived when they are part of a word or pseudo-word than when they are presented in isolation or in a random letter string (Reicher, 1969; McClelland & Johnston, 1977; Wheeler, 1970). In Reicher's seminal study of this phenomenon, known as the *word superiority effect* (*WSE*), observers were shown pattern-masked target letters embedded in a number of different contexts and were required to make a forced-choice response between two alternative letters. For instance, WEAR might be presented followed by a cue to judge whether the last letter was an R or a K; on another trial, the single letter R might be presented followed by the same response alternatives. Performance is more accurate for the R in WEAR than for the R presented alone.

The WSE depends on visual conditions. The effect is largest under conditions in which a distinct, high-contrast target is followed by a pattern mask with similar characteristics (the *pattern mask* condition); and it is considerably smaller, and can vanish altogether, when the target is low in contrast or otherwise degraded and is followed by a white, nonpatterned field (the *blank mask* condition; Johnston & McClelland, 1973).

MORSEL accounts for the WSE in much the same manner as does McClelland and Rumelhart's interactive-activation model (McClelland & Rumelhart, 1981). Namely, higher-order knowledge helps support letters embedded in words or pseudowords but not letters embedded in random letter strings or letters presented alone. In the interactive-activation model, word units feed back on letter units; in MORSEL, there is no explicit feedback from one level to the previous, only the letter-cluster units of the PO net which interact with one another. As I have shown previously (e.g., section 6.2.2), the PO net is

---

[8] In some empirical studies of the target redundancy effect, display size is fixed and distractor letters are included to fill out the display. For instance, three letters might have been presented on each trial, thereby requiring two distractors in the one-target condition and one in the two-target condition. MORSEL produces a redundancy effect under these circumstances as well.

effective in cleaning up noise in the input, but only to the extent that the target output is a tightly coupled coalition of letter-cluster units. The letter **R** in **WEAR** is supported by a coalition of six compatible neighbors—WE_R, W_AR, EAR, E_R*, AR*, and R**, but, following the representation proposed earlier for isolated letters, an **R** presented alone is supported by only three—**R, *R*, and R**. Larger coalitions are more self-reinforcing, and hence, better able to withstand the competition from alternative responses. Thus, orthographically regular strings like **WEAR** should benefit more than other stimuli from the operation of the PO net.

To verify this prediction, a simulation experiment was performed. Each trial of the simulation consisted of activating a set of letter-cluster units under certain assumptions and then observing which item was selected by the PO net. The stimuli studied were **WEAR** and the single letter **R**. On **WEAR** trials, units in the PO net included all clusters of **WEAR** and **WEAK**; on **R** trials, the PO net was composed of six units, the three for **R** and the three for **K**. Semlex units were not included, to make the point that semantic and lexical knowledge is not critical.

Following the distinction made by earlier investigators (McClelland & Rumelhart, 1981; Rumelhart, 1970; Turvey, 1973), I assume that the limitation in performance in the pattern mask condition is on the *duration* for which information is available to the system, while the limitation in the blank mask condition is on the *quality* of information presented. Thus, in the pattern mask condition, letter clusters were initially activated with high acuity, but after a brief time, arrival of the pattern mask interrupts processing by providing new iconic information that displaces the veridical letter-cluster activity. In the blank mask condition, the initial stimulus is highly degraded due to its low contrast; and because of the nature of the mask, the iconic trace persists beyond the offset of the stimulus.

The specific processing assumptions are as follows. In the pattern mask condition, letter clusters of **WEAR** (or **R**) were initially set to an activity level of 0.1 and clusters of **WEAK** (or **K**) to 0.0; these letter-cluster units fed activity to the PO net for three iterations, after which their activity was reset to 0.0 and Gaussian noise, $N(0,0.4)$, was added to the activity of each letter-cluster unit. The PO net was then allowed to settle, resulting in a pattern of activity consistent with either **WEAR** or **WEAK** (or **R** or **K**). In the blank mask condition, letter clusters of **WEAR** were initially set to an activity level of 0.1 and clusters of **WEAK** to 0.09; additionally, Gaussian noise, $N(0,.015)$, was added to the activity of each letter-cluster unit. The PO net then settled based on this input into one of the two response states. The noise levels of .4 and .015 were selected to attain a performance level of about 80% for word stimuli in the two conditions.

Table 6.2 shows the outcome of this simulation. The correct response is **WEAR** for the word stimuli and **R** for the letter stimuli. Each data point is the result of ten thousand trials and is quite reliable. A WSE is obtained in both the pattern and blank mask conditions, but the effect is much smaller in the latter. Parameter values such as the amount of noise, the number of iterations before the onset of the pattern mask, the letter-cluster unit activation levels, and parameters of the PO net did not affect the qualitative behavior of the system. However, the simulated WSE is smaller in magnitude than that reported in experimental studies; for example, Johnston and McClelland (1973) found a 15% word advantage for pattern masked displays. One explanation for the discrepancy is that I have oversimplified the situation by allowing only two possible outcomes of the PO net. With additional letter cluster units, perceptions other than the two response alternatives could arise, in which case the system would have to guess. One can readily imagine scenarios in which these guesses are more damaging for single-letter stimuli, thereby amplifying the WSE.[9]

---

[9] One further clarification of my simulation results is necessary. Johnston and McClelland (1973) found a significant difference in the blank mask condition between isolated letters and letters embedded in pound signs, e.g., ###R: When presentation conditions are matched, performance is better for isolated letters, leading to a WSE for words over letters in pound signs but not words over isolated letters. The difference between letters in pound signs and isolated letters is attributed to lateral interference arising from the pound signs; letters in pound signs, as well as letters in words, receive interference from the context in which they are embedded, which reduces their relative signal strength. On this account, my single letter stimuli correspond most closely to the letter-in-pound-sign stimuli because the activation level of spurious clusters (those supporting **K**) are the same in word and single letter conditions. To simulate the absence of lateral interference in the isolated letter condition, the mean activation level of spurious clusters must be reduced. As predicted, when **K** cluster activity is lowered from .09 to .088 for single letter stimuli, performance improves and the WSE is altogether eliminated.

6.3.3.1 The WSE and Inter-Letter Spacing

MORSEL makes a counterintuitive prediction regarding the WSE: as the spacing between letters of a string is increased, the advantage for letters in words should disappear. Increasing inter-letter spacing results in letters being encoded as isolated entities and not in terms of the adjacent letters: **W E A R** might be encoded as *W*, *E*, *A*, and *R*, rather than *WE, WE_R, and so forth. By removing the clusters that encode inter-letter dependencies from the representation, the benefits of the PO net are lost, and letters in words will be identified no more accurately than single letters or letters in random letter strings. Surprisingly, this counterintuitive proposition is supported experimentally, both in free report (Mewhort, Marchetti, & Campbell, 1982) and cued report (Holender, 1985).

6.3.3.2 The WSE and Attention

The WSE also vanishes if observers are precued with the location of the critical letter, i.e., the letter about which they will be required to make a judgement (Johnston & McClelland, 1974; Johnston, 1981). MORSEL has a straightforward interpretation of this result. Precuing location presumably serves to focus attention on the critical letter. When attention is focused on the **R** of **WEAR**, the spotlight allows activations stemming from **R** to propagate through the system but inhibits activations from the other letters. The **R** is thus processed in virtual isolation. As is the situation when the spacing between letters is increased, the **R** in **WEAR** yields a letter cluster activity pattern similar to that of an **R** presented alone, and performance in the two conditions is comparable.

Table 6.2 Word Superiority Effect Simulation

Stimulus	Pattern Mask (% Correct)	Blank Mask (% Correct)
Single Letter	74.9	79.7
Word	81.6	81.7

6.3.4 Importance of Word Boundaries

Word boundaries appear to be critical in perception. It is well known that letters at the ends of a string are reported more accurately than internal letters, either because the quality of information about internal letters is degraded by lateral interference (Townsend, Taylor, & Brown, 1971; Wolford & Hollingsworth, 1974) or because the positions of internal letters are poorly encoded (Estes, Allmeyer, & Reder, 1976; Mewhort & Campbell, 1978). I have already indicated that such effects are present in MORSEL (see sections 6.2.1 and 6.2.2). Beyond affording a perceptual advantage to end letters, boundaries serve to define the extent of a word. Readingtextwithoutspacescanbe-quitedifficult. Pollatsek and Rayner (1982) studied the effect of gaps between words by monitoring eye fixations and strategically filling the gap between certain words after a fixed amount of time into the fixation. One interesting result of this study is that the processing of a fixated word is disrupted considerably more by filling the gap immediately following the word's end with a random letter than with a random digit or dot pattern.

In MORSEL, removing gaps interferes with word identification. Compare MORSEL's response to the word CAN presented in isolation and to CAN embedded in a longer string of letters, say, S in front and B in back, as it appears in the fused sentence above. The patterns of letter-cluster activity in response to CAN and SCANB overlap on only *one* cluster—CAN; thus, there is little similarity between the two strings, and the pull out net will invariably fail to read out CAN when SCANB is given as input. The embedded word can be recognized correctly only if its boundaries are known and attention is focused on the region of interest. If, however, gaps between words are replaced by digits, a condition studied by Pollatsek and Rayner, recognition should not be as difficult. Consider CAN embedded in a 7 and an 8, 7CAN8. It is unclear what pattern of activity will emerge from BLIR-NET, but with a bit of retraining, the network could learn to treat all digits as blank space insofar as letter cluster activations are concerned, that is, to activate units like **C and AN* in response to 7CAN8. Such training is not feasible when words are embedded in random letters because the set of to-be-ignored elements is identical to the set of to-be-analyzed elements.

6.3.5 Recognition of Misspelled Words

People are quite able to recognize misspelled words, even out of context. Whether such performance will be mimicked by a model depends on how similar the representation of the incorrect spelling is to that of the correct spelling. In this regard, it is interesting to contrast representations of words based on position-specific letter channels (e.g., McClelland & Rumelhart, 1981; McClelland, 1984) and MORSEL's letter-cluster representation. Position-specific encodings have difficulty with misspellings formed by insertion or deletion of letters because such transformations cause misalignment of the letter channels. For example, if **DIMINISHED** is misspelled as **DIMISHED**, the correct and incorrect spellings share a common representation of the beginning of the word—**D** in position 1, **I** in position 2, etc.—but the similarity of their endings is not captured—the **S** is in position 7 of **DIMINISHED** but in position 5 of **DIMISHED**, etc. (Allowing for a bit of spatial slop does not solve this problem entirely, and it creates a host of additional problems.) In terms of MORSEL's letter-cluster representation, however, **DIMINISHED** and **DIMISHED** have a greater proportion of their elements in common because the letter-cluster representation encodes only relative, not absolute, letter position.

That **DIMISHED** and **DIMINISHED** have similar representations is not sufficient for the two to be identified as the same. Some means of filling in the missing letters of **DIMISHED** is necessary. The PO net provides a mechanism that can compensate for incorrect spellings, just as it compensates for other forms of noise. **DIMISHED** shares enough clusters in common with the correct spelling that the correct spelling is a plausible candidate for pull out. Additionally, **DIMINISHED** has a major advantage over **DIMISHED**: it is a word. Words have strong associations with the semlex units, which causes the PO net to prefer words over pseudowords, making **DIMINISHED** an even more viable candidate. So it seems that MORSEL should often compensate for misspellings, as long as the misspelling doesn't eradicate a large proportion of the clusters of the correct spelling.

When the PO net compensates for a spelling error, its output is indistinguishable from that when the correctly spelled word is presented. Thus, the error goes undetected. An error is more likely to be compensated for, and hence pass undetected, if it does not greatly alter the pattern of letter-cluster activity. Reversing the letters of a word, e.g., **DEHSINIMID**, fundamentally alters the pattern of activity, whereas substituting one letter for another does not. MORSEL makes a curious prediction regarding the detection of misspellings: errors involving the insertion or deletion of *repeated* letters in a word should be particularly difficult to detect. Consider **DIMINSHED** (the I has been omitted). Although the string does not directly activate clusters containing the missing I, e.g., INI and NIS, these clusters are the prime candidates for spurious activation due to the presence of other I's in the string (see section 2.5.1); for example, the cluster INI receives partial activation from the **IMI** of **DIMINSHED** (because the two are visually similar), as does NIS from the **INS** (because the two share the same letters but in a slightly rearranged order). As a result of these spurious activations, **DIMINSHED** and **DIMINISHED** yield quite similar patterns of activity, certainly more so than **DIMINISED** and **DIMINISHED**; hence, a missing I is less likely to be noticed than a missing **H**. A similar argument can be raised concerning the detection of inserted letters, e.g., **REVERESED**: for the same reason that **DIMINISHED** and **DIMINSHED** yield similar activity patterns, so do **REVERESED** and **REVERSED**, more so than, say, **REVERUSED** and **REVERSED**.

A simulation study was conducted to fortify these arguments. I examined the pattern of letter cluster activity resulting from the presentation of misspelled words. The misspelled words were formed either by deleting a letter or by inserting one or two consecutive letters. Half of the misspellings involved repeated letters. The stimuli are shown in table 6.3. The issue was whether misspellings involving repeated letters would be more difficult to detect than those involving nonrepeated letters. Difficulty of detection can be measured by presenting the misspelled word to BLIRNET and examining how strongly the incorrect spelling is activated relative to the correct spelling. The incorrect spelling will always be stronger than the correct, but the prediction is that for misspellings involving repeated letters this incorrect:correct ratio will be lower (closer to 1) because the patterns of activity for the correct and incorrect spellings are more similar.

The activation strength of the correct and incorrect spellings was derived from the activity of the letter-cluster units, according to a formula used by Mozer and Behrmann (1990a). This formula specifies that the strength of a particular spelling is the average activity of the letter clusters appropriate for that spelling—the target clusters—minus

Table 6.3 Stimuli Used in Misspelling Simulation

Deleted Letter			Inserted Letter(s)		
Correct Spelling	Repeated Letter	Nonrepeated Letter	Correct Spelling	Repeated Letter(s)	Nonrepeated Letter(s)
DIMINISHED	DIMINSHED	DIMINISED	REVERSED	REVERESED	REVERUSED
ELDERLY	ELDERY	ELDELY	COOPERATION	COOOPERATION	COODPERATION
SUNTANNING	SUNTANING	SUNTNNING	HABITUATED	HABITITUATED	HABITORUATED
NIGHTSHIRT	NIGHTSIRT	NIGHTHIRT	DECEMBER	DECEMEMBER	DECEMOLBER
CONSONANT	CONSNANT	CONONANT	BEHAVE	BEHAHVE	BEHARVE
CONSONANT	CONSOANT	CONSONNT	DEFENSE	DEFENSFE	DEFENSYE
REMEMBER	REMEBER	REMEMER	EVALUATION	EVALUALTION	EVALUASTION
DISCUSS	DISCUS	DISCSS	TENDENCY	TENEDENCY	TENIDENCY
SCISSOR	SCISOR	SCSSOR	KNOWING	KNOWNING	KNOWLING
SENSORY	SENORY	SESORY	FAMILIARITY	FAMILIARIATY	FAMILIARIOTY
POSSESS	POSESS	PSSESS	MOTIVATED	MOTIVATIED	MOTIVATUED
MISSPELLING	MISPELLING	MISSELLING	QUADRANT	QUADRUANT	QUADRYANT
APPROPRIATE	APPROPIATE	APPROPRATE	FREQUENCY	FREQUENECY	FREQUENTCY
SLOWDOWN	SLWDOWN	SOWDOWN	COMMAND	COMMANND	COMMAIND
BUBBLE	BUBLE	BUBBE	TENET	TENTET	TENFET

the proportion of activity in nontarget clusters, normalized to lie in the range [0,1]. This measure reaches 1 only if all target clusters are fully active and no nontarget cluster is active.

It was problematic to examine the actual output from BLIRNET because BLIRNET was trained to recognize only a small subset of the possible letter clusters. Instead, I used a simple algorithm to obtain activations similar to what BLIRNET would have produced in a full-scale implementation (extrapolating from the properties of BLIRNET noted in section 2.5.1). Basically, a letter cluster was activated to the extent that it matched a sequence of letters in the input string. Partial matches produced partial activations, depending on the visual similarity between letters. For example, the INI cluster was activated by presentation of **DIMINSHED**, primarily because INI matched IMI well—the N and M being visually similar—but also because INI partly matched INS. Further, a certain amount of positional uncertainty was included in the match process, permitting clusters representing slight permutations of the input string to become active. For example, the NIS cluster was activated by presentation of **DIMINSHED** because interchanging the N and its adjacent I yields **DIMNISHED**, in which the sequence NIS is present. This algorithm is described fully in Mozer and Behrmann (1990a, appendix 4).

Measuring the incorrect:correct spelling activity ratio, the results are quite striking. In the case of misspellings involving deleted letters, the ratio is 1.42 for nonrepeated letters but only 1.31 for repeated letters. In the case of misspellings involving inserted letters, the ratio is 1.34 for nonrepeated letters but only 1.29 for repeated letters. Both these differences are statistically reliable ($F(1,14)=18.7$, $p<.001$; $F(1,14)=4.80$, $p<.05$), and they are observed under a wide variety of assumptions about the nature of BLIRNET activations. Thus, misspellings involving repeated letters are more difficult to discriminate from the correct spelling, and hence are more likely to pass undetected.

Anecdotally, in a corpus of troublesome misspelling I have collected, many do fit the description predicted by MORSEL. Recently, however, I have discovered much stronger support from an empirical study (MacKay, 1969; 1987) showing that repeated-letter misspellings, both deletions and insertions, are more difficult to perceive and recall. The study further finds that perception of repeated-letter misspellings is more difficult when the repeated letters are close together, and that errors involving the second of two repeated letters are more difficult to detect than errors involving the first, e.g., **EDERLY** versus **ELDERY**. These further effects have not been simulated in MORSEL, but could readily be explained if long words were processed not as a whole but rather in smaller chunks. Such a strategy clearly seems beneficial in a misspelling detection task.

6.3.6 Integration of Information Across Fixations

Rayner and colleagues (Rayner, 1978; Rayner, McConkie, & Ehrlich, 1978; Rayner, McConkie, & Zola, 1980) have shown that a word or letter string appearing in parafoveal vision can facilitate the processing of a similar word appearing shortly thereafter in the fovea. Thus, information acquired from one region of the visual field can interact with information from another. Studies have explored the nature of the information preserved from one fixation to the next. Because letter case can be changed between fixations and have no effect on the degree of facilitation (McConkie & Zola, 1979; Rayner, McConkie, & Zola, 1980), the use of an integrative visual buffer (Irwin, Yantis, & Jonides, 1983) can be ruled out: presumably, if observers were storing overlapping visual information in an iconic buffer, then changing the case of every letter should seriously disrupt perceptual processing. Rayner, McConkie, and Zola (1980) propose that the information integrated consists of the *identities* of letters of the word (but only the beginning letters unless the word is near the fovea).

In MORSEL, the logical locus of information integration is BLIRNET's letter-cluster level. Presentation of a parafoveal stimulus causes activity in the letter-cluster units. If this activity persists, it would serve to prime the subsequent foveally presented word, causing pull out of that word to proceed more rapidly. The same sort of facilitation is expected in normal reading: as the reader processes the fixated word, information about other words on the page becomes partially activated (more so when attention is not sharply focused), allowing these words to be read out more rapidly when the focus shifts to them. I have assumed that letter-cluster units encode abstract letter identities, hence the predictions that letter case should not affect integration.

Key to the success of this account is the fact that in MORSEL, identity information and location information are decoupled: BLIRNET represents identities, the AM locations. If spatial location information was maintained in the letter-cluster representation, then summation of activities would not help to integrate information across fixations. Empirical support for the decoupling of identity and location information comes from a recent study of Pollatsek, Rayner, and Henderson (1990), who found that the degree of facilitation by a parafoveal stimulus is largely insensitive to whether the parafoveal and foveal stimuli appear in the same spatial location. Pollatsek et al. thus conclude that "the process of object identification is relatively insensitive to location information and that object information and location information are coded fairly independently" (p. 199).

6.3.7 Cost of Attentional Engagement

Speeded response to a visual stimulus is delayed by the presence of irrelevant stimuli, even when sensory interference, discriminability difficulties, and response conflict are ruled out as contributing factors (Eriksen & Hoffman, 1972; Eriksen & Eriksen, 1974; Eriksen & Schultz, 1978; Kahneman, Treisman, & Burkell, 1983). In the Kahneman et al. study, observers were asked to read as rapidly as possible a word that appeared unpredictably above or below the fixation point.

On half the trials, another object was presented on the opposite side of fixation, either a word or a word-sized patch of randomly placed black dots. The mere presence of the second object resulted in a reading time delay of about 30 msec. This delay was eliminated by precuing the location of the relevant stimulus. Surprisingly, delays are observed even when the display contains only one item (Eriksen & Hoffman, 1973, 1974; Hoffman, 1975). In these studies, a single letter was presented in a position that varied randomly around the fixation point. Unless the exact position of the letter was precued, identification reaction times were delayed by about the same magnitude as in the Kahneman et al. study.

There is a great burden on MORSEL to explain these delays, as they seem contrary to its spirit, for two reasons. First, BLIRNET posits parallelism, albeit capacity limited. BLIRNET should be able to process multiple items simultaneously, especially if the irrelevant items are not meaningful: meaningless dot patches should not propagate activation upwards through BLIRNET, and hence, should not interact with the processing of the relevant stimulus, a real word. Thus, the experimental finding of delays due to dot patches goes against the grain of the model. Second, one significant advantage to BLIRNET is that, unlike some other computational approaches to perception (e.g., Hinton, 1981a,b; Palmer, 1984), it does not require selection by location as a precursor to identification: it can analyze an item without knowing its location. The finding of delays in single-item displays where there is positional uncertainty seems to refute this ability in people.

Although BLIRNET cannot elucidate the reasons for such delays, another component of MORSEL can: the AM. Indeed, Kahneman et al. suggest that delays they observe are due to attentional factors. The general picture that emerges from the experimental work is that whenever one or more items is presented and the location of the relevant item is not known in advance, there is the mandatory involvement of an attentional process that takes some time to become fully engaged. This description is consistent with the operation of the AM. If location is known prior to stimulus onset, higher-level processes can orient attentional activation to that location. Otherwise, bottom-up activations from L_1 of BLIRNET and the other modules are needed to trigger attention. Triggering attention is not instantaneous; activation of the AM units builds gradually (see, for example, figures 4.4 and 4.5).

Until it reaches a certain level, reliable transmission of information through BLIRNET and the other modules is not possible. Thus, there is a temporal cost to the engagement of the AM, which is reflected in the empirically observed delays[10]

One aspect of MORSEL is puzzling with regard to these results. If higher-level processes are able to direct the AM to a cued location prior to stimulus onset, why not use the same technique to orient to a much broader spatial region—the entire visual field? That is, why shouldn't top-down connections activate each and every AM unit? This would allow stimulus information from all locations to be analyzed equally well without first having to engage attention. From a logical standpoint, this mode of operation would be beneficial in the experimental tasks described above, but the data suggest that such a mode is impossible. Other research supports the notion that there is a limited ability for a location to capture and hold attention in the absence of sensory stimulation (Hillyard, Munte, & Neville, 1985; Posner, 1980). This explains why advance knowledge of the specific location facilitates processing.

6.3.8 Stroop Interference Effects

In a task first studied by Stroop (1938), observers are asked to name the ink color in which a word is printed. Although the word itself is irrelevant to the task, the nature of the word influences performance: Observers are slower to name the ink color, and errors are more frequent, when the word is a color name and the name is incongruous with the ink color. For example, response to **BLUE** written in red ink is slower than to a neutral word, say **FOLK**.

MORSEL readily provides an account of this phenomenon which is based on the fact that the AM attends to locations, not feature dimensions. If MORSEL is to analyze information about the color of a word, attention must be focused at the word's location. This enables the

---

[10] This explanation of attentional engagement should not be misunderstood to imply that the AM must always select a single stimulus item: if the AM's parameters are set to allow a wide deployment of attention, several items may be included within the spotlight. This is what I mean when I refer to attention as being "unfocused": Unfocused attention is the state wherein attention has been engaged and it envelops all stimuli evenly.

color detection module to process color information and BLIRNET to process word-identity information. The results computed by these two modules are then passed to the PO net, which must select a single word identity and color. If the selection of word identity did not interact with the selection of color, the Stroop effect would not be observed. However, in MORSEL there is a locus of interaction: the semlex units. Semlex units are mutually excitatory with units representing color, as well as units representing word identities. When MORSEL processes the word **BLUE** in red ink, the letter-cluster units of **BLUE** become active in the PO net, as do the color units representing redness. The letter clusters of **BLUE** then activate the semlex units representing blueness, which in turn activate the color units representing blueness. Because the PO net must select a single color, there is a competition between redness and blueness. The stronger this competition is, the longer the PO net will take to make a selection. Consequently, response time will be slower when the word written in colored ink is an incongruous color name.[11]

In the Stroop task, an asymmetry between color and word naming is observed: the color naming task is interfered with more by word identity than a word naming task is interfered with by color identity. To explain this fact, one would have to posit that the connections between letter-cluster and semlex units are stronger than those between color and semlex units. Cohen, Dunbar, and McClelland (1990) have proposed a connectionist model of the Stroop task which is able to explain the asymmetry between word and color naming, as well as other, more subtle findings.

The Stroop task has not been simulated in MORSEL because doing so would require implementation of a color identification module. Nonetheless, there are related phenomena that are more amenable to simulation in the current implementation of MORSEL. The essence of the Stroop phenomenon—that observers are unable to prevent information known to be irrelevant from interfering with the processing of the relevant—is found in a task studied by Behrmann, Moscovitch, and Mozer (1990). In this task, observers are shown letter strings with

---

[11] This account makes the unintuitive prediction that if subjects are shown color words in brief exposures, they might produce cross-dimensional confusions in which a printed word is transformed into an ink color or vice-versa. This indeed occurs, as described in section 6.2.5.2.

the rightmost portion underlined, say GARM or EAST, and are asked to report whether the underlined portion—the *target*—is a word or not. The lexical status of the whole string—the *context*—is irrelevant to the task. Thus, the correct response to GARM is yes and to EAST is no. Four stimulus conditions were studied: target words embedded in word contexts (e.g., FARM), target words embedded in nonword contexts (e.g., GARM), target nonwords embedded in word contexts (e.g., EAST), and target nonwords embedded in nonword contexts (e.g., WAST). These four conditions are called *WIW* (for word in word), *WIN* (word in nonword), *NIW*, and *NIN*, respectively. Response times observed by Behrmann et al. are shown in the second column of table 6.4. Not surprisingly, the lexical status of the target had a significant effect on response time, with words being faster than nonwords. This is consistent with previous lexical decision studies (Rayner & Pollatsek, 1989). The interesting result was that the lexical status of the context also played a significant role: responses to word contexts were slower than to nonword contexts. No statistical interaction was found between lexical status of target and context. Thus, although subjects were told to attend to and respond on the basis of the underlined portion of the string, the irrelevant context influenced performance.

MORSEL predicts an influence of the irrelevant context in part because even if the underlining causes attention to be focused on the target, the context and target overlap in spatial location and it is impossible to process the target without also processing a portion of the context. This is analogous to the Stroop task, where it is impossible to process the color without also processing the word identity. A second reason for the influence of the irrelevant context is that in

Table 6.4 Embedded Target Experiment and Simulation

Condition	Response Time	
	Human Observers (RT in msec) from Behrmann et al.	MORSEL (avg. number of cycles to reach equilibrium)
word-in-word (WIW)	842	36.7
word-in-nonword (WIN)	802	32.7
nonword-in-word (NIW)	1003	59.5
nonword-in-nonword (NIN)	890	49.1

MORSEL, attention acts to inhibit, not completely suppress, the flow of information from unattended regions of the visual field. Thus, even assuming that MORSEL focuses attention narrowly on the underlined portion of the stimulus, the nonunderlined portion will receive some degree of analysis as well.

Consider the consequence of partial analysis of the unattended information. Presenting a stimulus like F<u>ARM</u> will cause the AM to focus on **ARM**, which in turn will cause BLIRNET to activate the letter clusters of **ARM** strongly and the clusters of **FARM** partially. Additionally, BLIRNET produces spurious partial activations of visually similar words. The task of the PO net then is to read out the target and suppress the context and other alternatives. To the extent that the context and other alternatives are strongly activated relative to the target, the PO net has a more difficult selection task; this is reflected in the PO net requiring a larger number of iterations to settle on a stable activity pattern. The PO net competition is also influenced by the lexical status of the items: if an item has a semlex representation, this representation serves to reinforce the item's orthographic representation. To use traditional terminology, the semlex representation provides *top-down support* to a particular candidate. This support can facilitate processing if the target is a word, or can impede processing if the context is a word. In the former case, the top-down and bottom-up evidence are consistent; in the latter case, the top-down evidence reinforces the context word, and thereby makes it more difficult to resolve the competition between target and context. This is the basis for predicting that MORSEL will respond more rapidly to words (**ARM** in **FARM** and **GARM**) than to nonwords (**AST** in **EAST** and **WAST**), and to strings presented in a nonword (**ARM** in **GARM** and **AST** in **WAST**) than to words presented in a word (**ARM** in **FARM** and **AST** in **EAST**).

Conducting a simulation to test these predictions is complicated by the fact that occasionally the PO net selects the context—say, **EAST**— or some other alternative instead of the target—**AST**. Human subjects in these experiments experience the same difficulty as well; this is one source of errors, as when subjects make the wrong lexical decision, responding to the context **EAST** instead of the target **AST**. Often, however, subjects become aware that the perceived string does not match the underlined portion of the stimulus string. Some type of *verification process* is required to detect the incongruity between perceived and the target strings. One simple possibility is the use of word length cues. However, because MORSEL does not encode word length explicitly, I propose an alternative means of verification. I assume a process (which is not modeled directly) that focuses on the first letter of the underlined portion of the stimulus string and matches it against the first letter of the string read out by the PO net. If the two letters disagree, MORSEL is triggered to reprocess the stimulus with the unattended information further suppressed.

I can now describe in greater detail the sequence of processing steps that MORSEL takes to perform the lexical decision task on the underlined portion of a stimulus string. When the string is first presented, the AM begins selection of the underlined portion. Simultaneously, BLIRNET begins processing the entire stimulus. Either because the AM has not yet had time to suppress the irrelevant portion of the string, or because the unattended portion is partly analyzed by BLIRNET, BLIRNET activates the context as well as the target. Operating on this input, the PO net must select one item as the response. I assume that the PO net continues to cycle until *equilibrium* is reached; this is the point at which the activity of each unit in the PO net changes by less than 1% from one cycle to the next, or a maximum of 50 cycles. Next, the verification process is carried out. If verification fails, the PO net is allowed to reprocess its input, but this time with the unattended information completely filtered. The model responds "yes"—i.e., the underlined portion is a word—if there is a coalition of semlex units with activity close to 1.0, indicating that the selected string has an associated lexical or semantic activity pattern and is hence a word. Otherwise, the model responds "no." The model's processing time is measured as the number of cycles the PO net requires to reach equilibrium. If verification fails and the PO net must reprocess the stimulus, the processing times from the first and second settlings of the PO net are added.

All four stimulus conditions were studied in our simulations: WIW, WIN, NIW, and NIN. The WIW stimuli were: **FARM**, **CLOCK**, **ESTATE**, **TREASON**, **QUART**, **CEREAL**, **TRACTOR**, **RESOURCE**, **RABBIT**, **MANDATE**, **UNIVERSE**, and **CARNATION**. These stimuli vary both in the length of the target and the context. Rather than generating different stimulus sets for the other three conditions, exactly the same stimuli were used but the context and/or target were redefined as nonwords. To elaborate, what distinguishes a word from a nonword in

MORSEL is that the word has an associated set of semlex units. Thus, I simply removed the semlex units for the target to transform the WIW stimuli into NIW stimuli, and so forth. This ensured that the four conditions were identical on all dimensions except for the lexical status of the target and context.

The details of the simulations are reported in Mozer and Behrmann (1990a, appendix 4). Several aspects of the simulations bear mention. Because it was not computationally feasible to simulate the PO net with its full complement of orthographic and semlex units, a PO net was specially constructed for each stimulus item. The PO net for a particular item consisted of the orthographic and semlex units necessary to represent the target, the context, and a variety of alternative responses visually similar to the presented stimulus (e.g., **WARM**, **FARCE**, and **BARM** for **FARM**). For the WIW condition, there was an average of 347 letter-cluster units, 336 semlex units, and 7876 connections; for the other conditions, there were slightly fewer semlex units and connections.

Each stimulus item was presented to MORSEL one hundred times. MORSEL can yield different responses on different trials due to two random factors—noise introduced in BLIRNET and the specific pattern of semlex unit connectivity. The third column of table 6.4 shows the average number of cycles required for the PO net to settle in each condition for correct responses. These numbers are in qualitative agreement with the human RT data obtained by Behrmann et al., in the sense that the rank orderings of the response times are identical. Responses to nonword targets are slower than to word targets, and responses to word contexts are slower than to nonword contexts. The correlation between the simulation and human data has a correlation coefficient of .98. Error rates produced by the model were below 6% in each condition.

Conducting an analysis of variance with stimulus items as the random factor, the main effects of target type and context type are both significant (target: $F(1,11)=42.8$, $p<.001$; context: $F(1,11)=13.5$, $p<.01$), while the interaction is not ($F(1,11)=3.3, p=.098$). Conducting specific comparisons of the WIW versus WIN conditions and the NIW versus NIN conditions, both indicate reliable effects (WIW/WIN: $F(1,11)=28.7$, $p<.001$; NIW/NIN: $F(1,11)=8.0$, $p<.02$). The qualitative pattern of results is quite insensitive to parameters of the PO net, the PO net equilibrium criteria, and the nature of the verification process. The main effects of context and target are statistically reliable for a wide range of parameter settings. However, some parameter settings cause the target × context interaction to become significant. The interaction can be prevented by increasing the strength of the bottom-up input from BLIRNET to the PO net relative to the top-down support from the semlex units. Adjusting this strength is legitimate because, as stated in section 3.3.3, I assume that subjects can exert deliberate control over the relative influence of semantics or lexicality depending on the specific nature of the task (e.g., whether nonwords are expected as well as words).

One could attempt to transform the simulated settling time of the PO net to an overall response time for MORSEL. However, the PO net's contribution is just a small fraction of the complete response time of MORSEL; one must also include the time to perform perceptual, verification, and response processing. Because this time does not depend on the stimulus condition, it can be represented by a single number. Taking this time to be 575 msec, and each cycle of the PO net to demand 7 msec, a nice quantitative match to the human data is obtained. However, one should not be terribly impressed given that two additional parameters were needed to fit just four data points! In any case, MORSEL clearly predicts the behavioral patterns shown by human observers and explains why stimulus information known to be irrelevant to a task can nonetheless harm performance.

6.4 Neuropsychological Phenomena

I now describe several acquired reading disorders—neglect, attentional, surface, and phonological dyslexia—and give an account of these disorders in MORSEL. The account of neglect dyslexia has been elaborated in some depth, whereas the accounts of attentional, surface, and phonological dyslexia are somewhat speculative, but provide interesting directions in which to extend MORSEL.

6.4.1 Neglect Dyslexia

The work summarized here has been conducted in collaboration with Marlene Behrmann. A complete description of the work, including details of the simulations, is found in Mozer and Behrmann (1990a, 1990b).

Neglect dyslexia is a reading impairment acquired as a consequence of brain injury. Neglect dyslexia patients may ignore the left side of an open book, the beginning words of a line of text, or the beginning letters of a single word, even when all the visual information appears in an intact region of their visual field (Bisiach & Vallar, 1988; Caplan, 1987; Ellis, Flude, & Young, 1987).[12] Neglect dyslexia, and the concomitant hemispatial neglect syndrome, is traditionally interpreted as a disturbance of selective attention (Heilman, Watson, & Valenstein, 1985; Kinsbourne, 1987; Mesulam, 1981; Posner & Petersen, 1990). One goal of studying neglect dyslexia is to better understand attentional selection in normal processing. Unfortunately, the literature on neglect dyslexia provides a seemingly contradictory source of data regarding the locus of the attentional deficit. Certain phenomena suggest that the deficit occurs early in processing, consistent with an early-selection view of attentional selection; other phenomena suggest that the deficit occurs much later in processing, following object identification, consistent with a late-selection view.

In favor of the early-selection view, neglect dyslexia has been shown to occur with respect to a retinal (or head- or body-centered) coordinate frame, as opposed to an intrinsic object-centered frame. Supporting evidence includes the following:

- Vertically presented words are not subject to neglect.

- rotation of words 180° leads to neglect with respect to the left of the retinal frame, not the object-centered frame. (However, see Barbut and Gazzaniga, 1987, and Hillis and Caramazza, 1989, for an alternative conceptualization.)

- Retinal location of a word affects performance: the further to the right a word is presented relative to fixation, the better it is reported (Behrmann, Moscovitch, Black, & Mozer, 1990; Ellis et al., 1987).

These findings suggest an attentional disruption occurring at an early stage of analysis for the following reason. The initial encoding of the

---

[12] All descriptions here refer to left-sided neglect, which results from right-hemisphere damage, because extrapersonal neglect appears to occur more frequently and be more severe following lesions to the right hemisphere than to the left (Black, Vu, Martin, & Szalai, 1990; De Renzi, 1982; but see Ogden, 1985, for evidence to the contrary).

visual world is certainly retinotopic, and one can argue on computational grounds that object recognition requires as a precondition a recoding of the perceptual data into an object-centered representation (Hinton, 1981a; Marr, 1982). Thus, if attentional selection operates on a retinotopic encoding, it must operate prior to object recognition. However, there is contradictory evidence indicating that the attentional disruption occurs at later stages of analysis. This evidence includes the following:

- Neglect is less severe for words than nonwords (Brunn & Farah, 1990; Sieroff, Pollatsek, & Posner, 1988).

- The nature of error responses depends on the morphemic composition of the stimulus (Behrmann et al., 1990).

- Extinction interacts with higher-order stimulus properties: if two words are presented that form a compound, e.g., COW and BOY, the patient is more likely to neglect the left word than in a control condition, e.g., SUN and FLY (Behrmann et al., 1990).

These paradoxical results rule out simple early and late selection views of attention. The early-selection view cannot explain why selection may depend on higher-order stimulus properties. The late-selection view is contrary to the finding that neglect depends on the position and orientation of the word in the visual field.

We have reconsidered the phenomena of neglect dyslexia within the framework of MORSEL, and demonstrated that a simple lesion to the AM produces the varied symptoms of neglect dyslexia. The lesion is in the bottom-up connections to the AM from the input feature maps. The damage is graded monotonically, most severe at the left extreme of the retina and least severe at the right. The consequence of the damage is to affect the probability that features present on the retinotopic input maps are detected by the AM. To the extent that features in a given location are not detected, the AM will fail to focus attention at that location. Note that this is not a perceptual deficit, in the sense that if attention can be mustered, features will be analyzed normally by BLIRNET.

To give the gist of the account, MORSEL and the hypothesized deficit are compatible with the early, peripheral effects observed in neglect dyslexia because the disruption directly affects a low-level representation. MORSEL is also compatible with the late, higher-order effects in neglect dyslexia: The PO net is able to reconstruct the elements of a string that are attenuated by the attentional system via semantic or lexical knowledge.

I now describe in detail the performance of neglect dyslexia patients and show that their behavior can be accounted for by the lesioned version of MORSEL. The patient descriptions and simulation results are grouped according to six basic phenomena. The first three—extinction, modulation of attention by task demands, and the effect of retinal presentation position on accuracy—appear to arise at an early stage of processing, while the last three—relative sparing of words versus nonwords, distinctions in performance within the class of words, and the influence of lexical status on extinction—appear more compatible with a deficit localized at later stages of processing. MORSEL provides a unifying framework to account for these disparate behaviors.

6.4.1.1 The Extinction Effect

A well-documented finding in the neglect literature is the *extinction* phenomenon, when a patient can detect a single contralesional stimulus but fails to report the stimulus when a second stimulus appears simultaneously in ipsilesional space. Extinction can occur when two words are presented simultaneously in the two visual fields. Sieroff and Michel (1987) demonstrated further that with a single word centered across the fovea and subtending the same visual angle as the two noncontiguous words, extinction of information in the contralesional hemifield is less severe. In a similar experiment, Behrmann et al. (1990) showed that a compound word (such as **PEANUT**) is read better when the two component morphemes (**PEA** and **NUT**) are physically contiguous than when they are separated by a single blank space. Further, when the two words are separated by a pound sign (**PEA#NUT**), performance is still better than in the spaced condition, despite possible perceptual complications introduced by the pound sign, lending additional support to the conclusion that extinction is strongly dependent on the physical separation between items in the display.

The phenomenon of extinction is consistent with the view that the visual attentional system attempts to select one of multiple items in the visual field; in neglect patients, the selection is heavily biased toward the rightmost item. This behavior is observed in MORSEL. In the unlesioned model, when two three-letter words are presented to the AM, attention selects the left word on 41.3% of trials and the right on 40.8%; some combination of the two words is selected on the remaining 17.9% of trials. In the lesioned model, the right word is nearly always selected because the bottom-up input to the AM from the retinotopic feature maps is degraded for the left word, thereby weakening its support. Table 6.5 shows the distribution of attention in the lesioned model for displays containing two three-letter words. Each row indicates the percent of presentations in which a given combination of letters is selected; 1, 2, and 3 are letters of the left word, 4, 5, and 6 letters of the right word. The right word is selected over 75% of the time, with the remainder of the presentations involving selection of the right word along with the rightmost portions of the left, or selections of only the rightmost portions of the right word. The AM clearly demonstrates extinction of the left item when two words are presented. However, when a single item is presented, either to the normal or the lesioned model, at least some portion of the item will always be attended (as discussed in more detail in section 6.4.1.3).

In the normal model, when two items are presented, one will be selected arbitrarily. If the AM is allowed to refocus on the same stimulus display, it will select the other item about half the time. Thus, simply by resetting the AM and allowing it to settle again, possibly with a slight inhibitory bias on the location just selected, both display items can be sampled. In the lesioned model, however, refocusing attention is unlikely to alter the selection. As long as the right item is present the left item is prevented from attracting attention; this masking does not occur in the normal model.

Table 6.5 Distribution of Attention in the Lesioned AM for Displays Containing Two Three-Letter Words

Letters Attended	Relative Likelihood of Attentional State
1 2 3 4 5 6	6.6%
2 3 4 5 6	9.7
3 4 5 6	0.1
4 5 6	76.2
5 6	7.2
6	0.2

Because the AM serves only to bias processing in BLIRNET toward the attended region, as opposed to completely filtering out the unattended information, MORSEL will not necessarily fail to detect the unattended information. This depends on the operation of the PO net, which attempts to combine the outputs of BLIRNET into a meaningful whole. Thus, one cannot directly translate the distribution of attention into a distribution of responses. Nonetheless, the strong right-sided bias will surely affect responses, particularly for simple stimuli which cannot benefit from the PO net's application of higher-order knowledge. For instance, in the task of detecting a single or a pair of simultaneously presented flashes of light, commonly used to test extinction, responses can only be based on the stimulus strength following attenuation by the AM.

6.4.1.2 Modulation of Attention by Task Demands

The strong predominance of right-biased responses in neglect patients can be modulated under certain conditions. Karnath (1988) showed that patients always reported the right-sided stimulus first when given the free choice in naming order of two bilaterally presented stimuli. The left-sided stimulus was often neglected in these cases. When patients were instructed to report the left-sided stimulus first, they were able to report both stimuli. A similar result in the domain of reading was found by Behrmann et al. (1990). One of their patients with neglect dyslexia (AH) reported the left-sided word on only 4% of trials when two words were presented simultaneously. When instructed to report the left-hand word first, AH reported both words correctly on 56% of trials. An overt attentional shift provided by cuing patients to a stimulus on the left has been shown to overcome the neglect deficit in other tasks too (Riddoch & Humphreys, 1983). These findings suggest that the distribution of attention can be influenced by task instructions.

In MORSEL, two sources of information can guide attention to locations: data driven and conceptually driven. These two sources simply add together to determine the selection of a location. In the lesioned model, the data-driven inputs for the left portion of the retina are weakened, but the conceptually driven inputs are undamaged; hence, sufficiently strong top-down guidance can compensate for the deficit in bottom-up control of attention. Simple simulation experiments readily demonstrate this result (Mozer & Behrmann, 1990b). This result makes the point that the deficit in MORSEL is attentional and not perceptual. A true perceptual deficit would occur if, for example, the connections within BLIRNET were lesioned. MORSEL's account of neglect dyslexia places the locus of damage outside of the recognition system; further, the effect of the damage on perception can be overcome via alternative routes—the conceptually driven inputs.

6.4.1.3 The Effect of Retinal Presentation Position on Accuracy

One finding in the literature compatible with a deficit at an early stage of processing is that performance changes as a function of stimulus location. Behrmann et al. (1990) presented words to a neglect dyslexia patient with their left edge immediately next to a central fixation point (the *near position*) or in the fourth character position to the right of fixation (the *far position*). Words appearing in the far position were still in the region of high acuity in the patient's intact visual field. The words were three to five letters in length. The patient reported only 28% of the words correctly in the near position, but 44% in the far position. Thus, performance improved as the stimuli were displaced farther into ipsilesional space. The effect of presentation position argues that attention must be operating at least partially in a retinotopic reference frame, as opposed to an object-centered frame. If neglect occurred with respect to an object-centered frame, the left side of an item might be neglected relative to the right, but the stimulus position in the visual field would not matter. The evidence for attention operating on a retinotopic frame supports an early selection view, i.e., the attentional system chooses among stimuli based on a low-level representation.

While this conclusion is clearly consistent with the architecture of MORSEL, it requires some explanation to see how MORSEL accounts for the effect of presentation position on accuracy. Consider first the normal model being shown a single word. Independent of word length, if the letters are arranged sufficiently close to each other, the AM will always select the region of retinotopic space corresponding to the entire word. In the lesioned model, however, the input strength of the left side of the word is less than the right side, often causing the left side to be suppressed in the AM selection process. Consequently, BLIRNET analyzes the word with a relative degradation of the left side. This degradation propagates through BLIRNET, and to the extent that it prevents the PO net from reconstructing the word's identity, accuracy will be higher in the normal model than in the lesioned model. The same reasoning applies with the lesioned model alone when considering presentation of a word on the relative right versus the left. The farther to the right the word appears, the stronger and more homogeneous its bottom-up input to the AM is, and the less likely the AM is to neglect the leftmost letters. Consequently, accuracy will be higher.

Figure 6.7 illustrates three examples of the AM suppressing the left side of a six-letter word: in the top row, the rightmost five letter positions are attended; in the middle row, four letters are attended; and in the bottom row, three letters are attended. Table 6.6 summarizes the distribution of attention for a six-letter word presented to the AM in each of three retinal positions. The standard position refers to the presentation position used in figure 6.7; the shifted positions refer to moving the word one or two letter positions (3 or 6 cells) to the right of the standard position. As expected, when the word is moved farther to the right, the AM is more likely to focus on its initial letters.

The AM's attentional focus affects BLIRNET's processing of a word and ultimately, the accuracy of report. Nonetheless, the detailed operation of BLIRNET was not simulated because BLIRNET did not have a sufficiently large set of letter clusters for the current simulations. Instead, its essential properties have been incorporated into a simple algorithm that determines letter-cluster activations for a particular input stimulus and attentional state, as was done in section 6.3.5.

The next stage in processing the stimulus is to feed the output of BLIRNET to the PO net, allow the PO net to settle, and then determine

Table 6.6 Distribution of Attention in the Lesioned AM for Displays Containing One Six-Letter Word

Letters Attended	Relative Likelihood of Attentional State		
	Standard Position	Shifted Right One Position	Shifted Right Two Positions
1 2 3 4 5 6	8.1%	18.2%	37.2%
2 3 4 5 6	14.6	24.5	31.9
3 4 5 6	30.1	33.7	25.8
4 5 6	33.0	20.0	5.0
5 6	13.9	3.6	0.1
6	0.3	0.0	0.0

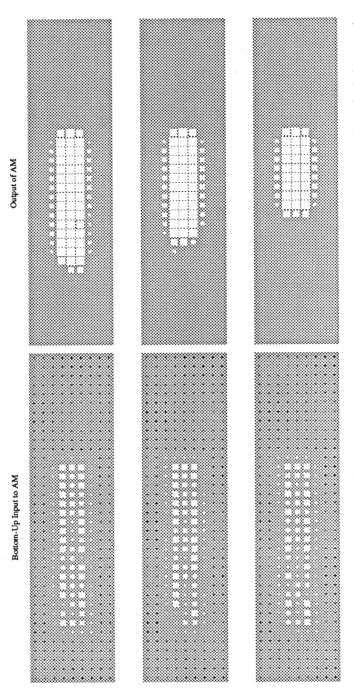

Figure 6.7 The bottom-up input to the lesioned AM and the resulting AM equilibrium state for three different presentations of a six-letter word. In the top row, the rightmost five letter positions are attended; in the middle row, four letters are attended; and in the bottom row, three letters are attended. (Reprinted with permission from "On the interaction of selective attention and lexical knowledge: A connectionist account of neglect dyslexia" by M. C. Mozer and M. Behrmann, in *Cognitive Neuroscience, 2,* p. 106. Copyright 1990 by MIT Press.)

which of a set of alternative responses best matches the final PO net activity pattern. When a stimulus, say **PARISH**, is fully attended, the PO net almost always reads out the correct response. When, say, only the last three letters of **PARISH** are attended, the PO net often is able to reconstruct the original word; other times it fabricates a left side, reading out instead **RADISH** or **POLISH** or **RELISH**; and occasionally it just reads out the attended portion, **ISH**, although the influence of the semlex units acts against the read out of nonwords.

To test the effect of stimulus presentation position in MORSEL, we conducted a simulation using 6 six-letter words. The probability of correct response was 49% for words presented in the standard position, 63% for words one position to the right, and 79% for words two positions to the right. Thus, the peripheral lesion in MORSEL does result in a retinotopic deficit as measured by reading performance. Performance is better than would be expected by examining the distribution of attention alone, thanks to the reconstruction ability of the PO net: Although the entire word is attended on only 8% of trials (for the standard position), the word is correctly reported far more frequently—49% of trials. Nonetheless, the retinal position of the stimulus does come into play; the PO net is not so effective that accuracy is absolute.

6.4.1.4 Relative Sparing of Words Versus Nonwords

A general finding in the neglect dyslexia literature is that the reading of words is less affected by neglect than the reading of pronounceable or unpronounceable nonwords (Behrmann et al., 1990; Brunn & Farah, 1990; Sieroff, 1989; Sieroff et al., 1988). MORSEL suggests that words gain an advantage by way of semantic or lexical support. Specifically, the PO net acts to recover the portion of a letter string suppressed by the AM using both orthographic knowledge (the connections among letter-cluster units) and semantic or lexical knowledge (the connections between letter cluster and semlex units). This gives words an advantage over pseudowords, which lack the support of semantic and lexical knowledge, and an even greater advantage over nonpronounceable nonwords, which lack the support of orthographic, semantic, and lexical knowledge.

A simulation study was conducted using the lesioned version of MORSEL to compare performance on twelve five-letter words and twelve five-letter pseudowords. The two conditions differ in that the words have an associated representation in the semlex units whereas the pseudowords do not. The lesioned MORSEL correctly reported 39% of words but only 7% of pseudowords. In comparison, the neglect dyslexia patient HR studied by Behrmann et al. (1990) correctly reported 66% of words and 5% of pseudowords for stimuli of four to six letters.[13]

To summarize the implications of the current simulation, MORSEL provides a mechanism by which semantic or lexical knowledge can help compensate for noisy sensory data. This results in differential performance for words versus pseudowords because pseudowords do not benefit from such knowledge.

6.4.1.5 Distinctions in Performance Within the Class of Words

Studies examining the lexical status of a letter string have shown a difference in accuracy between words and nonwords, but recent work has found a more subtle influence of psycholinguistic variables on performance. Behrmann et al. (1990) compared performance on words that have a morpheme embedded on the right side—for example, **PEANUT**, which contains the morpheme **NUT**, and **TRIANGLE**, which contains **ANGLE**—and words having no right-embedded morphemes—for example, **PARISH** and **TRIBUNAL**. Although the patient studied by Behrmann et al. showed no difference in accuracy for the two stimulus types, a distinction was found in the nature of the errors produced. The upper portion of table 6.7 summarizes the responses of the patient for words that contain right-embedded morphemes (hereafter, *REM words*) and words that do not (*control words*). Words were presented in two positions, either immediately to the right of fixation (the *near condition*) or several letter spaces further to the right (the *far condition*). Responses were classified into three categories: *correct responses*, *neglect errors* (in which the right morpheme or its syllable control is reported, i.e., **NUT** for **PEANUT** or

---

[13] Little effort was taken to obtain quantitative fits to the data because the quantitative data reported in Behrmann et al. is self-contradictory: the patient performs quite well in one experiment but then poorly with similar stimulus materials in another. This is because experiments were conducted some weeks apart, and therefore reflect different stages of recovery of the patient and different overall levels of arousal and motivation.

Table 6.7 Distribution of Responses on Word Reading Task

Neglect Dyslexia Patient (from Behrmann et al., 1990)

Response Type	Near Condition		Far Condition	
	REM Wds (PEANUT)	Control Wds (PARISH)	REM Wds (PEANUT)	Control Wds (PARISH)
Correct	43%	40%	79%	76%
Neglect Error	39	4	13	4
Other Error	18	56	9	20

Simulation of Lesioned MORSEL

Response Type	Near Condition		Far Condition	
	REM Wds (PEANUT)	Control Wds (PARISH)	REM Wds (PEANUT)	Control Wds (PARISH)
Correct	39%	44%	75%	76%
Neglect Error	32	0	9	0
Other Error	29	56	16	24

ISH for **PARISH**), and all *other errors.* The other errors consist mainly of responses in which the rightmost letters have been reported correctly but alternative letters have been substituted on the left to form an English word, for example, **IRISH** or **POLISH** for **PARISH** (these errors have been termed *backward completions*). In both near and far conditions, overall accuracy is comparable for REM and control words, but neglect errors are the predominant error response for REM words and backward completions for control words.

Our simulation study used twelve compound words and twelve control words—half six letters and half seven—from the stimulus set of Behrmann et al. (1989). The distribution of responses produced by lesioned MORSEL is shown in the lower portion of table 6.7. Comparing the upper and lower portions of the table, it is evident that the model produces the same pattern of results as the patient. The difference in accuracy between near and far conditions confirms the previous finding concerning the effect of retinal presentation position. Overall accuracy is about the same for REM and control words. Neglect errors are frequent for REM words, whereas backward completion errors (the primary error type in the "other error" category for the simulation as well as the patient) are most common for control words. The only discrepancies between the patient and simulation data are that MORSEL produces about a 5% lower neglect error rate uniformly across all conditions and a slight accuracy advantage for control words. These discrepancies are addressed in Mozer and Behrmann (1990a).

The difference in performance for the two word classes is explained by the action of the semlex units. These units support neglect responses for REM words but not control words. The same effect was responsible for the basic word advantage in the word/pseudoword simulations. However, in the present simulation, the influence of semlex units acts not to increase the accuracy of report for one stimulus type but to bias the network toward one type of error response over another when the perceptual data is not strong enough to allow the PO net to reconstruct the target.

6.4.1.6 The Influence of Lexical Status on Extinction

The last two sections presented experimental results that were explained by MORSEL in terms of an interaction between attentional selection and higher-order stimulus properties. However, the tie to attentional selection is somewhat indirect because the stimuli were single words or pseudowords and attention is generally thought of as selecting between two competing items, not selecting between portions of a single item.

Using the extinction paradigm, Behrmann et al. (1990) have been able to show that the ability of a neglect dyslexia patient to select the leftmost of two words is indeed influenced by the relation between the words. When the patient was shown pairs of semantically unrelated three-letter words separated by a space, e.g., SUN and FLY, and was asked to read both words, the left word was reported on only 12% of trials; when the two words could be joined to form a compound word, e.g., COW and BOY, the left word was read on 28% of trials. (On all trials where the left word was reported, the right word was also reported.) Thus, it would seem that the operation of attention to select among stimuli interacts with higher-order stimulus properties.

One natural interpretation of this interaction is that the attentional system is directly influenced by semantic or lexical knowledge, as proposed by late-selection theories of attention. MORSEL provides an alternative account in which attention operates at an early stage, but because unattended information is partially processed, later stages can alter the material selected. Thus, one need not posit a direct influence of higher-order knowledge on attentional selection to obtain behavior in which the two interact.

To describe how MORSEL can account for the interaction, I begin with a description of the lesioned model's behavior and then turn to simulation results. When two items are presented to the lesioned AM, usually the right word is selected (table 6.5). Consequently, BLIRNET strongly activates the clusters of **BOY** when **COW** and **BOY** are presented, partially activates the clusters of **COW** and, because BLIR-NET has some difficulty keeping track of the precise ordering of letters, weakly activates clusters representing a slight rearrangement of the stimulus letters, OWB and WB_Y. These latter clusters support the word **COWBOY**. The overall pattern of letter cluster activity is thus consistent with **COWBOY** as well as **BOY**. Because both words receive support from the semlex units, the PO net can potentially read out either; thus, in the case of **COWBOY**, the left morpheme is read out along with the right. When the two morphemes cannot be combined to form a word, however, the semlex units do not support the joined-morpheme response, and the PO net is unlikely to read the two morphemes out together.

There is another avenue by which the left morpheme may be read out: the patient may be able to shift attention to the left and reprocess the display. In the experiment of Behrmann et al., this seems a likely possibility because all trials contained two words and the patient's task was to report the entire display contents. Although the patient was not explicitly told that two words were present, the observation of both words on even a few trials may have provided sufficient incentive to try reporting more than one word per trial. The patient may therefore have had a top-down control strategy to shift attention left-ward. MORSEL is likewise able to refocus attention to the left on some trials using top-down control (Mozer & Behrmann, 1990b). This will cause an increase in reports of the left morpheme both for related and unrelated stimulus pairs.

Twelve word pairs were used in the simulation; six were *related morphemes*, which can be joined to form a compound word, and six were *unrelated morphemes*, which do not combine in this manner. The left morpheme was reported on 14.1% of trials for related morphemes but only 2.8% for unrelated morphemes. Thus, the strength of semantic or lexical knowledge is sufficient to recover the extinguished information on the left for two morphemes that can be combined to form a word. Assuming that top-down control of the AM allows MORSEL to shift attention to the left and reprocess the display on some proportion of the trials, δ, we can obtain a good quantitative fit to the data. We arbitrarily pick δ to be 10%, which makes the total percent of trials in which the left morpheme is reported 24.1% for related morphemes and 12.8% for unrelated morphemes. These results are in line with the patient data obtained by Behrmann et al.— 28% and 12%.

Interestingly, on trials in which just the right morpheme is reported, MORSEL occasionally produces left neglect errors, for example, reporting **ROY** for **BOY**. Behrmann et al.'s patient made similar errors. Thus, both left-item extinction and left-sided neglect can be observed on a single trial.

MORSEL makes further predictions concerning the factors that influence extinction for morpheme pairs, including the following (which have yet to be tested on neglect patients). First, the physical separation between the two morphemes is important: the further apart the morphemes are, the less activation BLIRNET will produce for the internal clusters of the joined morpheme—e.g., OWB and W_OY of **COWBOY**. This will reduce the likelihood of the PO net reading out **COWBOY**. Patients have been shown to perform better when there is no space between two morphemes than when there is a fixed space (Behrmann et al., 1990; Sieroff & Michel, 1987), but these studies have not manipulated spacing as a continuous variable. Interitem spacing could explain the result of Sieroff et al. (1988) that performance on **COW BOY** (with *two* spaces between the words) is no better than on **BOY COW**, in apparent contradiction to the effect of related morphemes obtained by Behrmann et al. The second factor that may influence extinction is semantic relatedness of the two morphemes. The particular effect we have simulated depends not on the two morphemes being semantically related, but on the fact that they can be joined to form a lexical item. Semantic relatedness alone may allow for a reduction in extinction, but it would not be by exactly the same mechanism (Mozer & Behrmann, 1990a).

6.4.1.7 Discussion

Previous neuropsychological studies of neglect dyslexia have advanced disparate explanations of the deficit. For example, the fact that stimulus position, orientation, and physical features are important determinants of performance has been taken as support for the fact that the attentional deficit arises at peripheral stages of processing (Behrmann et al., 1990; Ellis et al., 1987). This interpretation is incomplete, however, since it does not explain why lexical and morphemic effects also play an important role in performance. A second group of explanations have been proposed to account for the superiority of words over nonwords and for the role of morphemic composition in reading. One theory falling into this latter group postulates that reading of words is automatic and attention-free and is thus immune from attentional deficits (LaBerge & Samuels, 1974; Sieroff et al., 1988), whereas nonwords are subject to such deficits because they necessarily require attention. Clearly, these two types of explanations draw on entirely different theoretical perspectives.

While researchers have recognized the need for a unified explanation that can take into account both early and later stages of processing, MORSEL provides the first explicit, computational proposal. A single lesion—to the connections that help draw attention to objects in the visual field—is sufficient to account for a remarkable range of behaviors, some of which are compatible with a deficit at an early stage of processing and others which might naturally be interpreted as arising at later stages of the system. Although the lesion in MORSEL is indeed at an early stage of processing, higher-order knowledge at later stages may compensate for the peripheral dysfunction.

6.4.2 Attentional Dyslexia

Having provided a detailed account of phenomena surrounding neglect dyslexia, I turn to another acquired reading disorder, attentional dyslexia, and sketch an account in the framework of MORSEL.

As documented by Shallice and Warrington (1977) and Shallice (1988), attentional dyslexia patients correctly read single words presented in isolation, as well as single letters, but performance falters when multiple items are present. For instance, when several words appear simultaneously, letters from one word often migrate to the homologous position of another word. For example, **WIN FED** might be read as **FIN FED**. These *letter migration errors* have also been observed with normal subjects under conditions of brief masked exposure of multiple words (see section 6.2.3). Although patients have no difficulty processing multiple letters as part of a word, as evidenced by normal performance on reading single words, when the task focuses on the letters instead of the word, a deficit is observed. Patients are, for example, unable to name the constituent letters of a visually presented word. The difficulty is clearly in processing a letter when surrounded by other letters, because naming performance is near perfect on individually presented letters. Even when a target letter is flanked by digits that are of a different color and do not have to be reported (e.g., the target V in 1 3 V 4 7), patients still make some errors. A striking feature of the disorder is that the category of the irrelevant flankers affects performance: If the flanking symbols are letters—members of the same category (e.g., H L V R C), performance is much poorer. This category effect cannot be due to interference occurring at the response production stage: When the target is a digit and is surrounded by other digits, interference is marked but when the target digit is replaced by dots which the patient is to count, performance is significantly better. Thus, when the output demands are equated, there is still a significant effect of the category of the flankers in relation to the targets.

Acquired attentional dyslexia has only been reported in the two patients described by Shallice and Warrington (1977). However, Geiger and Lettvin (1987) have described a group of developmental dyslexic readers who show many of the same characteristics as the acquired attentional dylexics. When letters are presented foveally and in isolation, their subjects are able to identify the letters with no difficulty. If, however, the foveal letters are presented simultaneously with letters in the parafovea, the dyslexic subjects are significantly worse than control subjects at reporting letters closest to fixation. Geiger and Lettvin (1987) suggest that while normal readers learn a strategy for suppressing information that is not fixated, the dyslexic subjects do not. Shaywitz and Waxman (1987) propose a related explanation in terms of an impairment in covert attentional shifts (in the absence of explicit eye movements).

Rayner, Murphy, Henderson, and Pollatsek (1989) report a similar phenomenon in their subject, SJ, an adult with developmental dyslexia. Although SJ could read whole words and could report the constituent letters (unlike the subjects of Shallice & Warrington, 1977), letters in parafoveal vision interfered with his processing of the currently fixated word. The deficit could not be attributed to an impairment in overt eye movements: Although SJ's average eye fixations were longer than normal and he made more fixations than normal, he did not show an abnormal pattern of eye movements. Interestingly, SJ's reading performance improved when information outside of the fixated window region was replaced with Xs or with random letters.

The common finding of all these studies is that the presence of extraneous information in the visual field interferes with processing of the relevant information. As with neglect dyslexia, a straightforward explanation can be proposed in terms of damage to the attentional system: The damage in attentional dyslexia results in difficulty focusing on a single item in a multi-item display. Consequently, information which ought to be filtered out still gains access to higher levels of processing, thereby overloading the system and interfering with the processing of the relevant information.

In MORSEL, two different types of damage to the AM could yield this deficit. First, there are many ways that internal parameters of the AM could be garbled which would result in attention capturing everything present in the visual field (figure 6.8). Second, if the AM is prevented from reaching equilibrium, attention will be distributed over multiple items. This is because the AM initially activates all locations where items appear and then narrows its focus over time. In the case of developmental dyslexia, a plausible reason why the AM cannot reach equilibrium is that the time course of attentional settling is slowed. This behavior is readily modeled in the AM by scaling down all connection strengths proportionately. Consequently, under conditions of brief exposure or speeded response, the AM will not have sufficient time to focus on a single item.

When multiple items are attended in MORSEL, they are simultaneously processed by BLIRNET and interference among the items can occur. One manifestation of this interference in attentional dyslexia patients is the letter migration phenomenon. Detailed simulations of letter migrations are reported in section 6.2.3. Basically, migrations occur in these simulations when two words are presented simultaneously and processing time is limited so as to prevent the AM from selecting a single word. As a result, BLIRNET activates letter clusters of both words simultaneously, and the PO net occasionally recombines clusters of the two words into a single migration response. Note that if one of the words is replaced by a string of Xs or random letters,

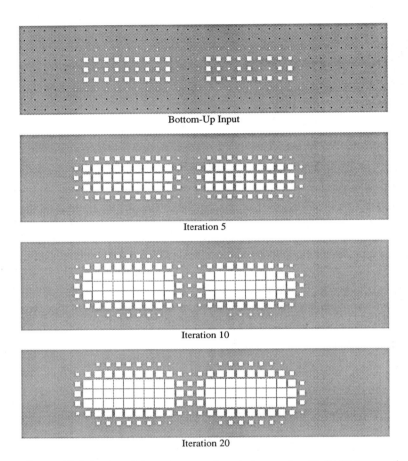

Bottom-Up Input

Iteration 5

Iteration 10

Iteration 20

Figure 6.8 Behavior of the AM on two three-letter words with θ=.25 (see section 4.1.2 for an explanation of θ). Rather than selecting one word or another, as would the model with θ set to the standard value of .5, the AM settles on both simultaneously.

there should be less interference because there is less ambiguity in the resulting pattern of letter-cluster activity. Thus, MORSEL can account for the improved reading performance of Rayner et al.'s subject SJ.

Letter migration errors are just one illustration of interference caused by the presence of multiple items. Another is observed when individual letters are processed simultaneously, for example H L V R C. While BLIRNET may be capable of identifying multiple letters in parallel, performance degrades with multiple letters because of interactions within BLIRNET that produce unpredictable spurious activations. For instance, V and L might result in some activation of the letter N. Consequently, it becomes more difficult to discern what is actually present from the pattern of activity produced by BLIRNET. This explains why performance on a target letter is better when the letter is presented in isolation than when embedded in other items.

What remains is to explain the category effect—why performance is so much worse for a letter flanked by irrelevant letters than digits. MORSEL's account is based on the fact that the output of BLIRNET specifies letter and word identities, but no location information. Localization is achieved when the AM focuses on single objects. When the AM is unable to do so, location information cannot be recovered. Consequently, when the target and flankers are all of the same category, for example, H L V R C, MORSEL will generally be able to detect the individual items but will be unable to determine which is the target. In support of this explanation, Shallice and Warrington note that when their patients made an error, there was a strong tendency for the reported letter to be one of the flankers (36% of errors for one patient, 77% for another). Note that localization is irrelevant when the target and flankers are members of different categories, for example, 1 3 V 4 7. In this example, it is trivial to determine which item to report on the basis of identity alone because there is only one letter present. Thus, MORSEL explains why performance improves when the target and flankers are of different categories.

The final phenomenon regarding attentional dyslexia that needs to be explained is why patients are unable to name the constituent letters of a visually presented word. This requires a bit of elaboration as to how MORSEL would read letter-by-letter. The pattern of activity produced by BLIRNET in response to an isolated letter is quite different than for the same letter in the context of a word. For example, an isolated E yields activity in the letter clusters **E, *E*, and E**, whereas the E in, say, FED yields activity in **_E, FE_*, E_**, *_ED, *FE, FED, and ED*. While the former pattern of activity is tied to the verbal response "E," the latter is not. Thus, to report letters of a word individually, it is necessary to process them individually. This involves sequentially focusing attention on single letters, thereby suppressing activation from the neighbors and obtaining a pattern of activity identical to that which would be obtained by a single letter presented in isolation. Because the damaged attentional system is unable to focus on individual letters, letter-by-letter reading is impossible.

6.4.3   Surface and Phonological Dyslexia

In this final section, I speculate on two further acquired disorders of reading, *phonological* and *surface dyslexia*. Phonological dyslexia is a selective impairment in the ability to read pronounceable nonwords (*pseudowords*) relative to the ability to read words. Patients often transform pseudowords into visually similar words, or are unable to form any response. Surface dyslexia is a selective difficulty in reading aloud exception words (e.g., **YACHT**), relative to regularly spelled words and pseudowords. Patients often regularize the exception words, that is, apply English spelling-to-sound rules to words that violate the rules (e.g., pronouncing **YACHT** as "yakt").

These disorders have given rise to much speculation as to the nature of the processes that carry out the transformation from an orthographic representation to a phonological one. The predominant account, the *dual-route model* (see Coltheart, 1985, for a review), posits that there are two routes from the printed letter string to a phonological representation, a *lexical* and a *nonlexical* procedure. The lexical procedure looks up the phonological representation corresponding to a word's orthographic representation in a table of lexical items. The nonlexical procedure converts orthography to phonology by a system of spelling-to-sound rules. According to the dual-route model, reading nonwords aloud is achieved using the nonlexical procedure, reading exception words by the lexical procedure, and regularly spelled words by either procedure. Phonological dyslexia results when the nonlexical procedure is disrupted, surface dyslexia when the lexical procedure is disrupted.

MORSEL provides an elaboration of the dual-route model. On MORSEL's account, orthographic information obtained from the visual stimulus is represented by the letter-cluster units. Because MORSEL has no representation of phonology, an additional set of units must be introduced—the *phonological units*. These units might represent the phonological analogue of letter cluster units, what Rumelhart and McClelland (1986) call *Wickelphones*. (See Rumelhart and McClelland's paper for a description of this representation, as well as a possible improvement, the *Wickelfeature* representation.) Phonological units interact with the letter-cluster and semlex units of the PO net, as depicted in figure 6.9. Letter-cluster and semlex units are reciprocally connected, and phonological units are innervated by

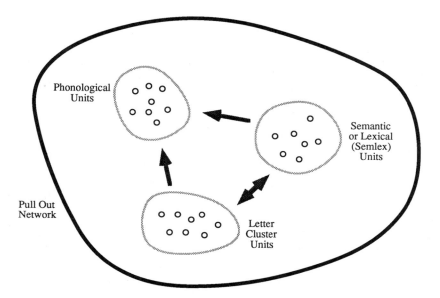

Figure 6.9 A proposal for how MORSEL might incorporate a phonological representation. Arrows indicate the flow of activity.

both letter-cluster and semlex units. (Ultimately, it may be necessary to posit reciprocal connections from the phonological units as well.) With regard to reading aloud, two pathways are critical: the letter-cluster-to-phonological (*LC-P*) and semlex-to-phonological (*S-P*) connections. LC-P connections represent low-order statistics of grapheme-phoneme correspondence, whereas S-P connections represent the higher-order statistics. Low-order statistics are what one might call "regularities" of the correspondence—how an individual letter cluster directly maps to a Wickelphone. Higher-order statistics embody special cases, exceptions of the correspondence—how a letter cluster in the context of other clusters might map to a Wickelphone.

With this machinery in place, an account of phonological and surface dyslexia is possible. This account depends on the assumption, motivated by other concerns (see section 3.3.3), that processes external to MORSEL modulate the overall strength of the link between semlex and letter-cluster units. Disruption of these external processes have two possible side effects: intensification or inhibition of the S-LC link. If the link strength is intensified to an extreme, symptoms of phonological dyslexia will arise for the following reason. When sem-lex units have a large influence over letter-cluster units, nonword inputs are likely to be turned into words; if this influence becomes overwhelming, all inputs will be turned into words, or perhaps activity in the PO net will be shut off altogether due to the incompatibility of bottom-up and top-down influences.

If, instead, the S-LC link were completely choked off, symptoms of surface dyslexia would arise. The semlex units, no longer having a source of input, are effectively cut out of the picture. Consequently, the phonological units would depend on the LC-P pathway for activation. The knowledge embodied by these connections would be sufficient only to activate the phonological representations of regular words and pseudowords. Irregular words would tend to become regularized, or possibly the LC-P connections would be too inconsistent to permit any response whatsoever.

This account makes two further predictions. First, in the case of phonological dyslexia, the letter-cluster representation is distorted as well as the phonemic by the overinfluential semlex units, hence the claim that not only should patients be unable to read nonwords aloud, but they should be unable to copy nonwords except in a letter-by-letter fashion. I know of no evidence for or against this prediction. Second, in the case of surface dyslexia, choking off the S-LC pathway should result in the loss of semantic information. Coltheart (1985) describes the patient MP of Bub, Canceliere, & Kertesz (1985) who appears to show this deficit. Indeed, loss of semantics is a central feature of one type of surface dyslexia (Shallice & McCarthy, 1985).

I have analyzed the complex syndromes of phonological and surface dyslexia only superficially, but the approach suggested by MOR-SEL is a possible refinement of the dual-route model. Although MORSEL's account is still dual route in that there are two pathways leading to the phonological code, MORSEL divides up the processing task somewhat differently and potentially avoids the need for an explicit lexical representation. More important, in MORSEL the two pathways are not independent processing systems but are intertwined and interactive.

This type of account has broader implications for cognitive neuropsychology. Until recently, the predominant theoretical paradigm in the field was to construct models consisting of box-and-arrow flow diagrams with the underlying assumption that damage affects a single component without influencing the functioning of other components. MORSEL and related connectionist models of neuropsychological phenomena (Hinton & Shallice, 1989; Patterson, Seidenberg, & McClelland, 1989) suggest an alternative approach in which the consequences of damage to a component cannot be predicted by analyzing the components in isolation because *interactions* among components yield complex, nontransparent effects. Indeed, one of the basic lessons of connectionism is that it is precisely the interactions among components that produce interesting behavior, whether the components are regarded as individual processing units or larger processing modules.

7 Evaluation of MORSEL

An evaluation of MORSEL is not complete unless its deficiencies are also noted. In the sections that follow, I point to shortcomings and some directions in which MORSEL is currently being extended.

7.1 Shortcomings of MORSEL

7.1.1 The Details are Surely Wrong

I have no strong commitment to the nuts and bolts of MORSEL. In fact, I believe that many of the details are wrong. The input representation is not rich enough. The letter-cluster representation should be augmented with information about overall word shape or length. The connectivity of BLIRNET is somewhat ad hoc and could be improved with modern connectionist learning algorithms. The AM dynamics are too brittle. The PO net requires a more rigorous computational foundation (cf., Hopfield, 1982). The temporal dynamics of the PO net needs work; it is not sufficiently responsive to changes in its input. Nonetheless, I have experimented with a variety of alternatives to the mechanisms reported here, and have been pleased to discover that the qualitative behavior of MORSEL was remarkably insensitive to the details.

7.1.2 Lack of Flexibility in Object Recognition

MORSEL is not as flexible as people in recognizing objects. Words can be read under many permutations: take a line of text, rotate it 45 degrees, or even 180 degrees; arrange the letters vertically instead of horizontally; double the size of the letters, or vary the size of each letter individually; insert gaps between letters, or even arbitrary symbols; present letters one at a time by scanning a line of text with a peep hole; and so on. Certainly, some of these variations are not processed by ordinary means, as indicated by slowed response times. However, other variations, such as global scale and orientation adjustments, seem quite natural.

MORSEL can be modified to yield scale invariance (see section 7.2.1) but affords no easy solution to the problem of orientation invariance. It is not clear that a complete solution is in order: objects in unknown orientations cannot be recognized as readily as objects in known orientations (Jolicoeur, 1990; Rock, 1973), but once the orientation is known, recognition is relatively straightforward regardless of orientation. This second fact is easily demonstrated by tilting a book at an angle. Once the orientation of the book has been determined, reading of individual words is greatly facilitated. This suggests that what MORSEL requires is a means of analyzing an object with respect to a frame of reference. Hinton (1981a, 1981b) has emphasized that imposing a frame of reference on an object can be critical in perception. His model of object recognition provides an example of the sort of normalization mechanism that is missing from MORSEL.

7.1.3 Letter-Cluster Frequency Effects

MORSEL derives explanatory power from the assumption that the letter-cluster units represent not just arbitrary sequences like VQX, *YY, or U_29, but rather familiar sequences like ION, *IN, or T_D*. This assumption is critical in accounting for aspects of letter transposition errors (section 6.2.2), letter migration errors (section 6.2.3), and the word superiority effect (section 6.3.3). The specific assumption I have adopted is that the letter-cluster level consists of the 6000 or so most frequently occurring clusters in English words, weighted by word frequency. Some low frequency clusters are therefore excluded, such as U_W* (found only in the word **SQUAW**), YH_W (**ANYHOW**), and PSC (**HOPSCOTCH**). This affects the performance of the PO net. The PO net works best when all potential letter clusters of a string are found among the letter-cluster units. Missing clusters mean fewer interactions in the PO net, which impairs the net's ability to suppress noise. Thus, words containing predominantly high-frequency clusters are read out more easily than words containing low-frequency clusters (see section 3.3.1).

Unfortunately, this facet of MORSEL is at odds with the experimental literature. McClelland and Johnston (1977) have reported that differences in letter-cluster frequency do not systematically influence the accuracy of perception of letters in words or pseudowords. The notion of letter-cluster units need not be abandoned, however. One way to reconcile MORSEL with the empirical results is to suppose that there is a letter-cluster unit for every letter sequence that occurs in English. Of the 56,966 possible letter clusters made up of three letters in four consecutive positions, 24,419 are found in English words (computation based on Kučera & Francis, 1967). Installing these clusters in MORSEL will not affect the model's differential performance on word-like strings as compared to random-letter strings, which is desirable, but will eliminate the experimentally unsupported difference in performance between word-like strings containing high- versus low-frequency clusters.

Alternatively, letter-cluster frequency effects may be eliminated by a training procedure proposed in section 7.2.3 where letter-cluster units learn what patterns to respond to on their own, rather than being assigned a meaning in advance. The consequence of this procedure is that the units will respond in an even more distributed manner: each unit might come to represent several letter clusters, and each letter cluster might be represented by several units (just as Wickelphones are represented by several Wickelfeatures in the Rumelhart and McClelland, 1986, verb model). Further, the units learn patterns that are useful in discriminating one word from another; these patterns will not necessarily correspond to the high-frequency clusters. It therefore seems quite plausible that a training procedure that establishes a representation of letter strings will eliminate letter-cluster frequency effects, but without altering the basic nature of the letter-cluster unit responses.

7.1.4 Loss of Location Information is Too Severe

When displays are brief and attention is unfocused, MORSEL has no means of determining what appeared where because all information about absolute locations has been discarded by the operation of BLIR-NET and the other processing modules. For example, if two words are presented, letter-cluster units appropriate for each word will be activated. As these units do not encode the spatial source of their activation, MORSEL will be unable to pin the words down to a location. Consequently, many word migration errors are expected. While word migration errors do occur (see section 6.2.5), they are relatively rare. Perhaps MORSEL can be salvaged by the suggestion that even in brief displays, the system has enough time to partially focus attention, establishing a gradient of attention. Words will be pulled out in accordance with this gradient (the most active first), giving MORSEL some ability to recover at least the relative arrangement of words.

Another way out of this bind is to adopt the suggestion of Pashler and Badgio (1985, 1987), who argue that the visual system has the ability "to redirect visual attention to the location where a token of an active [letter or digit] identity is present," that is, to recover information about the location of an item given its identity. LaBerge and Brown (1989) and Farah, Brunn, Wong, Wallace, and Carpenter (1990) have also argued for the ability to map from an object-based to a retinotopic attentional representation in order to focus on task-relevant objects or parts of objects. We have begun work on incorporating a mechanism that accomplishes this mapping into MORSEL (Mozer, Pashler, & Miyata, 1990). This mechanism is applied after BLIRNET has identified multiple objects in parallel. Given some letter deemed to be of interest (the *target*), the mechanism causes the AM to shift attention to the location where that letter appears. Attention shifting is direct in the sense that the mechanism does not need to scan the display sequentially; it can home in on the target letter regardless of the amount of information in the display. This mechanism allows for the object-based direction of attention, in contrast to the location-based direction currently available in MORSEL.

The location-recovery mechanism uses the back propagation algorithm of Rumelhart, Hinton, and Williams (1986), albeit in a somewhat unconventional manner. Back propagation is usually used to adjust *weights* in a network in order to obtain a desired pattern of output activity when a particular input is presented. Instead, we have used back propagation to adjust *activities* of the AM units to obtain a pattern of activity in which only the target letter is highly active. The back propagation procedure therefore provides suggestions to the AM about how attention might be modulated to focus on the target letter. These suggestions are used, in conjunction with the AM activation dynamics, to rapidly focus on the target. Because this procedure can be repeated to determine the location of any previously identified letter, it allows for a *dynamic* binding of letter identity and location, in contrast to the static binding performed by the visual STM.

This mechanism can operate only when visual stimulus information is available because the back propagation algorithm requires that units in all layers of the network maintain their activity during the back propagation phase. If the visual stimulus is removed, activities decay, and the recovery of location information is prevented. Interestingly, the mechanism makes the prediction that terminating a display by a pattern mask (which presumably causes the immediate replacement of elementary feature activations with features of the pattern mask) will more seriously disrupt the recovery of location information than other means of limiting performance (e.g., degraded stimulus quality). This prediction has been simulated, but has yet to be empirically tested.

7.2 Extensions to MORSEL

7.2.1 Scale-Invariant Recognition

I believe that it is a simple matter to expand BLIRNET to perform scale invariant recognition. The basic idea is to add units in the intermediate layers of BLIRNET with both larger and smaller receptive fields than those of existing units but with identical connectivity. The effect is to have units tuned to the same sets of features but at various scales. This proposal for achieving scale invariance is analogous to the means by which BLIRNET achieves translation invariance: For translation invariance, BLIRNET requires isomorphic units operating at each location; for scale invariance, it requires isomorphic units operating at each scale. Just as successively higher layers of BLIRNET collapse across space, so should higher layers collapse across scale, so that by the penultimate layer, BLIRNET has factored out not only the explicit representation of location but also size. The scheme requires that connection strengths be replicated not only across the retinotopic map, but across the scale map as well. However, these connection strengths are prewired and do not change as a function of experience.

7.2.2 Beyond Letter and Word Recognition

I have promoted MORSEL as a model of two-dimensional object recognition, yet have discussed primarily the recognition of upper-case letters and words. Extending MORSEL beyond letter and word recognition is straightforward. One means of doing so is by including additional processing modules. For instance, a color detection module and a letter-case detection module would allow other attributes of letters to be identified. MORSEL can also be extended by training BLIRNET to recognize other shapes. Because the internal layers of BLIRNET are not tuned specifically for letter and word recognition, BLIRNET is a general architecture that can be used to achieve translation-invariant recognition of arbitrary two-dimensional line drawings. To do so, an output representation must be determined for the shapes of interest, and BLIRNET must learn to recognize these shapes just as it learned to recognize words. Introducing more complex shapes may require that the set of elementary features be elaborated (e.g., to include units detecting corners, T-junctions, etc.), but this does not affect the operation of BLIRNET.

7.2.3 A Multi-Stage Attentional Mechanism

Neurophysiological data from Moran and Desimone (1985) suggest an intriguing and computationally powerful modification to MORSEL's attentional mechanism. Moran and Desimone trained monkeys to attend to a stimulus at one location in the visual field and ignore a stimulus at another. Visually responsive cells in prestriate area V4 and inferior temporal cortex were found to dramatically reduce their response to the unattended stimulus, but only when the attended stimulus was also within the cell's receptive field. MORSEL simply cannot account for this result. In MORSEL, units that would correspond to those studied by Moran and Desimone are found in the higher layers of BLIRNET. The response of these units is modulated by attention because the AM suppresses the flow of activity from unattended stimuli at an early stage of BLIRNET. However, the suppression of unattended stimuli occurs *regardless* of their proximity to attended stimuli, in contradiction to Moran and Desimone's finding.

Reconsidering this finding in light of MORSEL, I have proposed a modification to the AM that will make MORSEL both consistent with the neurophysiological data and a more computationally powerful model (Mozer, 1990; see also Treisman & Gormican, 1988, for a similar idea). The modification is based on the observation that attention is necessary in MORSEL to suppress interference among multiple items presented simultaneously. Interference occurs when features of two items converge on the same detector in BLIRNET. At low layers of BLIRNET, such collisions occur only for features of two nearby items, while at higher layers, features from increasingly distant items collide because the unit receptive fields broaden. From this perspective, there is no need to suppress unattended information unless it collides with the attended. Consequently, attention should be applied in stages corresponding to the layers of BLIRNET. At each stage, the system only needs to suppress features of unattended items that will collide with the attended item at the next layer of BLIRNET.

Whether an unattended item is suppressed at a given stage will depend on its proximity to the attended item, consistent with the Moran and Desimone data. Further, because an unattended item will be processed to a fairly high level if it is physically distant from the attended item, this scheme is an improvement over the current implementation of MORSEL: it allows greater analysis of unattended information *at no cost.* It thus makes better use of the dedicated computational resources in BLIRNET, assuming that activations in the intermediate layers of BLIRNET can be used to influence behavior in some manner.

The implementation of this scheme is a straightforward extension of MORSEL. It involves having an attentional stage corresponding to each layer of BLIRNET, compared to the current model which has just one stage corresponding to the input layer of BLIRNET. Each attentional stage operates much as the AM, except that competition among attentional units should be local, with the range of competitive interactions determined by the receptive field sizes in BLIRNET. Thus, at a given attentional stage, items in relatively distant locations can be attended simultaneously.

This scheme makes a highly counterintuitive prediction. Because increasing the distance between relevant and irrelevant items allows for increased analysis of the irrelevant item, it should *facilitate* incidental detection of higher-order properties of irrelevant items (within the limits of visual acuity). This prediction is not only counterintuitive but is the opposite of that made by gradient models of attention (LaBerge & Brown, 1989). Unfortunately, testing the prediction is a bit tricky as the analysis of the irrelevant items cannot be measured directly. This is because irrelevant items are eventually filtered out, and hence are not available for direct, conscious report. However, an indirect priming paradigm might be useful for testing the prediction.

7.2.4 Towards a Realistic Training Scenario

The procedure by which MORSEL learns to recognize words is unnatural. A collection of letter-cluster units is created in advance, and a teacher instructs MORSEL to associate visual patterns with a subset of these units. When children learn to read, they are not shown a word and then told, "Whenever you see this word you should activate neurons 14, 97, 148, and 512." The absurdity of this point stems from the fact that children are given no explicit instruction as to the internal representation they should construct in response to a stimulus. Is there a more realistic training scenario for MORSEL, one that provides the system with information analogous to that which a child receives, and also one that yields a letter-cluster-type internal representation? In this section, I sketch an idea that seems to be on the right track.

Children learn to read after they have mastered other aspects of language and cognition, such as auditory word recognition and attaching semantic properties to objects. Thus, I assume that in MORSEL's initial state, phonological and semantic units are already in place (see figure 6.9). Phonological units are activated by a spoken word, semantic units by visual images of objects. On the view I wish to present, the goal of learning to read is to form associations between the visual images of printed words and the corresponding phonological and/or semantic (hereafter, *PS*) representation. The PS representation is assumed to have been activated prior to presentation of a word by a teacher who has either spoken the word or has pointed to the relevant object.

The architecture of the system I propose is no different than the current configuration of MORSEL: The visual input maps through several layers to a set of untrained letter-cluster units, which in turn map to the PS units. The only difference between this new training procedure and the one previously described is that the letter-cluster units function as hidden units rather than output units because the error signal to the system is injected at the PS level. Using the back propagation algorithm, the response properties of the letter-cluster units can be adjusted toward the goal of activating the appropriate PS representation in response to a visual stimulus.

The letter-cluster units resulting from this training regimen should detect letter-cluster-type patterns, for the following reason. There are far fewer letter-cluster units than words, so the letter-cluster units cannot be tuned to specific words. Just as a word-level representation won't suffice, neither will a letter-level representation: BLIRNET discards enough positional information that a letter-level representation cannot maintain the relative positions of the letters; additional context is necessary. Thus, the resulting letter-cluster representation must be intermediate between the letter and word levels.

This point can be argued in another way. When learning to read, children scan words sequentially, letter by letter. Suppose that during training, MORSEL behaves as a letter-by-letter reader, focusing attention on each letter in turn. If the spotlight of attention is broad enough to include some neighboring letters, the input to MORSEL will then consist of a sequence of spatially constrained snapshots of the word being read. For example, presentation of **DEAR** might result in the sequence of inputs *DE, DEA, EAR, AR*—the asterisk indicating an end of word delimiter. I have developed a learning algorithm that constructs a letter-cluster-type representation based on input sequences of this sort (Mozer, 1989, 1990).

Consider the simple task of training a network to recognize four words: **DEAR, DEAN, BEAR,** and **BEAN**. Output of the network consists of four units, one for each word (this might correspond to a localist semantic or lexical representation). Between the input and output layers is a hidden layer, consisting of two units. Each hidden unit is connected back to itself, so that once it becomes active, it remains so until the end of the sequence. The training signal to the network comes at the end of the sequence. To discriminate among the four words, the network must discover the distinction between **D** and **B** in position 1 and between **R** and **N** in position 4. It would be sensible if one hidden unit responded to, say, *DE or **DEA** and the other to **AR*** or **EAR**. What in fact happens, though, is that one unit responds to a *mixture* of *DE and **DEA**—with the corresponding letters superimposed on one another—and the other to a mixture of **AR*** and **EAR**. Thus, although the hidden units respond to letter-cluster-type patterns, the resulting representation is somewhat more distributed than the letter-cluster representation built into MORSEL. The algorithm used in this simple problem has been successful at learning to discriminate among a much larger class of strings (Mozer, 1989, 1990), and fits nicely with the scenario described above for training MORSEL's letter-cluster units. Further developmental studies of MORSEL's acquisition of reading skills should prove useful in clarifying representational issues.

7.3 The Successes of MORSEL

Although its name suggests something small in scale, MORSEL is intended to embody a significant chunk of the visual system. Evaluating a model of this scope is difficult. MORSEL is a clear success on several grounds, however.

- It is a significant feat that MORSEL can perform translation-invariant recognition and multiple-object recognition, let alone that it does so without knowledge replication (cf. Fukushima & Miyake, 1982) and compares favorably to other connectionist models (see section 2.1 and appendix A).

- MORSEL explains a wide spectrum of psychological phenomena in the domain of letter and word perception and spatial attention. MORSEL also makes empirical predictions, several of which have been experimentally confirmed (e.g., Behrmann, Moscovitch, & Mozer, 1990; Mozer, 1989). In chapter 6, I perhaps downplayed the predictive aspect of MORSEL because it was difficult to distinguish between data taken into consideration when constructing the model and data that are natural consequences of the model. With a model as broad as MORSEL, the distinction does not seem critical. Nonetheless, it is impressive that MORSEL has provided a framework for interpreting a wider range of phenomena than it was originally designed to accommodate. For instance, the data on misspelling detection (section 6.3.5), visual search (section 6.3.1), and neglect dyslexia (section 6.4.1) were either not available or were not known to me when MORSEL was originally designed, yet the simulations of these phenomena required no modifications of the model beyond specifying some details that were irrelevant in earlier work.

- Even after five years of effort, MORSEL still has many interesting directions in which it might be extended to become an even broader and more complete model of visual perception and attention. Several of these directions are described in section 7.2. Despite its generality and extensibility, MORSEL is sufficiently specific that it can be falsified by future empirical research.

- Even though MORSEL is surely wrong in many details, it has been a valuable exercise to consider the overall architecture of the system—how various components interact, such as form recognition and attention, as opposed to just how the individual components operate in isolation.

Psychological models of visual perception and attention have tended toward two extremes. At one extreme are models that provide an explicit account of a circumscribed phenomenon—concrete, mathematically or computationally well-defined, but narrow in scope. At the other extreme are models that provide a general architecture for understanding a range of phenomena, but whose breadth is obtained at the expense of detail. MORSEL straddles the gap between these extremes. Several recent computational models are also situated in an intermediate position, notably the work of Chapman (1990a) and Grossberg (1988; Grossberg & Mingolla, 1985). By adopting a broad-ranging yet computationally detailed perspective, these models are far richer than the data they purport to explain. They deliver an integrated, computational theory of visual information processing.

Appendix A: A Comparison of Hardware Requirements

In this appendix, I compare the hardware requirements of BLIRNET to two models that perform somewhat the same function, PABLO (McClelland, 1985, 1986a) and mapping networks (Hinton, 1981a, 1981b).

A.1 BLIRNET Versus PABLO

PABLO has only been implemented in a fairly small simulation. I will consider how much hardware is required of PABLO for it to process information in a retina the size of BLIRNET's. First, however, it is necessary to match the two models in terms of their representations. Local representations were used in PABLO primarily for expository purposes. It would be unfair to penalize PABLO on this ground. Thus, for an equitable comparison, distributed representations must be considered. Suppose PABLO used the same representation of words as BLIRNET, namely 6000 letter-cluster units. Equating the output representations of the two models is simple, but equating the input representations is more problematic because BLIRNET's input is at the elementary feature level whereas PABLO's is at the letter level. Even with a more highly processed input representation, however, PABLO compares unfavorably to BLIRNET. PABLO's input representation is a distributed encoding of letters, with four units per letter,[1] for a total of $4 \times 26 = 104$ units.

Now the two models must be matched in terms of the scale of implementation. The essential question to ask is how many distinct

---

[1] One unit is activated by a particular letter preceded by a blank, one by a letter preceded by any other letter, one by a letter followed by a blank, and one by a letter followed by any other letter. Thus, the presentation of any letter, either alone or in context, will result in the activation of two letter units.

letter positions there are on BLIRNET's retina. Given a 36×6 cell retina with each letter occupying a 3×3 region, there are $34 \times 4 = 136$ locations in which a letter might appear. However, these locations are highly overlapping; it would be unfair to expect that PABLO had a processing subsystem for each of these locations. Being a bit more conservative, one could estimate the number of *discrete* letter locations, that is, the maximum number of letters that can be simultaneously placed on the retina without overlap, at $12 \times 2 = 24$.

A.1.1 Number of Units

The total number of units in BLIRNET is

$$\sum_{l=1}^{6} feature\_types_l \times x\_dimension_l \times y\_dimension_l \, ,$$

where l is the layer number. With 6000 letter cluster units, this amounts to

$$5 \times 36 \times 6 + 45 \times 12 \times 3 + 180 \times 6 \times 1 + 720 \times 3 \times 1$$
$$+ \, 720 \times 1 \times 1 + 6000 \times 1 \times 1 = 12,660$$

units. PABLO requires one set of programmable letter units and one set of programmable word units for each of the 24 possible letter locations, in addition to one set each of central letter and central word units. Further, there is one connection activation unit for each pairing of letter and word units. Thus, the total number of units amounts to $(24 + 1) \times (104 + 6000) + 104 \times 6000 = 776,600$, easily an order of magnitude more than contained in BLIRNET.[2]

A.1.2 Number of Connections

BLIRNET also fares well in terms of the number of connections, but the computation of this number is somewhat elaborate. The total number of connections in BLIRNET is

---

[2] McClelland points out that the connection activation units could in principle be implemented as connections rather than processing units. Even excluding these units, the total number of units in the system is $(24 + 1) \times (104 + 6000) = 152,600$, which still leaves an order of magnitude difference between PABLO and BLIRNET.

$$\sum_{l=2}^{6} x\_receptive\_field\_dim_l \times y\_receptive\_field\_dim_l \times$$
$$non\_zero\_connection\_density_l \times feature\_types_{l-1} \times$$
$$x\_dimension_l \times y\_dimension_l \times feature\_types_l$$
$$= 5.83 \times 3.33 \times .348 \times 5 \times 12 \times 3 \times 45 + 3.67 \times 3 \times .139 \times$$
$$45 \times 6 \times 1 \times 180 + 3.33 \times 1 \times .067 \times 180 \times 3 \times 1 \times 720 +$$
$$3 \times 1 \times .00139 \times 720 \times 1 \times 1 \times 720 + 1 \times 1 \times 1 \times 720 \times$$
$$1 \times 1 \times 6000 = 4,538,005.$$

Unfortunately, the connectivity of PABLO is even more complex. Before making an estimate, the maximum word length must be specified. Although words of up to 12 letters may be presented, the critical length of interest is only 4 letters because the letter clusters are made up of 4-letter sequences. With this number in mind, let us begin. PABLO requires complete connectivity between programmable letter and programmable word units, each word unit being connected to 4 letter slots $(104 \times 6000 \times 4 \times 24 = 59,904,000)$; connections between central letter and central word units $(104 \times 6000 = 624,000)$; connections between programmable letter and central letter units $(104 \times 24 = 2496)$; connections from central word units to two connection activation units, representing a single letter, for each of four letter positions $(6000 \times 2 \times 4 = 48,000)$; and connections from each connection activation unit to its corresponding connection within each programmable module $(4 \times 104 \times 6000 \times 24 = 59,904,000)$. The grand total here is 120,482,496, nearly 1.5 orders of magnitude greater than that required by BLIRNET.

This figure can be adjusted up or down, depending on the extent to which one wishes to defend PABLO. I believe the figure to be fairly conservative, however. The adjustments down are relatively minor, e.g., eliminating the connection activation units removes 48,000 connections, and eliminating detectors near the edge of the retina due to boundary effects may cut down the total by 10%. However, adjustments upwards are potentially far more devastating. For instance, I assumed that PABLO was concerned simply with recognizing position-specific letter clusters, which allowed me to set the word length to 4 consecutive letters. If we were interested in having each programmable word network identify all letter clusters in a word, rather than only those in the local region, the word length would have to be upped to 12. Another blow against PABLO is the fact that I've omitted all recurrent connections among programmable word units. While the pull-out net of MORSEL serves a corresponding function, MORSEL requires only one pull-out net, whereas PABLO requires recurrent connections within each set of programmable word units.

McClelland (1986b) has argued that selective programming of the local networks might significantly reduce the size of a model like PABLO. Essentially, he suggests that the central structure could program local networks to recognize only the *relevant* patterns, rather than turning on connections to *all* known patterns. Consequently, each local network needn't have a full complement of word units but only as many word units as there are patterns that might be recognized simultaneously. On first reading this argument is persuasive, and if correct would significantly reduce the number of units and connections required by PABLO. However, the argument appears flawed because the proposed solution creates an enormous mapping problem, which McClelland fails to address. This mapping problem has two components: (a) How is the mapping between central word units and connection activation units performed, given that there is no longer a fixed correspondence? (b) How is the output of a programmable word unit to be interpreted, given that its meaning is dependent on the visual input? These issues must be settled before McClelland's (1986b) optimistic estimates of PABLO's resource requirements can be seriously considered.

In summary, MORSEL is far more economical than PABLO, both in the number of units and the number of connections. Despite my attempt to compare similar versions of the two models, they are not exactly comparable. MORSEL must perform more analysis because it takes as input a primitive featural description of the visual input, whereas PABLO operates on a letter-level description. In its favor, though, PABLO may have greater processing capacity, particularly for displays containing dissimilar words.

A.2 BLIRNET Versus Mapping Networks

Comparing BLIRNET and Hinton's mapping network is difficult. A direct unit-for-unit comparison is unfair because BLIRNET uses the conventional semilinear units while the mapping scheme uses sigma-pi units (Rumelhart, Hinton, & McClelland, 1986), which are computationally far more powerful (Durbin & Rumelhart, 1989). Rumelhart (personal communication, 1987) has experimented with a more conventional architecture that implements a mapping network, and it is possible to compare this architecture to BLIRNET. Rumelhart's network consists of four layers: a *retina* comparable to L_1 of BLIRNET, a *location* map, a *hidden* layer that receives input from the retina and the location map, and an *output* layer that is supposed to contain a normalized representation of a portion of the retina. Basically, the location map specifies the region of the retina to be mapped onto the output layer, yielding a location-invariant representation of a visual pattern.

The question at hand is, how many hidden units are needed to perform this mapping? The hidden units in Rumelhart's network are performing an analogous function to the units in layers L_2–L_4 of BLIRNET, because these layers operate on the retina, L_1, to build a normalized representation of sorts in L_5. The total number of units in layers L_2–L_4 of BLIRNET is

$$\sum_{l=2}^{4} feature\_types_i \times x\_dimension_i \times y\_dimension_i$$
$$= 45 \times 18 \times 3 + 180 \times 9 \times 1 + 720 \times 3 \times 1 = 6210 .$$

The number of units required in Rumelhart's network depends on the number of positions a word can appear in. Following the earlier conservative calculation, assume there are 12 discrete horizontal and 2 discrete vertical letter positions on BLIRNET's retina (although the true number of overlapping positions is far greater). A word can thus begin in any of these 24 positions. Rumelhart's simulation experiments suggest that the number of hidden units required, h, is $O\,(number\_mappings \times number\_features\_mapped)$. Here, the number of mappings is simply 24, but the number of features that need to be mapped depends on the maximum word length. In horizontal position i, the maximum word length is $13 - i$, and each letter of a word is represented by $3 \times 3 \times 5 = 45$ features. Thus, h is on the order of

$$\sum_{i=1}^{12} 2 \times (13 - i) \times 45 = 7020,$$

about the same number of units as required by BLIRNET.

I do not have sufficient information to estimate the number of nonzero connections in Rumelhart's network at present. In the worst case, every hidden unit will be connected to every input and output, for a total of $36 \times 6 \times 5 \times 7020 \times 2 = 15,163,200$ connections. At best, and probably closer to the truth, each hidden unit represents the conjunction of a particular mapping and a particular input feature, and thus should be connected to exactly one input unit and one output unit, for a total of $7020 \times 2 = 14,040$ connections. In comparison, BLIRNET requires 218,008 connections using the estimate from section A1.1.2.

cluster	freq	d'	cluster	freq	d'	cluster	freq	d'
ME_*	1	5.36	L_D*	4	3.84	THE	4	3.48
M_N*	2	5.24	LED	4	3.84	*C_L	6	3.47
IN_T	7	4.90	VE*	4	3.84	*MA	32	3.47
ER_A	1	4.58	UND	5	3.81	B_E*	6	3.47
AL_Y	11	4.56	C**	1	3.79	CAL	6	3.47
A_LY	11	4.55	*NO	5	3.78	BL_*	6	3.46
Y**	17	4.54	IN*	5	3.78	HAN	11	3.46
**K	2	4.52	D_NG	20	3.77	MAN	8	3.46
*UN	3	4.52	DI_G	20	3.77	RAN	16	3.46
KIN	2	4.52	IC*	1	3.77	AB_E	6	3.45
RY*	1	4.51	LIT	7	3.77	ABL	6	3.45
O_AL	7	4.49	ON_E	8	3.76	ION	68	3.45
L_Y*	12	4.47	CON	11	3.75	LLE	2	3.44
LLY	12	4.45	E_Y*	2	3.75	**W	31	3.43
TIV	2	4.37	TIC	2	3.75	*TH	4	3.43
NA_I	16	4.35	AN*	5	3.73	O_**	45	3.41
LY*	13	4.30	A_D*	12	3.71	**I	20	3.40
INA	8	4.27	O_S*	29	3.67	*C_M	6	3.38
NAL	8	4.26	N**	56	3.66	*_IC	2	3.36
I_NS	25	4.21	IO_S	26	3.65	*CH	14	3.36
ITY	1	4.18	TH_R	1	3.64	NC_*	16	3.36
N_TI	18	4.16	**U	4	3.63	E_ED	17	3.35
OO_*	1	4.13	*CO	20	3.63	ON_*	40	3.35
*DO	6	4.12	NIN	5	3.63	*M_R	16	3.34
NT*	25	4.12	*HA	10	3.61	ED*	116	3.34
*IN	17	4.11	*S_U	1	3.59	*_OU	3	3.33
IVE	3	4.11	*_OM	9	3.58	*M_S	15	3.33
TY*	1	4.11	CHA	12	3.58	CE*	18	3.33
ON*	38	4.09	COM	4	3.58	N_IN	38	3.33
ASS	1	4.08	*_AM	3	3.56	MIN	21	3.32
I_Y*	2	4.08	ALL	17	3.55	OUS	1	3.32
IV_*	3	4.08	NTI	28	3.54	*_HA	13	3.31
ONS	28	4.08	NS*	44	3.52	*_NT	30	3.31
LL_*	13	3.99	*WA	17	3.51	OUN	3	3.31
*MO	5	3.98	I_G*	178	3.51	T_ON	55	3.31
ND*	15	3.95	AR*	12	3.50	TI_N	55	3.31
EN*	7	3.92	I_AL	1	3.50	PRO	5	3.30
NAT	18	3.92	G**	181	3.49	*_RO	5	3.29
ONA	10	3.88	NG*	181	3.49	*AN	11	3.29
V_**	4	3.85	HE_*	2	3.48	ST*	27	3.29
I_N*	34	3.84	IO_*	36	3.48	*_UN	4	3.28

cluster	freq	d'	cluster	freq	d'	cluster	freq	d'
C_S*	3	3.28	D_**	2	3.02	ILL	2	2.84
MEN	25	3.28	H**	1	3.02	N_E*	25	2.84
*SO	12	3.27	INS	7	3.02	NED	16	2.84
*WI	12	3.27	ISH	1	3.02	ANT	36	2.83
**_V	1	3.26	ORS	3	3.02	N_SS	7	2.83
O_ED	8	3.26	T**	62	3.02	PAR	10	2.83
R_D*	30	3.26	**O	16	3.01	T_D*	60	2.83
RED	30	3.26	*_HO	1	3.01	TA_I	8	2.83
UN_E	9	3.26	ENE	5	3.01	TED	60	2.83
IAN	2	3.25	PE_*	3	3.01	GS*	18	2.82
STO	14	3.24	*P_O	6	3.00	N_ED	32	2.82
VE_*	1	3.24	A_LE	8	3.00	O_IN	14	2.82
*_EM	4	3.23	EM_N	6	3.00	RI_G	67	2.82
**J	1	3.22	LE*	11	3.00	*FO	10	2.81
*MI	18	3.22	DEN	5	2.99	ERI	41	2.81
DIN	25	3.22	E_IN	37	2.99	IS_E	18	2.81
ANS	7	3.21	GRA	13	2.99	R**	82	2.81
NE*	29	3.21	RIC	1	2.99	RE*	26	2.81
*_HI	2	3.20	*_HE	6	2.98	**H	32	2.80
D**	135	3.19	BLE	9	2.98	AT_*	21	2.80
TIO	57	3.19	*LO	3	2.97	E_CE	7	2.80
**_P	7	3.18	AND	24	2.97	E_T*	39	2.80
CHE	2	3.18	E_ER	5	2.97	O_E*	24	2.80
*M_N	33	3.17	*_OO	2	2.96	**V	6	2.78
S_S*	5	3.17	FOR	7	2.96	ECT	4	2.78
*EN	11	3.16	TO_*	5	2.96	TTE	18	2.78
S_ON	16	3.16	OR*	6	2.95	AT_D	22	2.77
C_**	19	3.15	*HE	14	2.94	END	25	2.77
I_T*	9	3.15	*O_E	12	2.94	LI_E	13	2.77
**N	16	3.14	TE*	24	2.94	**_N	44	2.76
*S_O	10	3.13	*AL	6	2.93	*CA	33	2.76
A_T*	10	3.13	INT	42	2.93	ELE	2	2.76
LL*	4	3.13	NCE	23	2.93	ER*	63	2.76
HER	6	3.12	ONE	22	2.93	IA_*	1	2.76
ING	204	3.12	*_ND	10	2.92	ITI	3	2.76
RO_E	5	3.12	E**	125	2.92	CAT	4	2.75
M_NT	23	3.10	SI_N	16	2.92	ERA	15	2.75
ANC	15	3.09	**B	53	2.91	RE_S	7	2.75
ER_O	5	3.09	*D_S	6	2.91	RS*	63	2.75
A_CE	15	3.08	*GR	14	2.91	**_C	4	2.74
DIS	3	3.08	CE_*	6	2.91	*C_A	20	2.74
ER_N	35	3.08	IC_*	3	2.91	*DI	8	2.74
I_AT	14	3.08	*TO	16	2.90	EL_*	2	2.74
ME_T	24	3.08	CTI	8	2.90	R_NG	69	2.74
**M	75	3.07	AL*	3	2.89	*PA	20	2.73
*BO	8	3.07	O_T*	4	2.88	*PO	14	2.73
*ME	18	3.07	TOR	20	2.88	DER	33	2.73
ENC	6	3.07	*_OS	5	2.87	L_**	30	2.73
SE*	8	3.07	EA_*	6	2.87	ND_R	33	2.73
A_IO	40	3.06	*G_A	15	2.86	A_IS	6	2.72
AN_I	17	3.06	TON	11	2.86	ARD	5	2.72
IT_*	4	3.06	*BE	14	2.85	EN_I	32	2.72
AT_O	40	3.05	*HO	3	2.85	IL_*	2	2.72
LE_*	7	3.05	N_D*	16	2.85	*B_R	13	2.71
*BR	4	3.04	R_EN	10	2.85	A_**	21	2.71
DS*	2	3.04	*TA	10	2.84	I_E*	26	2.71

cluster	freq	d'	cluster	freq	d'	cluster	freq	d'
*CL	3	2.70	**D	31	2.55	RES	53	2.43
T_IN	5	2.70	*_LE	8	2.55	RI_E	9	2.43
NER	12	2.69	*SI	21	2.55	**_S	2	2.42
PRE	13	2.69	O_ES	21	2.55	*A_T	19	2.42
IES	6	2.68	TI_E	14	2.55	E_AT	21	2.42
IN_*	206	2.68	IST	27	2.54	E_EN	16	2.42
IN_I	7	2.68	N_**	295	2.54	EST	59	2.42
R_ED	7	2.68	NT_R	43	2.54	TRI	4	2.42
*_AL	14	2.67	OVE	4	2.54	**R	66	2.40
IE_*	6	2.67	T_RS	43	2.54	*_AI	15	2.40
NTE	82	2.67	TAT	13	2.54	EN_*	26	2.40
RIE	5	2.67	*SC	1	2.52	I_IN	12	2.40
RIN	75	2.67	*TR	9	2.52	NE_S	12	2.40
TRA	5	2.67	E_S*	79	2.52	OR_*	18	2.40
SSI	6	2.66	STE	50	2.52	T_S*	14	2.40
TI_G	83	2.66	**_H	22	2.51	**E	20	2.39
**G	17	2.65	*_OL	5	2.51	*S_A	31	2.39
*DE	9	2.65	*P_E	15	2.51	E_TS	16	2.39
AN_*	23	2.65	*PE	16	2.51	N_ER	83	2.39
E_SI	16	2.65	*RE	35	2.51	RA_E	26	2.39
ERE	27	2.65	DE_*	17	2.51	A_E*	36	2.38
R_S*	12	2.65	LA_E	15	2.51	ATI	65	2.38
PER	12	2.64	*H_R	8	2.50	ER_E	9	2.38
RE_*	43	2.64	*LI	27	2.50	IN_S	44	2.38
STR	3	2.64	A**	2	2.50	*_IL	7	2.37
*AR	5	2.63	GE_*	2	2.50	*LE	11	2.37
ES_E	14	2.63	LAN	14	2.50	S**	236	2.37
I_ED	10	2.63	SS*	18	2.50	*S_L	10	2.36
*_AC	1	2.62	T_ES	3	2.50	C_NT	17	2.36
*C_R	14	2.62	VER	4	2.50	*SP	1	2.35
ER_*	63	2.62	A_S*	13	2.49	EN_S	15	2.35
I_TI	8	2.62	*BA	18	2.48	**S	126	2.34
L_S*	4	2.62	*CR	15	2.48	ENS	18	2.34
O_D*	1	2.62	*FA	12	2.48	RE_E	12	2.34
RA_I	27	2.62	G_**	22	2.48	*_IS	19	2.33
*SH	4	2.61	INE	44	2.48	E_SE	14	2.33
I_**	9	2.61	NT_*	22	2.48	A_ER	19	2.32
ORE	27	2.61	T_ER	19	2.48	AN_S	14	2.32
S_ER	38	2.61	T_RE	30	2.48	AT_R	19	2.32
T_RI	32	2.61	*_AS	19	2.47	ENT	70	2.32
*LA	18	2.60	*BU	4	2.47	*S_E	7	2.31
L**	8	2.60	AL_*	6	2.47	**C	98	2.30
T_NG	84	2.60	ALI	2	2.47	E_TI	48	2.30
*_ET	7	2.59	STA	22	2.47	RAT	49	2.30
A_ED	25	2.59	*FL	2	2.46	*S_R	15	2.29
LAT	18	2.59	*RO	2	2.46	*TE	26	2.29
NDE	36	2.59	AST	23	2.46	ILI	4	2.29
*FI	15	2.57	I_ER	8	2.46	*PR	22	2.28
ERS	64	2.57	TI_*	7	2.45	SI_E	5	2.28
NG_*	21	2.57	*_ON	35	2.44	SIN	20	2.28
NTS	20	2.57	*C_N	27	2.44	TIN	99	2.28
R_TI	26	2.57	*RA	23	2.44	*S_I	14	2.27
REC	3	2.57	AIN	16	2.44	AN_E	45	2.27
*_IT	16	2.56	*_EE	7	2.43	*B_A	9	2.26
R_ST	32	2.56	*T_R	17	2.43	*S_N	27	2.26
T_R*	43	2.56	OR_E	11	2.43	TS*	25	2.26

cluster	freq	d'	cluster	freq	d'	cluster	freq	d'
I_ES	23	2.25	O**	3	2.13	L_NG	18	1.99
ORT	9	2.25	TE_*	114	2.13	LI_G	18	1.99
O_ER	12	2.24	TES	25	2.13	**_O	106	1.97
ARI	20	2.23	ER_I	8	2.12	**F	45	1.97
GE*	3	2.23	S_IN	49	2.12	E_TE	51	1.96
**A	35	2.22	AR_I	11	2.11	NES	33	1.96
*_IR	12	2.22	E_**	252	2.11	R_**	106	1.96
EAR	14	2.22	LS*	2	2.11	*_ES	40	1.95
ES_*	39	2.22	STI	42	2.11	ST_N	51	1.95
R_TE	31	2.22	A_IN	47	2.10	**P	81	1.93
**L	60	2.21	ART	20	2.10	A_TE	49	1.93
*_EC	3	2.21	EA_E	17	2.10	*_OR	39	1.90
ES*	60	2.21	IND	15	2.10	**_U	15	1.89
I_TE	54	2.21	*_LA	13	2.09	*_RE	32	1.88
ELL	2	2.20	*SU	1	2.09	ATE	73	1.88
N_S*	61	2.20	A_TI	31	2.09	*SE	23	1.87
*_IN	76	2.19	T_**	50	2.08	*_EA	27	1.85
*_US	6	2.19	U_E*	1	2.08	*T_A	11	1.84
TE_S	55	2.19	EN_E	46	2.07	I_S*	16	1.81
TER	127	2.19	LE_S	8	2.06	SE_*	8	1.81
ES_I	21	2.18	*_AN	62	2.05	*FR	3	1.79
RE_I	2	2.18	*_RA	31	2.05	*_EN	67	1.78
RE_T	47	2.18	AR_*	21	2.05	*_AR	53	1.74
IS_*	6	2.17	I_LE	1	2.05	**_I	134	1.69
TEN	35	2.17	LIN	27	2.05	R_IN	20	1.68
*_EL	8	2.16	*F_R	15	2.04	*_AT	56	1.67
*ST	40	2.16	REA	13	2.04	*_ER	25	1.67
AR_E	9	2.16	S_**	54	2.04	**_L	30	1.65
L_IN	4	2.15	A_ES	25	2.02	URE	2	1.65
*_UR	5	2.14	NE_*	42	2.02	**_R	82	1.51
*P_R	26	2.14	**_T	43	2.01	*_RI	11	1.43
*SA	17	2.14	ESS	25	2.01	**_A	227	1.27
IN_E	54	2.14	LES	11	2.01	**_E	191	1.19
ST_R	54	2.14	**T	74	1.99			

References

Allport, D. A. (1977). On knowing the meaning of words we are unable to report: The effects of visual masking. In S. Dornic (Ed.), *Attention and performance VI*. Hillsdale, NJ: Erlbaum.

Anderson, J. A., & Hinton, G. E. (1981). Models of information processing in the brain. In G. E. Hinton & J. A. Anderson (Eds.), *Parallel models of associative memory* (pp. 9–48). Hillsdale, NJ: Erlbaum.

Baddeley, A. D. (1986). *Working memory*. New York: Oxford University Press.

Barbut, D., & Gazzaniga, M. (1987). Disturbances in conceptual space involving language and speech. *Brain, 110*, 1487–1496.

Beck, J., & Ambler, B. (1973). The effects of concentrated and distributed attention on peripheral accuity. *Perception and Psychophysics, 14*, 225–230.

Behrmann, M., Moscovitch, M., Black, S. E., & Mozer, M. C. (1990). Perceptual and conceptual mechanisms in neglect dyslexia: Two contrasting case studies. *Brain, 113*, 1163–1183.

Behrmann, M., Moscovitch, M., & Mozer, M. C. (1990). Directing attention to words and nonwords in normal subjects and in a computational model: Implications for neglect dyslexia. *Cognitive Neuropsychology*. Accepted for publication.

Bergen, J. R., & Julesz, B. (1983). Parallel versus serial processing in rapid pattern discrimination. *Nature, 303*, 696–698.

Bisiach, E., & Vallar, G. (1988). Hemineglect in humans. In F. Boller & J. Grafman (Eds.), *Handbook of neuropsychology, Volume 1* (pp. 195–222). North Holland, Amsterdam: Elsevier Science Publishers, BV.

Bjork, E. L., & Estes, W. K. (1971). Detection and placement of redundant signal elements in tachistoscopic displays of letters. *Perception and Psychophysics, 9,* 439–442.

Black, S. E., Vu, B., Martin, D., & Szalai, J. (1990). Evaluation of a bedside battery for hemispatial neglect in acute stroke. *Journal of Experimental and Clinical Neuropsychology, 12,* 109. (abstract)

Bradshaw, J. L. (1974). Peripherally presented and unreported words may bias the perceived meaning of a centrally fixated homograph. *Journal of Experimental Psychology, 6,* 1200–1202.

Briand, K. A., & Klein, R. M. (1987). Is Posner's "beam" the same as Treisman's "glue"?: On the relation between visual orienting and feature integration theory. *Journal of Experimental Psychology: Human Perception and Performance, 13,* 228–241.

Broadbent, D. E. (1958). *Perception and communication.* London: Pergamon.

Brunn, J. L., & Farah, M. J. (1990). The relation between spatial attention and reading: Evidence from the neglect syndrome. *Cognitive Neuropsychology.* (in press)

Bub, D., Canceliere, A., & Kertesz, A. (1985). Whole-word and analytic translation of spelling to sound in a non-semantic reader. In K. E. Patterson, J. C. Marshall, & M. Coltheart (Eds.), *Surface dyslexia: Cognitive and neuropsychological studies of phonological reading.* London: Erlbaum.

Butter, C. M. (1987). Varieties of attention and disturbances of attention: A neuropsychological analysis. In M. Jeannerod (Ed.), *Neurophysiological and neuropsychological aspects of spatial neglect* (pp. 1–24). Amsterdam: North Holland.

Caplan, B. (1987). Assessment of unilateral neglect: A new reading test. *Journal of Experimental and Clinical Neuropsychology, 9,* 359–364.

Carpenter, G. A., & Grossberg, S. (1987). A massively parallel architecture for a self-organizing neural pattern recognition machine. *Computer Vision, Graphics, and Image Processing, 37,* 54–115.

Carpenter, G. A., & Grossberg, S. (1988). The ART of adaptive pattern recognition by a self-organizing neural network. *Computer, 21,* 77–88.

Carr, T. H., Davidson, B. J., & Hawkins, H. L. (1978). Perceptual flexibility in word recognition: Strategies affect orthographic computation but not lexical access. *Journal of Experimental Psychology: Human Perception and Performance, 4,* 674–690.

Cavanaugh, P. (1984). Image transforms in the visual system. In P. Dodwell & T. Caelli (Eds.), *Figural Synthesis* (pp. 185–218). Hillsdale, NJ: Erlbaum.

Chapman, D. (1990a). *Vision, instruction, and action* (Technical Report 1204). Massachusetts Institute of Technology, Artificial Intelligence Laboratory.

Chapman, D. (1990b). *Intermediate vision: Architecture, implementation, and use* (Technical Report TR-90-6). Palo Alto, CA: Teleos Research.

Cohen, J. D., Dunbar, K., & McClelland, J. L. (1990). On the control of automatic processes: A parallel distributed processing model of the Stroop effect. *Psychological Review, 97,* 332–361.

Colegate, R. L., Hoffman, J. E., & Eriksen, C. W. (1973). Selective encoding from multielement visual displays. *Perception & Psychophysics, 14,* 217–224.

Collins, A. M., & Quillian, M. R. (1969). Retrieval time from semantic memory. *Journal of Verbal Learning and Verbal Behavior, 8,* 240–247.

Collins, J. F., & Eriksen, C. W. (1967). The perception of multiple simultaneously presented forms as a function of foveal spacing. *Perception & Psychophysics, 2,* 369–373.

Coltheart, M. (1985). Cognitive neuropsychology and the study of reading. In M. I. Posner & O. S. M. Marin (Eds.), *Attention and performance XI* (pp. 3–37). Hillsdale, NJ: Erlbaum.

Connor, J. M. (1972). Effects of increased processing load on parallel processing of visual displays. *Perception & Psychophysics, 12,* 121–128.

Crick, F. (1984). The function of the thalamic reticular complex: The searchlight hypothesis. *Proceedings of the National Academy of Sciences, 81,* 4586–4590.

Crick, F. H. C., & Asanuma, C. (1986). Certain aspects of the anatomy and physiology of the cerebral cortex. In J. L. McClelland & D. E. Rumelhart (Eds.), *Parallel distributed processing: Explorations in the microstructure of cognition. Volume II: Psychological and biological models* (pp. 333–371). Cambridge, MA: MIT Press/Bradford Books.

De Renzi, E. (1982). *Disorders of space exploration and cognition.* New York: Wiley.

Desimone, R. (1989, August). *ATTENTION!: Neural mechanisms in extrastriate cortex in monkeys.* Paper presented at the Symposium on Cognitive Neuroscience at the Eleventh Annual Conference of the Cognitive Science Society, Ann Arbor, MI.

Deutsch, J. A., & Deutsch, D. (1963). Attention: Some theoretical considerations. *Psychological Review, 70,* 80–90.

Duncan, J. (1980). The locus of interference in the perception of simultaneous stimuli. *Psychological Review, 87,* 272–300.

Duncan, J. (1987). Attention and reading: Wholes and parts in shape recognition. In M. Coltheart (Ed.), *Attention and performance XII* (pp. 39–62). Hillsdale, NJ: Erlbaum.

Duncan, J., & Humphreys, G. W. (1989). Visual search and stimulus similarity. *Psychological Review, 96,* 433–458.

Durbin, R., & Rumelhart, D. E. (1989). Product units: A computationally powerful and biologically plausible extension to backpropagation networks. *Neural Computation, 1,* 133–142.

Egeth, H., Jonides, J., & Wall, S. (1972). Parallel processing of multielement displays. *Cognitive Psychology*, *3*, 674–698.

Egeth, H. E., Virzi, R. A., & Garbart, H. (1984). Searching for conjunctively defined targets. *Journal of Experimental Psychology: Human Perception and Performance*, *10*, 32–39.

Ellis, A. W., Flude, B., & Young, A. W. (1987). Neglect dyslexia and the early visual processing of letters in words and nonwords. *Cognitive Neuropsychology*, *4*, 439–464.

Eriksen, B. A., & Eriksen, C. W. (1974). Effects of noise letters upon the identification of a target letter in a nonsearch task. *Perception & Psychophysics*, *16*, 143–149.

Eriksen, C. W. (1966). Independence of successive inputs and uncorrelated error in visual form perception. *Journal of Experimental Psychology*, *62*, 26–35.

Eriksen, C. W., & Hoffman, J. E. (1972). Temporal and spatial characteristics of selective encoding from visual displays. *Perception and Psychophysics*, *12*, 201–204.

Eriksen, C. W., & Hoffman, J. E. (1973). The extent of processing of noise elements during selective coding from visual displays. *Perception and Psychophysics*, *14*, 155–160.

Eriksen, C. W., & Hoffman, J. E. (1974). Selective attention: Noise suppression or signal enhancement? *Bulletin of the Psychonomic Society*, *4*, 587–589.

Eriksen, C. W., & Lappin, J. S. (1965). Internal perceptual system noise and redundancy in simultaneous inputs in form identification. *Psychonomic Science*, *2*, 351–352.

Eriksen, C. W., & Schultz, D. W. (1978). Temporal factors in visual information processing. In J. Requin (Ed.), *Attention and performance VII* (pp. 3–23). Hillsdale, NJ: Erlbaum.

Eriksen, C. W., & Spencer, T. (1969). Rate of information processing in visual perception: Some results and methodological considerations. *Journal of Experimental Psychology Monograph*, *79*, (2, part 2).

Eriksen, C. W., & Yeh, Y.-Y. (1985). Allocation of attention in the visual field. *Journal of Experimental Psychology: Human Perception and Performance, 11,* 583–597.

Estes, W. K. (1972). Interactions of signal and background variables in visual processing. *Perception & Psychophysics, 12,* 278–286.

Estes, W. K. (1982). Similarity-related channel interactions in visual processing. *Journal of Experimental Psychology: Human Perception and Performance, 8,* 353–380.

Estes, W. K., Allmeyer, D. H., & Reder, S. M. (1976). Serial position functions for letter identification at brief and extended exposure durations. *Perception and Psychophysics, 19,* 1–15.

Farah, M. J., Brunn, J. L., Wong, A. B., Wallace, M. A., & Carpenter, P. A. (1990). Frames of reference for allocating attention to space: Evidence from the neglect syndrome. *Neuropsychologia.*

Feldman, J. A. (1980). A connectionist model of visual memory. In G. E. Hinton & J. A. Anderson (Eds.), *Parallel models of associative memory* (pp. 49–81). Hillsdale, NJ: Erlbaum.

Feldman, J. A., & Ballard, D. H. (1982). Connectionist models and their properties. *Cognitive Science, 6,* 205–254.

Fodor, J. A. (1983). *The modularity of mind.* Cambridge, MA: MIT Press.

Fodor, J. A., & Pylyshyn, Z. W. (1988). Connectionism and cognitive architecture: A critical analysis. *Cognition, 28,* 3–71.

Folk, C. L., & Egeth, H. E. (1989). Does the identification of simple features require parallel processing? *Journal of Experimental Psychology: Human Perception and Performance, 15,* 97–110.

Frick, R. W. (1987). The homogeneity effect in counting. *Perception & Psychophysics, 41,* 8–16.

Friedman, R. B. (1980). Identity without form: Abstract representations of letters. *Perception and Psychophysics, 28,* 53–60.

Fukushima, K. (1987). A neural network model for selective attention. In M. Caudill & C. Butler (Eds.), *Proceedings of the IEEE First Annual International Conference on Neural Networks, Volume II* (pp. 11–18). San Diego, CA: IEEE Publishing Services.

Fukushima, K., & Miyake, S. (1982). Neocognitron: A new algorithm for pattern recognition tolerant of deformations and shifts in position. *Pattern Recognition, 15,* 455–469.

Gardner, G. T. (1973). Evidence for independent parallel channels in tachistoscopic perception. *Cognitive Psychology, 4,* 130–155.

Geiger, G., & Lettvin, J. Y. (1987). Peripheral vision in persons with dyslexia. *New England Journal of Medicine, 316,* 1238–1243.

Green, D. M., & Swets, J. A. (1966). *Signal detection theory and psychophysics.* New York: Wiley.

Grossberg, S. (1976). Adaptive pattern classification and universal recoding. I: Parallel development and coding of neural feature detectors. *Biological Cybernetics, 23,* 121–134.

Grossberg, S. (1982). *Studies of mind and brain.* Reidel: Dordrecht, Holland.

Grossberg, S. (1988). *Neural networks and natural intelligence.* Cambridge, MA: MIT Press.

Grossberg, S., & Mingolla, E. (1985). Neural dynamics of perceptual grouping: Textures, boundaries, and emergent segmentations. *Perception & Psychophysics, 38,* 141–171.

Hebb, D. O. (1949). *The organization of behavior.* New York: Wiley.

Heilman, K. M., Watson, R. T., & Valenstein, E. (1985). Neglect and related disorders. In K. M. Heilman & E. Valenstein (Eds.), *Clinical neuropsychology* (2nd ed.). New York: Oxford University Press.

Hillis, A. E., & Caramazza, A. (1989). *The effects of attentional deficits on reading and spelling* (Technical Report 44). Baltimore, MD: Cognitive Neuropsychology Laboratory, Johns Hopkins University.

Hillyard, S. A., Munte, T. F., & Neville, H. J. (1985). Visual-spatial attention, orienting, and brain physiology. In M. I. Posner & O. S. M. Marin (Eds.), *Attention and performance XI* (pp. 63–84). Hillsdale, NJ: Erlbaum.

Hinton, G., & Shallice, T. (1989). *Lesioning a connectionist network: Investigations of acquired dyslexia* (Technical Report CRG-TR-89-3). Toronto, Canada: University of Toronto, Department of Computer Science, Connectionist Research Group.

Hinton, G. E. (1980). Implementing semantic networks in parallel hardware. In G. E. Hinton & J. A. Anderson (Eds.), *Parallel models of associative memory* (pp. 161–187). Hillsdale, NJ: Erlbaum.

Hinton, G. E. (1981a). A parallel computation that assigns canonical object-based frames of reference. In *Proceedings of the Seventh International Joint Conference on Artificial Intelligence* (pp. 683–685).

Hinton, G. E. (1981b). Shape representation in parallel systems. In *Proceedings of the Seventh International Joint Conference on Artificial Intelligence* (pp. 1088–1096).

Hinton, G. E., & Lang, K. (1985). Shape recognition and illusory conjunctions. In *Proceedings of the Ninth International Joint Conference on Artificial Intelligence* (pp. 252–259).

Hinton, G. E., McClelland, J. L., & Rumelhart, D. E. (1986). Distributed representations. In D. E. Rumelhart & J. L. McClelland (Eds.), *Parallel distributed processing: Explorations in the microstructure of cognition. Volume I: Foundations* (pp. 77–109). Cambridge, MA: MIT Press/Bradford Books.

Hoffman, J. E. (1975). Hierarchical stages in the processing of visual information. *Perception & Psychophysics, 18,* 348–354.

Holender, D. (1985). Disruptive effect of precueing on the identification of letters in masked words: An attentional interpretation. In M. I. Posner & O. S. M. Marin (Eds.), *Attention and performance XI* (pp. 613–629). Hillsdale, NJ: Erlbaum.

Hopfield, J. J. (1982). Neural networks and physical systems with emergent collective computational abilities. *Proceedings of the National Academy of Sciences, 79*, 2554–2558.

Humphreys, G. W., Evett, L. J., & Quinlan, P. T. (1990). Orthographic processing in visual word identification. *Cognitive Psychology.* (in press)

Humphreys, G. W., Quinlan, P. T., & Riddoch, M. J. (1989). Grouping processes in visual search: Effects with single- and combined-feature targets. *Journal of Experimental Psychology: General, 118*, 258–279.

Irwin, D. E., Yantis, S., & Jonides, J. (1983). Evidence against visual integration across saccadic eye movements. *Perception & Psychophysics, 34*, 49–57.

Johnston, J. C. (1981). Effects of advance precueing of alternatives on the perception of letters alone and in words. *Journal of Experimental Psychology: Human Perception and Performance, 7*, 560–572.

Johnston, J. C., Hale, B. L., & van Santen, J. P. H. (1983). *Resolving letter position uncertainty in words* (TM 83-11221-19). Murray Hill, NJ: Bell Labs.

Johnston, J. C., & McClelland, J. L. (1973). Visual factors in word perception. *Perception & Psychophysics, 14*, 365–370.

Johnston, J. C., & McClelland, J. L. (1974). Perception of letters in words: Seek not and ye shall find. *Science, 184*, 1192–1194.

Johnston, J. C., & McClelland, J. L. (1980). Experimental tests of a hierarchical model of word identification. *Journal of Verbal Learning and Verbal Behavior, 19*, 503–524.

Johnston, W. A., & Dark, V. J. (1986). Selective attention. *Annual Review of Psychology, 37*, 43–75.

Jolicoeur, P. (1990). Orientation congruency effects on the identification of disoriented shapes. *Journal of Experimental Psychology: Human Perception and Performance, 16*, 351–364.

Jonides, J. (1981). Voluntary versus automatic control over the mind's eye movement. In J. Long & A. Baddeley (Eds.), *Attention and performance IX* (pp. 187–203). Hillsdale, NJ: Erlbaum.

Julesz, B. (1981). Textons, the elements of texture perception, and their interactions. *Nature, 290,* 91–97.

Kahneman, D., & Treisman, A. (1984). Changing views of attention and automaticity. In R. Parasuraman, R. Davies, & J. Beatty (Eds.), *Varieties of attention* (pp. 29–61). New York: Academic Press.

Kahneman, D., Treisman, A., & Burkell, J. (1983). The cost of visual filtering. *Journal of Experimental Psychology: Human Perception and Performance, 9,* 510–522.

Kanwisher, N. G. (1987). Repetition blindness: Type recognition without token individuation. *Cognition, 27,* 117–143.

Kanwisher, N. G. (1990). Binding and type-token problems in human vision. In *Proceedings of the 12th Annual Conference of the Cognitive Science Society.* Hillsdale, NJ: Erlbaum.

Kanwisher, N. G., & Potter, M. C. (1989). Repetition blindness: The effects of stimulus modality and spatial displacement. *Memory and Cognition, 17,* 117–124.

Kanwisher, N. G., & Potter, M. C. (1990). Repetition blindness: Levels of processing. *Journal of Experimental Psychology: Human Perception and Performance, 16,* 30–47.

Karnath, H. O. (1988). Deficits of attention in acute and recovered hemi-neglect. *Neuropsychologia, 26,* 27–43.

Kinsbourne, M. (1981). Single channel theory. In D. H. Holding (Ed.), *Human skills.* Chichester, Sussex: Wiley.

Kinsbourne, M. (1987). Mechanisms of unilateral neglect. In M. Jeannerod (Ed.), *Neurophysiological and neuropsychological aspects of spatial neglect* (pp. 69–86). Amsterdam: North Holland.

Kleiss, J. A., & Lane, D. M. (1986). Locus and persistence of capacity limitations in visual information processing. *Journal of Experimental Psychology: Human Perception and Performance*, *12*, 200–210.

Koch, C., & Ullman, S. (1985). Shifts in selective visual attention: towards the underlying neural circuitry. *Human Neurobiology*, *4*, 219–227.

Krumhansl, C. L., & Thomas, A. C. (1977). Effect of level of confusability on reporting letters from briefly presented visual displays. *Perception and Psychophysics*, *21*, 269–279.

Kučera, H., & Francis, W. N. (1967). *Computational analysis of present-day American English*. Providence, RI: Brown University Press.

LaBerge, D. (1983). Spatial extent of attention to letters and words. *Journal of Experimental Psychology: Human Perception and Performance*, *9*, 371–379.

LaBerge, D., & Brown, V. (1989). Theory of attentional operations in shape identification. *Psychological Review*, *96*, 101–124.

LaBerge, D., & Samuels, S. J. (1974). Toward a theory of automatic information processing in reading. *Cognitive Psychology*, *6*, 293–323.

Lawrence, D. H. (1971). Two studies of visual search for word targets with controlled rates of presentation. *Perception & Psychophysics*, *10*, 85–89.

Le Cun, Y., Boser, B., Denker, J. S., Hendersen, D., Howard, R. E., Hubbard, W., & Jackel, L. D. (1990). Backpropagation applied to handwritten zip code recognition. *Neural Computation*, *1*, 541–551.

Linsker, R. (1988). Self-organization in a perceptual network. *Computer*, *21*, 105–117.

Luce, R. D. (1959). *Individual choice behavior*. New York: Wiley.

MacKay, D. G. (1969). The repeated letter effect in misspellings of dysgraphics and normals. *Perception & Psychophysics*, *5*, 102–106.

MacKay, D. G. (1987). *The organization of perception and action: A theory of language and other cognitive skills.* New York: Springer-Verlag.

Marcel, A. J. (1983a). Conscious and unconscious perception: Experiments on visual masking and word recognition. *Cognitive Psychology, 15,* 197–237.

Marcel, A. J. (1983b). Conscious and unconscious perception: An approach to the relations between phenomenal experience and perceptual processes. *Cognitive Psychology, 15,* 238–300.

Marr, D. (1969). A theory of cerebellar cortex. *Journal of Physiology, 202,* 437–470.

Marr, D. (1982). *Vision.* San Francisco: Freeman.

McClelland, J. L. (1985). Putting knowledge in its place: A scheme for programming parallel processing structures on the fly. *Cognitive Science, 9,* 113–146.

McClelland, J. L. (1986a). The programmable blackboard model of reading. In J. L. McClelland & D. E. Rumelhart (Eds.), *Parallel distributed processing: Explorations in the microstructure of cognition. Volume II: Psychological and biological models* (pp. 122–169). Cambridge, MA: MIT Press/Bradford Books.

McClelland, J. L. (1986b). Resource requirements of standard and programmable nets. In D. E. Rumelhart & J. L. McClelland (Eds.), *Parallel distributed processing: Explorations in the microstructure of cognition. Volume I: Foundations* (pp. 460–487). Cambridge, MA: MIT Press/Bradford Books.

McClelland, J. L., & Johnston, J. C. (1977). The role of familiar units in perception of words and nonwords. *Perception and Psychophysics, 22,* 249–261.

McClelland, J. L., & Mozer, M. C. (1986). Perceptual interactions in two-word displays: Familiarity and similarity effects. *Journal of Experimental Psychology: Human Perception and Performance, 12,* 18–35.

McClelland, J. L., & Rumelhart, D. E. (1981). An interactive activation model of context effects in letter perception: Part I. An account of basic findings. *Psychological Review*, *88*, 375–407.

McClelland, J. L., Rumelhart, D. E., & Hinton, G. E. (1986). The appeal of parallel distributed processing. In D. E. Rumelhart & J. L. McClelland (Eds.), *Parallel distributed processing: Explorations in the microstructure of cognition. Volume I: Foundations* (pp. 3–44). Cambridge, MA: MIT Press/Bradford Books.

McConkie, G. W., & Rayner, K. (1975). The span of the effective stimulus during a fixation in reading. *Perception & Psychophysics*, *17*, 578–586.

McConkie, G. W., & Zola, D. (1979). Is visual information integrated across successive fixations in reading? *Perception and Psychophysics*, *25*, 221–224.

McCulloch, W. S., & Pitts, W. H. (1943). A logical calculus of ideas immanent in nervous activity. *Bulletin of Mathematical Biophysics*, *5*, 115–133.

Mesulam, M-M. (1981). A cortical network for directed attention and unilateral neglect. *Annals of Neurology*, *10*, 309–325.

Mewhort, D. J., Marchetti, F. M., & Campbell, A. J. (1982). Blank characters in tachistoscopic recognition: Space has both a symbolic and a sensory role. *Canadian Journal of Psychology*, *36*, 559–575.

Mewhort, D. J. K., & Campbell, A. J. (1978). Processing spatial information and the selective-masking effect. *Perception & Psychophysics*, *24*, 93–101.

Miikkulainen, R. (1990). A distributed feature map model of the lexicon. In *Proceedings of the 12th Annual Conference of the Cognitive Science Society* (pp. 447–454). Hillsdale, NJ: Erlbaum.

Milner, P. M. (1974). A model for visual shape recognition. *Psychological Review*, *81*, 521–535.

Minsky, M., & Papert, S. (1988). *Perceptrons* (Expanded edition). Cambridge, MA: MIT Press.

Moran, J., & Desimone, R. (1985). Selective attention gates visual processing in the extrastriate cortex. *Science, 229*, 782–784.

Mozer, M. C. (1983). Letter migration in word perception. *Journal of Experimental Psychology: Human Perception and Performance, 9*, 531–546.

Mozer, M. C. (1987). *The perception of multiple objects: A parallel, distributed processing approach.* Unpublished doctoral dissertation, University of California, San Diego.

Mozer, M. C. (1988). A connectionist model of selective attention in visual perception. In *Proceedings of the Tenth Annual Conference of the Cognitive Science Society* (pp. 195–201). Hillsdale, NJ: Erlbaum.

Mozer, M. C. (1989). A focused back-propagation algorithm for temporal pattern recognition. *Complex Systems, 3*, 349–381.

Mozer, M. C. (1989). Types and tokens in visual letter perception. *Journal of Experimental Psychology: Human Perception and Performance, 15*, 287–303.

Mozer, M. C. (1990). Discovering faithful 'Wickelfeature' representations in a connectionist network. In *Proceedings of the 12th Annual Conference of the Cognitive Science Society* (pp. 356–363). Hillsdale, NJ: Erlbaum.

Mozer, M. C. (April 1990). *Improving a computational model of attention with constraints from single-cell recordings.* Poster presented at a conference on Recent Advances in the Analysis of Attention, Eugene, OR.

Mozer, M. C., & Behrmann, M. (1990a). On the interaction of selective attention and lexical knowlege: A connectionist account of neglect dyslexia. *Cognitive Neuroscience, 2*, 96–123.

Mozer, M. C., & Behrmann, M. (1990b). Reading with attentional impairments: A brain-damaged model of neglect and attentional dyslexias. In N. Sharkey & R. Reilly (Eds.), *Connectionist approaches to natural language processing.* Hillsdale, NJ: Erlbaum.

Mozer, M. C., Pashler, H., & Miyata, Y. (April 1990). *Recovering the "where" from the "what": A connectionist mechanism to direct attention to objects.* Paper presented at a conference on Recent Advances in the Analysis of Attention, Eugene, OR.

Mullin, P. A., & Egeth, H. E. (1989). Capacity limitations in visual word perception. *Journal of Experimental Psychology: Human Perception and Performance, 15,* 111–123.

Nakayama, K., & Silverman, G. H. (1986). Serial and parallel processing of visual feature conjunctions. *Nature, 320,* 264–265.

Navon, D. (1989). Attentional selection: Early, late, or neither? *European Journal of Cognitive Psychology, 1,* 47–68.

Neisser, U. (1964). Visual search. *Scientific American, 210,* 94–102.

Neisser, U. (1967). *Cognitive psychology.* New York: Appleton-Century-Crofts.

Nissen, M. J. (1985). Accessing features and objects: Is location special? In M. I. Posner & O. S. M. Marin (Eds.), *Attention and performance XI* (pp. 205–219). Hillsdale, NJ: Erlbaum.

Norman, D. A. (1968). Toward a theory of memory and attention. *Psychological Review, 75,* 522–536.

Norman, D. A. (1986). Reflections on cognition and parallel distributed processing. In J. L. McClelland & D. E. Rumelhart (Eds.), *Parallel distributed processing: Explorations in the microstructure of cognition. Volume II: Psychological and biological models* (pp. 531–546). Cambridge, MA: MIT Press/Bradford Books.

Norman, D. A., & Shallice, T. (1985). Attention to action: Willed and automatic control of behavior. In R. J. Davidson, G. E. Schwartz, & D. Shapiro (Eds.), *Consciousness and self regulation: Advances in research, Vol. IV.* New York: Plenum Press.

Ogden, J. A. (1985). Anterior-posterior interhemispheric differences in the loci of lesions producing visual hemineglect. *Brain and Cognition, 4,* 59–75.

Palmer, S. E. (1984). The psychology of perceptual organization: A transformational approach. In A. Rosenfeld & J. Beck (Eds.), *Human and machine vision.* New York: Academic.

Pashler, H. (1984). Evidence against late selection: Stimulus quality effects in previewed displays. *Journal of Experimental Psychology: Human Perception and Performance, 10,* 429–448.

Pashler, H. (1987). Detecting conjunctions of color and form: Reassessing the serial search hypothesis. *Perception & Psychophysics, 41,* 191–201.

Pashler, H. (1987). Target-distractor discriminability in visual search. *Perception & Psychophysics, 41,* 285–292.

Pashler, H., & Badgio, P. C. (1985). Visual attention and stimulus identification. *Journal of Experimental Psychology: Human Perception and Performance, 11,* 105–121.

Pashler, H., & Badgio, P. C. (1987). Attentional issues in the identification of alphanumeric characters. In M. Coltheart (Ed.), *Attention and performance XII: The psychology of reading* (pp. 63–82). Hillsdale, NJ: Erlbaum.

Patterson, K. E., Seidenberg, M. S., & McClelland, J. L. (1989). Connections and disconnections: Acquired dyslexia in a computational model of the reading process. In R. G. M. Morris (Ed.), *Parallel distributed processing: Implications for psychology and neurobiology.* Oxford: Oxford University Press.

Pinker, S., & Prince, A. (1988). On language and connectionism. *Cognition, 28,* 73–193.

Pollack, J. B. (1988). Recursive auto-associative memory: Devising compositional distributed representations. In *Proceedings of the Tenth Annual Conference of the Cognitive Science Society* (pp. 33–39). Hillsdale, NJ: Erlbaum.

Pollatsek, A., & Rayner, K. (1982). Eye movement control in reading: The role of word boundaries. *Journal of Experimental Psychology: Human Perception and Performance, 8,* 817–833.

Pollatsek, A., Rayner, K., & Henderson, J. M. (1990). Role of spatial location in integration of pictorial information across saccades. *Journal of Experimental Psychology: Human Perception and Performance, 16*, 199–210.

Posner, M., & Petersen, S. E. (1990). The attention system of the human brain. *Annual Review of Neuroscience, 13*, 25-42.

Posner, M. I. (1978). *Chronometric explorations of mind*. Hillsdale, NJ: Erlbaum.

Posner, M. I. (1980). Orienting of attention. *Quarterly Journal of Experimental Psychology, 32*, 3–25.

Posner, M. I., & Cohen, Y. (1984). Components of visual orienting. In H. Bouma & D. Bouwhuis (Eds.), *Attention and performance X* (pp. 531–556). Hillsdale, NJ: Erlbaum.

Posner, M. I., Snyder, C. R. R., & Davidson, B. J. (1980). Attention and the detection of signals. *Journal of Experimental Psychology: General, 109*, 160–174.

Prince, A., & Pinker, S. (1988). Wickelphone ambiguity. *Cognition, 30*, 189–190.

Prinzmetal, W. (1981). Principles of feature integration in visual perception. *Perception & Psychophysics, 30*, 330–340.

Prinzmetal, W., & Banks, W. P. (1983). Perceptual capacity limits in visual detection and search. *Bulletin of the Psychonomic Society, 21*, 263–266.

Prinzmetal, W., & Millis-Wright, M. (1984). Cognitive and linguistic factors affect visual feature integration. *Cognitive Psychology, 16*, 305–340.

Rayner, K. (1975). The perceptual span and peripheral cues in reading. *Cognitive Psychology, 7*, 65–81.

Rayner, K. (1978). Foveal and parafoveal cues in reading. In J. Requin (Ed.), *Attention and performance VII* (pp. 149–161). Hillsdale, NJ: Erlbaum.

Rayner, K., McConkie, G. W., & Ehrlich, S. (1978). Eye movements and integrating information across fixations. *Journal of Experimental Psychology: Human Perception and Performance*, *4*, 529–544.

Rayner, K., McConkie, G. W., & Zola, D. (1980). Integrating information across eye movements. *Cognitive Psychology*, *12*, 206–226.

Rayner, K., Murphy, L. A., Henderson, J. M., & Pollatsek, A. (1989). Selective attentional dyslexia. *Cognitive Neuropsychology*, *6*, 357–378.

Rayner, K., & Pollatsek, A. (1989). *The psychology of reading*. Englewood Cliffs, NJ: Prentice-Hall.

Reicher, G. M. (1969). Perceptual recognition as a function of meaningfulness of stimulus material. *Journal of Experimental Psychology*, *81*, 274–280.

Riddoch, M. J., & Humphreys, G. W. (1983). The effect of cueing on unilateral neglect. *Neuropsychologia*, *21*, 589–599.

Rock, I. (1973). *Orientation and form*. New York: Academic Press.

Rosenbloom, P., & Newell, A. (1987). Learning by chunking: A production system model of practice. In D. Klahr, P. Langley, & R. Neches (Eds.), *Production system models of learning and development* (pp. 221–285). Cambridge, MA: MIT Press.

Rosenfeld, R., & Touretzky, D. S. (1988). Coarse-coded symbol memories and their properties. *Complex Systems*, *2*, 463–484.

Rumelhart, D. E. (1970). A multicomponent theory of the perception of briefly exposed visual displays. *Journal of Mathematical Psychology*, *7*, 191–216.

Rumelhart, D. E., Hinton, G. E., & McClelland, J. L. (1986). A general framework for parallel distributed processing. In D. E. Rumelhart & J. L. McClelland (Eds.), *Parallel distributed processing: Explorations in the microstructure of cognition. Volume I: Foundations* (pp. 45–76). Cambridge, MA: MIT Press/Bradford Books.

Rumelhart, D. E., Hinton, G. E., & Williams, R. J. (1986). Learning internal representations by error propagation. In D. E. Rumelhart & J. L. McClelland (Eds.), *Parallel distributed processing: Explorations in the microstructure of cognition. Volume I: Foundations* (pp. 318–362). Cambridge, MA: MIT Press/Bradford Books.

Rumelhart, D. E., & McClelland, J. L. (1982). An interactive activation model of context effects in letter perception: Part II. The contextual enhancement effect and some tests and extensions of the model. *Psychological Review, 89,* 60–84.

Rumelhart, D. E., & McClelland, J. L. (1986). On learning the past tenses of English verbs. In J. L. McClelland & D. E. Rumelhart (Eds.), *Parallel distributed processing: Explorations in the microstructure of cognition. Volume II: Psychological and biological models* (pp. 216–271). Cambridge, MA: MIT Press/Bradford Books.

Rumelhart, D. E., & Zipser, D. (1985). Feature discovery by competitive learning. *Cognitive Science, 9,* 75–112.

Sandon, P. A. (1990). Simulating visual attention. *Cognitive Neuroscience, 2,* 213–231.

Sandon, P. A., & Uhr, L. M. (1988). An adaptive model for viewpoint-invariant object recognition. In *Proceedings of the Tenth Annual Conference of the Cognitive Science Society* (pp. 209–215). Hillsdale, NJ: Erlbaum.

Schneider, W. (1985). Toward a model of attention and the development of automatic processing. In M. I. Posner & O. S. M. Marin (Eds.), *Attention and performance XI.* Hillsdale, NJ: Erlbaum.

Schneider, W., & Shiffrin, R. M. (1977). Controlled and automatic human information processing: I. Detection, search and attention. *Psychological Review, 84,* 1–66.

Shallice, T. (1988). *From neuropsychology to mental structure.* Cambridge, England: Cambridge University Press.

Shallice, T., & McCarthy, R. (1985). Phonological reading: From patterns of impairment to possible procedures. In K. Patterson, J. C. Marshall, & M. Coltheart (Eds.), *Surface dyslexia: Cognitive and neuropsychological studies of phonological reading* (pp. 361–394). London: Erlbaum.

Shallice, T., & McGill, J. (1978). The origins of mixed errors. In J. Requin (Ed.), *Attention and performance VII* (pp. 193–208). Hillsdale, NJ: Erlbaum.

Shallice, T., & Warrington, E. K. (1977). The possible role of selective attention in acquired dyslexia. *Neuropsychologia, 15*, 31–41.

Shaywitz, B. A., & Waxman, S. G. (1987). Dyslexia. *New England Journal of Medicine, 316*, 1268–1270.

Shiffrin, R. M., & Gardner, G. T. (1972). Visual processing capacity and attentional control. *Journal of Experimental Psychology, 93*, 72–83.

Shiffrin, R. M., & Schneider, W. (1977). Controlled and automatic human information processing: II. Perceptual learning, automatic attending, and a general theory. *Psychological Review, 84*, 127–190.

Sieroff, E. (1989). *Perception of visual letter strings in a case of left neglect: Manipulation of the word form.* Manuscript submitted for publication.

Sieroff, E., & Michel, F. (1987). Verbal visual extinction in right/left hemisphere lesion patients and the problem of lexical access. *Neuropsychologia, 25*, 907–918.

Sieroff, E., Pollatsek, A., & Posner, M. I. (1988). Recognition of visual letter strings following injury to the posterior visual spatial attention system. *Cognitive Neuropsychology, 5*, 451–472.

Singh, J. (1966). *Great ideas in information theory, language, and cybernetics.* New York: Dover Publications.

Smolensky, P. (1986). Information processing in dynamical systems: Foundations of Harmony Theory. In D. E. Rumelhart & J. L. McClelland (Eds.), *Parallel distributed processing: Explorations in the microstructure of cognition. Volume 1: Foundations* (pp. 194–281). Cambridge, MA: MIT Press/Bradford Books.

Smolensky, P. (1990). Tensor product variable binding and the representation of symbolic structures in connectionist networks. *Artificial Intelligence.* (in press)

St. John, M. F., & McClelland, J. L. (1986). Reconstructive memory for sentences: A PDP approach. In *Proceedings of the Ohio University Inference Conference.*

Steinman, S. B. (1987). Serial and parallel search in pattern vision. *Perception, 16,* 389–398.

Stroop, J. R. (1938). Factors affecting speed in serial verbal reactions. *Psychological Monographs, 50 (whole no. 225),* 38–48.

Thibadeau, R., Just, M. A., & Carpenter, P. A. (1982). A model of the time course and content of reading. *Cognitive Science, 6,* 157–203.

Touretzky, D. S. (1986). BoltzCONS: Reconciling connectionism with the recursive nature of stacks and trees. In *Proceedings of the Eighth Annual Conference of the Cognitive Science Society* (pp. 522–530). Hillsdale, NJ: Erlbaum.

Touretzky, D. S. (1989). Analyzing the energy landscapes of distributed winner-take-all networks. In D. S. Touretzky (Ed.), *Advances in neural information processing systems 1* (pp. 626–633). San Mateo, CA: Morgan Kaufmann.

Touretzky, D. S., & Hinton, G. E. (1985). Symbols among the neurons: Details of a connectionist inference architecture. In *Proceedings of the Ninth International Joint Conference on Artificial Intelligence* (pp. 238–243).

Touretzky, D. S., & Hinton, G. E. (1988). A distributed connectionist production system. *Cognitive Science, 12,* 423–466.

Townsend, J. T., Taylor, S. G., & Brown, D. R. (1971). Lateral masking for letters with unlimited viewing time. *Perception & Psychophysics, 10,* 375–378.

Treisman, A. (1969). Strategies and models of selective attention. *Psychological Review, 76,* 282–299.

Treisman, A. (1988). Features and objects: The 14th Bartlett memorial lecture. *Quarterly Journal of Experimental Psychology, 40A,* 201–237.

Treisman, A. (April 1990). *Paper presented at a conference on Recent Advances in the Analysis of Attention, Eugene, OR.*

Treisman, A., & Gelade, G. (1980). A feature integration theory of attention. *Cognitive Psychology, 12,* 97–136.

Treisman, A., & Gormican, S. (1988). Feature analysis in early vision: Evidence from search asymmetries. *Psychological Review, 95,* 15–48.

Treisman, A., & Schmidt, H. (1982). Illusory conjunctions in the perception of objects. *Cognitive Psychology, 14,* 107–141.

Treisman, A., & Souther, J. (1985). Search asymmetry: A diagnostic for preattentive processing of separable features. *Journal of Experimental Psychology: General, 114,* 285–310.

Treisman, A., & Souther, J. (1986). Illusory words: The roles of attention and of top-down constraints in conjoining letters to form words. *Journal of Experimental Psychology: Human Perception & Performance, 12,* 3–17.

Treisman, A., Sykes, M., & Gelade, G. (1977). Selective attention and stimulus integration. In S. Dornic (Ed.), *Attention and performance VI* (pp. 333–361). Hillsdale, NJ: Erlbaum.

Turvey, M. (1973). On peripheral and central processes in vision: Inferences from an information-processing analysis of masking with patterned stimuli. *Psychological Review, 80,* 1–52.

Uhr, L. (1987). *Highly parallel, hierarchical, recognition cone perceptual structure* (Technical Report 688). Madison, WI: Computer Sciences Department, University of Wisconsin.

Ungerleider, L. G., & Mishkin, M. (1982). Two cortical visual systems. In D. J. Ingle, M. A. Goodale, & R. J. W. Mansfield (Eds.), *Analysis of visual behavior*. Cambridge, MA: MIT Press.

van der Heijden, A. H. C. (1975). Some evidence for a limited-capacity parallel self-terminating process in simple visual search tasks. *Acta Psychologica, 39*, 21–41.

van der Heijden, A. H. C., Hagenaar, R., & Bloem, W. (1984). Two stages in postcategorical filtering and selection. *Memory & Cognition, 12*, 458–469.

Van Essen, D. C., & Maunsell, J. H. R. (1983). Hierarchical organization and functional streams in the visual cortex. *Trends in Neuroscience, 6*, 370–375.

Virzi, R. A., & Egeth, H. E. (1984). Is meaning implicated in illusory conjunctions? *Journal of Experimental Psychology: Human Perception and Performance, 10*, 573–580.

Wheeler, D. (1970). Processes in word recognition. *Cognitive Psychology, 1*, 59–85.

Wickelgren, W. (1966). Phonemic similarity and interference in short-term memory for single letters. *Journal of Experimental Psychology, 71*, 396–404.

Wickelgren, W. (1969). Context-sensitive coding, associative memory, and serial order in (speech) behavior. *Psychological Review, 76*, 1–15.

Widrow, B., & Hoff, M. E. (1960). Adaptive switching circuits. *Institute of Radio Engineers, Western Electronic Show and Convention, Convention Record, Part 4*, 96–104.

Widrow, B., & Stearns, S. D. (1985). *Adaptive signal processing*. Englewood Cliffs, NJ: Prentice-Hall.

Widrow, B., Winter, R. G., & Baxter, R. A. (1987). Learning phenomena in layered neural networks. In M. Caudill & C. Butler (Eds.), *Proceedings of the IEEE First Annual International Conference on Neural Networks, Volume II* (pp. 411–429). San Diego, CA: IEEE Publishing Services.

Wiesmeyer, M., & Laird, J. (1990). A computer model of 2D visual attention. In *Proceedings of the 12th Annual Conference of the Cognitive Science Society* (pp. 582–589). Hillsdale, NJ: Erlbaum.

Willows, D. M., & MacKinnon, G. E. (1973). Selective reading: Attention to the "unattended" lines. *Canadian Journal of Psychology, 27*, 292–304.

Winer, B. J. (1962). *Statistical principles in experimental design.* New York: McGraw-Hill.

Wolfe, J. M., Cave, K. R., & Franzel, S. L. (1989). Guided search: An alternative to the feature integration model for visual search. *Journal of Experimental Psychology: Human Perception and Performance, 15*, 419–433.

Wolford, G., & Hollingsworth, S. (1974). Lateral masking in visual information processing. *Perception & Psychophysics, 16*, 315–320.

Wolford, G., & Shum, K. H. (1980). Evidence for feature perturbations. *Perception & Psychophysics, 27*, 409–420.

Woodworth, R. S. (1938). *Experimental psychology.* New York: Holt.

Zemel, R. S., Mozer, M. C., & Hinton, G. E. (1989). TRAFFIC: A model of object recognition based on transformations of feature instances. In D. S. Touretzky, G. E. Hinton, & T. J. Sejnowski (Eds.), *Proceedings of the 1988 Connectionist Models Summer School* (pp. 452–461). San Mateo, CA: Morgan Kaufmann.

Zemel, R. S., Mozer, M. C., & Hinton, G. E. (1990). TRAFFIC: Recognizing objects using hierarchical reference frame transformations. In *Advances in neural network information processing systems II.* San Mateo, CA: Morgan Kaufmann.

Index